THE MAJOR
LANGUAGES
OF
EAST AND
SOUTH-EAST ASIA

THE MAJOR LANGUAGES Edited by Bernard Comrie

The Major Languages of Western Europe

The Major Languages of Eastern Europe (Forthcoming)

The Major Languages of East and South-East Asia

The Major Languages of The Middle East, South Asia and Africa (Forthcoming)

THE MAJOR LANGUAGES OF EAST AND SOUTH-EAST ASIA

EDITED BY
BERNARD COMRIE

ROUTLEDGE
London

First published as part of
The World's Major Languages in 1987 by
Croom Helm Ltd

Reprinted with revisions and additional material in 1990 by
Routledge
11 New Fetter Lane, London EC4P 4EE

© 1987 and 1990 Selection, introduction and editorial matter Bernard Comrie, chapter 1 David Strecker, chapter 2 Thomas John Hudak, chapter 3 Đình-Hoà Nguyên, chapter 4 Scott DeLancey, chapter 5 Charles N Li and Sandra A Thompson, chapter 6 Julian K Wheatley, chapter 7 Masayoshi Shibatani, chapter 8 Nam-Kil Kim, chapter 9 Ross Clark, chapter 10 DJ Prentice, chapter 11 Paul Schachter.

All rights reserved. No part of this book may be reprinted or reproduced or utilized in any form or by any electronic, mechanical or other means, now known or hereafter invented, including photocopying and recording, or in any information storage or retrieval system, without permission in writing from the publishers.

British Library Cataloguing in Publication Data
Available on request

ISBN 0-415-04739-0

Typeset in 10 on 12pt Times by Computype, Middlesex
Printed and bound in Great Britain by Mackays of Chatham

Contents

Preface	vii
List of Abbreviations	ix
Introduction	1
BERNARD COMRIE, UNIVERSITY OF SOUTHERN CALIFORNIA	

1	**Tai Languages**	19
	DAVID STRECKER, CINCINNATI	
2	*Thai*	29
	THOMAS JOHN HUDAK, UNIVERSITY OF KENTUCKY	

3	**Vietnamese**	49
	ĐÌNH-HOÀ NGUYÊN, SOUTHERN ILLINOIS UNIVERSITY AT CARBONDALE	

4	**Sino-Tibetan Languages**	69
	SCOTT DELANCEY, UNIVERSITY OF OREGON	
5	*Chinese*	83
	CHARLES N. LI AND SANDRA A. THOMPSON, BOTH UNIVERSITY OF CALIFORNIA SANTA BARBARA	
6	*Burmese*	106
	JULIAN K. WHEATLEY, CALIFORNIA STATE UNIVERSITY FRESNO	

7	**Japanese**	127
	MASAYOSHI SHIBATANI, KOBE UNIVERSITY	

8	**Korean**	153
	NAM-KIL KIM, UNIVERSITY OF SOUTHERN CALIFORNIA	

9	**Austronesian Languages**	171
	ROSS CLARK, UNIVERSITY OF AUCKLAND	

10	*Malay (Indonesian and Malaysian)* D.J. PRENTICE, UNIVERSITY OF LEIDEN	185
11	*Tagalog* PAUL SCHACHTER, UNIVERSITY OF CALIFORNIA LOS ANGELES	208

Language Index 231

Preface

The text of this book has been extracted from that of *The World's Major Languages* (Routledge, 1987). The aim of that book was to make available information on some fifty of the world's major languages and language families, in a form that would be accessible and interesting both to the layman with a general interest in language and to the linguist eager to find out about languages outside his or her specialty. Not all of those interested in major languages of the world, however, have an interest that includes all parts of the world, and it therefore seemed advisable to publish portions of the original text in a series of paperbacks — *The Major Languages*. Readers interested in only one part of the world now have access to discussion of those languages without having to acquire the whole volume.

Perhaps the most controversial problem that I, in the original volume had to face was the choice of languages to be included. My main criterion was, admittedly, a very subjective one; what languages do I think the reader would expect to find included? In answering this question I was, of course, guided by more objective criteria, such as the number of speakers of individual languages, whether they are official languages of independent states, whether they are widely used in more than one country, whether they are the bearers of long-standing literary traditions. These criteria often conflict — thus Latin, though long since deprived of native speakers, was included because of its immense cultural importance — and I bear full responsibility, as editor, for the final choice.

The notion of 'major language' is obviously primarily a social characterisation, and the fact that a language was not included implies no denigration of its importance as a language in its own right: every human language is a manifestation of our species' linguistic faculty and any human language may provide an important contribution to our understanding of language as a general phenomenon. In the recent development of general linguistics, important contributions have come from the Australian Aboriginal languages Walbiri (Warlpiri) and Dyirbal (Jirrbal). Other editors might well have come up with different selections of languages, or have used somewhat different criteria. When linguists learned in 1970 that the last speaker of Kamassian, a Uralic language originally spoken in Siberia, had kept her language alive for decades in her prayers — God being the only other speaker of her language — they may well have wondered whether, for this person, *the* world's major language was not Kamassian.

Contributors were presented with early versions of my own chapters on Slavonic languages and Russian as models for their contributions, but I felt it inappropriate to lay down strict guidelines as to how each individual chapter should be written, although I did ask authors to include at least some material on both the structure of their language and its social background. The main criterion that I asked contributors to follow was: tell the reader what you consider to be the most interesting facts about your language. This has necessarily meant that different chapters highlight different phenomena, e.g. the chapter on English the role of English as a world language, the chapter on Arabic the writing system, the chapter on Turkish the grammatical system. But I believe that this variety lent strength to the original volume, since within the space limitations of what is quite a sizable book it would have been impossible to do justice in a more comprehensive and homogeneous way to each of over fifty languages and language families.

The criterion for dividing the contents of the original volume among the four new books has been my assessment of likely common and divergent interests: if the reader is interested in language X, then which of the other major languages of the world is he or she likely to be most interested in? In part, my decisions have been governed by consideration of genetic relatedness (for instance, all Romance languages, including Rumanian, are included in *The Major Languages of Western Europe*), in part by consideration of areal interests (so that *The Major Languages of The Middle East, South Asia and Africa* includes the Indo-Iranian languages, along with other languages of the Middle East and South Asia). Inevitably, some difficulties arose in working out the division, especially given the desire not to have too much overlap among volumes, since a reader might want to acquire more than one of the paperback volumes. In fact, the only overlap among the volumes is in the Introduction, substantial parts of which are the same for all volumes, and in the fact that the chapter on Indo-European languages is included in both of the European volumes (given that most of the languages of both western and eastern Europe are Indo-European).

Editorial support in the preparation of my work on the original volume was provided by the Divison of Humanities of the University of Southern California, through the research fund of the Andrew W. Mellon Professorship, which I held during 1983–4, and by the Max Planck Institute for Psycholinguistics (Nijmegen, The Netherlands), where I was a visiting research worker in the summer of 1984. I am particularly grateful to Jonathan Price for his continuing willingness to consult with me on all details of the preparation of the text.

Bernard Comrie
Los Angeles

Abbreviations

abilit.	abilitative	conj.	conjunction
abl.	ablative	conjug.	conjugation
abstr.	abstract	conjv.	conjunctive
acc.	accusative	cont.	contemplated
acr.	actor	cop.	copula
act.	active	cp	class prefix
act.n.	action nominal	crs.	currently relevant state
adj.	adjective	Cz.	Czech
adv.	adverb	Da.	Danish
Alb.	Albanian	dat.	dative
Am.	American	dbl.	double
anim.	animate	decl.	declension
aor.	aorist	def.	definite
Ar.	Arabic	dent.	dental
Arm.	Armenian	deriv. morph.	derivational morpheme
art.	article	de-v.	deverbal
Ashk.	Ashkenazi(c)	dir.	direct
asp.	aspirated	disj.	disjunctive
AT	actor-trigger	Dor.	Doric
athem.	athematic	drc.	directional
aux.	auxiliary	DT	dative-trigger
Av.	Avestan	du.	dual
ben.	beneficiary	dur.	durative
BH	Biblical Hebrew	d.v.	dynamic verb
BN	B-Norwegian	E.	Eastern
Boh.	Bohemian	Eng.	English
BP	Brazilian Portuguese	ENHG	Early New High German
Br.	British		
BT	beneficiary-trigger	EP	European Portuguese
c.	common	erg.	ergative
Cast.	Castilian	ex.	existential-possessive
Cat.	Catalan	f.	feminine
caus.	causative	fact.	factive
cc	class concord	foc.	focus
Cent.	Central	Fr.	French
cl.	class(ifier)	fut.	future
clit.	clitic	g.	gender
comp.	comparative	gen.	genitive

ABBREVIATIONS

ger.	gerund(ive)	neg.	negative
Gk.	Greek	NHG	New High German
Gmc.	Germanic	nm.	nominal
Go.	Gothic	NN	N-Norwegian
gr.	grade	nom.	nominative
GR	Gallo-Romance	noms.	nominalisation
gutt.	guttural	NP	New Persian
H	High	nt.	neuter
Hier. Hitt.	Hieroglyphic Hittite	Nw.	Norwegian
Hitt.	Hittite	O.	Oscan
hon.	honorific	OArm.	Old Armenian
IE	Indo-European	obj.	object
imper.	imperative	obl.	oblique
imperf.	imperfect(ive)	OBs.	Old Burmese
inanim.	inanimate	Oc.	Occitan
incl.	inclusive	OCS	Old Church Slavonic
indef.	indefinite	OE	Old English
indic.	indicative	OFr.	Old French
indir.	indirect	OFri.	Old Frisian
infin.	infinitive	OHG	Old High German
inst.	instrumental	OIc.	Old Icelandic
intr.	intransitive	OIr.	Old Irish
inv.	inversion particle	OIran.	Old Iranian
irr.	irrational	OLat.	Old Latin
It.	Italian	OLith.	Old Lithuanian
IT	instrument-trigger	ON	Old Norse
i.v.	intransitive verb	OP	Old Persian
L	Low	opt.	optative
lab.	labial	OPtg.	Old Portuguese
Lat.	Latin	orig.	original(ly)
Latv.	Latvian	OS	Old Saxon
LG	Low German	OV	object–verb
lig.	ligature	p.	person
lingu.	lingual	pal.	palatal
lit.	literally	part.	participle
Lith.	Lithuanian	pass.	passive
loc.	locative	pat.	patient
m.	masculine	PDr.	Proto-Dravidian
MBs.	Modern Burmese	perf.	perfect(ive)
ME	Middle English	pers.	person
med.	medio-passive	PGmc.	Proto-Germanic
MH	Middle Hebrew	PIE	Proto-Indo-European
MHG	Middle High German	PIt.	Proto-Italic
mid.	middle	Pkt.	Prakrit
MidFr.	Middle French	pl.	plural
ModE	Modern English	Po.	Polish
ModFr.	Modern French	pos.	position
MoH	Modern Hebrew	poss.	possessive
Mor.	Moravian	prep.	preposition
MP	Middle Persian	prepl.	prepositional
n.	noun	pres.	present
necess.	necessitative	pret.	preterit

prim.	primary	st.	standard
prog.	progressive	su.	subject
pron.	pronoun	subj.	subjunctive
PT	patient-trigger	sup.	superlative
Ptg.	Portuguese	s.v.	stative verb
Q	question	SVO	subject–verb–object
rat.	rational	Sw.	Swedish
recip.	reciprocal	tap.	tense/aspect pronoun
refl. pron.	reflexive pronoun	tg.	trigger
rel.	relative	them.	thematic
rep.	reported	Tk.	Turkish
res.	result	Toch.	Tocharian
Ru.	Runic	top.	topic
Rum.	Rumanian	tr.	transitive
Rus.	Russian	transg.	transgressive
Sard.	Sardinian	t.v.	transitive verb
SCr.	Serbo-Croat	U.	Umbrian
sec.	secondary	v.	verb
Seph.	Sephardi(c)	v.n.	verbal noun
sg.	singular	vd.	voiced
S-J	Sino-Japanese	Ved.	Vedic
Skt.	Sanskrit	VL	Vulgar Latin
Slk.	Slovak	vls.	voiceless
SOV	subject–object–verb	VO	verb–object
Sp.	Spanish	voc.	vocative
spec.	species	VSO	verb–subject–object

* The asterisk is used in discussion of historical reconstructions to indicate a reconstructed (non-attested) form. In synchronic discussions, it is used to indicate an ungrammatical item; (*X) means that inclusion of X makes the item ungrammatical; *(X) means that omission of X makes the item ungrammatical.

In the chapter on Vietnamese, a subscript numeral n after a word in the English translation indicates that that word glosses the nth word in the Vietnamese example.

INTRODUCTION

Bernard Comrie

1 Preliminary Notions

How many languages are there in the world? What language(s) do they speak in India? What languages have the most speakers? What languages were spoken in Australia, or in California before European immigration? When did Latin stop being spoken, and when did French start being spoken? How did English become such an important world language? These and other similar questions are often asked by the interested layman. One aim of the volumes of *The Major Languages* series is to provide answers to these and related questions, or in certain cases to show why the questions cannot be answered as they stand. The chapters concentrate on an individual language or group of languages, and in this Introduction I want rather to present a linking essay which will provide a background against which the individual chapters can be appreciated.

After discussing some preliminary notions in this section, section 2 of the Introduction provides a rapid survey of the languages spoken in East and South-East Asia today. Since the notion of 'major language' is primarily a social notion — languages become major (such as English), or stop being major (such as Sumerian) not because of their grammatical structure, but because of social factors — section 3 discusses some important sociolinguistic notions, in particular concerning the social interaction of languages.

1.1 How Many Languages?

Linguists are typically very hesitant to answer the first question posed above, namely: how many languages are spoken in the world today? Probably the best that one can say, with any hope of not being contradicted, is that at a very conservative estimate some 4,000 languages are spoken today. Laymen are often surprised that the figure should be so high, but I would emphasise that this is a conservative estimate. But why is it that linguists are not able to give a more accurate figure? There are several different reasons conspiring to prevent them from doing so, and these will be outlined below.

One is that many parts of the world are insufficiently studied from a linguistic viewpoint, so that we simply do not know precisely what languages are spoken there. Our knowledge of the linguistic situation in remote parts of the world has improved dramatically in recent years – New Guinea, for instance, has changed from being almost a blank linguistic map to the stage where most (though still not all) of the languages can be pinpointed with accuracy: since perhaps as many as one fifth of the world's languages are spoken in New Guinea, this has radically changed any estimate of the total number of languages. But there are still some areas where uncertainty remains, so that even a detailed index of the world's languages such as Voegelin and Voegelin (1977) lists several languages with accompanying question marks, or queries whether one listed language might in fact be the same as some other language but under a different name.

A second problem is that it is difficult or impossible in many cases to decide whether two related speech varieties should be considered different languages or merely different dialects of the same language. With the languages of Europe, there are in general established traditions of whether two speech varieties should be considered different languages or merely dialect variants, but these decisions have often been made more on political and social grounds rather than strictly linguistic grounds.

One criterion that is often advanced as a purely linguistic criterion is mutual intelligibility: if two speech varieties are mutually intelligible, they are different dialects of the same language, but if they are mutually unintelligible, they are different languages. But if applied to the languages of Europe, this criterion would radically alter our assessment of what the different languages of Europe are: the most northern dialects and the most southern dialects (in the traditional sense) of German are mutually unintelligible, while dialects of German spoken close to the Dutch border are mutually intelligible with dialects of Dutch spoken just across the border. In fact, our criterion for whether a dialect is Dutch or German relates in large measure to social factors — is the dialect spoken in an area where Dutch is the standard language or where German is the standard language? By the same criterion, the three nuclear Scandinavian languages (in the traditional sense), Danish, Norwegian and Swedish, would turn out to be dialects of one language, given their mutual intelligibility. While this criterion is often applied to non-European languages (so that nowadays linguists often talk of the Chinese languages rather than the Chinese dialects, given the mutual unintelligibility of, for instance, Mandarin and Cantonese), it seems unfair that it should not be applied consistently to European languages as well.

While native speakers of English are often surprised that there should be problems in delimiting languages from dialects — since present-day dialects of English are in general mutually intelligible (at least with some familiarisation), and even the language most closely related genetically to English, Frisian, is mutually unintelligible with English — the native speaker of English would be hard put to interpret a sentence in Tok Pisin, the English-based pidgin of much of Papua New Guinea, like *sapos ol i karamapim bokis bilong yumi, orait bai yumi paitim as bilong ol* 'if they cover our box, then we'll spank them', although each word, except perhaps *i*, is of English origin ('suppose all ?he cover-up-him box belong you-me, all-right by you-me fight-him arse belong all').

In some cases, the intelligibility criterion actually leads to contradictory results, namely when we have a dialect chain, i.e. a string of dialects such that adjacent dialects are readily mutually intelligible, but dialects from the far ends of the chain are not mutually intelligible. A good illustration of this is the Dutch-German dialect complex. One could start from the far south of the German-speaking area and move to the far west of the Dutch-speaking area without encountering any sharp boundary across which mutual intelligibility is broken; but the two end points of this chain are speech varieties so different from one another that there is no mutual intelligibility possible. If one takes a simplified dialect chain A–B–C, where A and B are mutually intelligible, as are B and C, but A and C are mutually unintelligible, then one arrives at the contradictory result that A and B are dialects of the same language, B and C are dialects of the same language, but A and C are different languages. There is in fact no way of resolving this contradiction if we maintain the traditional strict difference between language and dialects, and what such examples show is that this is not an all-or-nothing distinction, but rather a continuum. In this sense, it is impossible to answer the question how many languages are spoken in the world.

A further problem with the mutual intelligibility criterion is that mutual intelligibility itself is a matter of degree rather than a clearcut opposition between intelligibility and unintelligibility. If mutual intelligibility were to mean 100 per cent mutual intelligibility of all utterances, then perhaps no two speech varieties would be classified as mere dialect variants; for instance, although speakers of British and American English can understand most of one another's speech, there are areas where intelligibility is likely to be minimal unless one speaker happens to have learned the linguistic forms used by the other, as with car (or auto) terms like British *boot, bonnet, mudguard* and their American equivalents *trunk, hood, fender*. Conversely, although speakers of different Slavonic languages are often unable to make full sense of a text in another Slavonic language, they can usually make good sense of parts of the text, because of the high percentage of shared vocabulary and forms.

Two further factors enter into the degree of mutual intelligibility between two speech varieties. One is that intelligibility can rise rapidly with increased familiarisation: those who remember the first introduction of American films into Britain often recall that they were initially considered difficult to understand, but increased exposure to American English has virtually removed this problem. Speakers of different dialects of Arabic often experience difficulty in understanding each other at first meeting, but soon adjust to the major differences between their respective dialects, and Egyptian Arabic, as the most widely diffused modern Arabic dialect, has rapidly gained in intelligibility throughout the Arab world. This can lead to 'one-way intelligibility', as when speakers of, say, Tunisian Arabic are more likely to understand Egyptian Arabic than vice versa, because Tunisian Arabic speakers are more often exposed to Egyptian Arabic than vice versa. The second factor is that intelligibility is to a certain extent a social and psychological phenomenon: it is easier to understand when you want to understand. A good example of this is the conflicting assessments different speakers of the same Slavonic language will often give about the intelligibility of some other Slavonic language, correlating in large measure with whether or not they feel well-disposed to speakers of the other language.

The same problems as exist in delimiting dialects from languages arise, incidentally, on the historical plane too, where the question arises: at what point has a language changed sufficiently to be considered a different language? Again, traditional answers are often contradictory: Latin is considered to have died out, although its descendants, the Romance languages, live on, so at some time Latin must have changed sufficiently to be deemed no longer the same language, but a qualitatively different language. On the other hand, Greek is referred to in the same way throughout its attested history (which is longer than that of Latin and the Romance languages combined), with merely the addition of different adjectives to identify different stages of its development (e.g. Ancient Greek, Byzantine Greek, Modern Greek). In the case of the history of the English language, there is even conflicting terminology: the oldest attested stages of English can be referred to either as Old English (which suggests an earlier stage of Modern English) or as Anglo-Saxon (which suggests a different language that is the ancestor of English, perhaps justifiably so given the mutual unintelligibility of Old and Modern English).

A further reason why it is difficult to assess the number of languages spoken in the world today is that many languages are on the verge of extinction. While it has probably been the case throughout mankind's history that languages have died out, the historically recent expansion of European population to the Americas and Australia has resulted in a greatly accelerated rate of language death among the indigenous languages of these areas. Perusal of Voegelin and Voegelin (1977) will show a number of languages as 'possibly extinct' or 'possibly still spoken', plus an even greater number of languages with only a handful of speakers — usually of advanced age — so that a language may well be dying out somewhere in the world as I am writing these words. When a language dies, this is sometimes an abrupt process, such as the death of a fluent speaker who happened to have outlived all other speakers of the language; more typically, however, the community's facility with the language decreases, as more and more functions are taken over by some other language, so that what they speak, in terms of the original language of the community, is only a part of that language. Many linguists working on Australian Aboriginal languages have been forced, in some cases, to do what has come to be called 'salvage linguistics', i.e. to elicit portions of a language from someone who has neither spoken nor heard the language for decades and has perhaps only a vague recollection of what the language was like.

1.2 Language Families and Genetic Classification
One of the basic organisational principles of this volume, both in section 2 of the Introduction and in the arrangement of the individual chapters, is the organisation of languages into language families. It is therefore important that some insight should be provided into what it means to say that two languages belong to the same language family (or equivalently: are genetically related).

It is probably intuitively clear to anyone who knows a few languages that some languages are closer to one another than are others. For instance, English and German are closer to one another than either is to Russian, while Russian and Polish are closer to one another than either is to English. This notion of similarity can be made more precise, but for the moment the relatively informal notion will suffice. Starting in the late eighteenth century, a specific hypothesis was proposed to account for such similarities, a hypothesis which still forms the foundation of research into the history and relatedness of languages. This hypothesis is that where languages share some set of features in common, these features are to be attributed to their common ancestor. Let us take some examples from English and German.

In English and German we find a number of basic vocabulary items that have the same or almost the same form, e.g. English *man* and German *Mann*. Likewise, we find a number of bound morphemes (prefixes and suffixes) that have the same or almost the same form, such as the genitive suffix, as in English *man's* and German *Mann(e)s*. Although English and German are now clearly different languages, we may hypothesise that at an earlier period in history they had a common ancestor, in which the word for 'man' was something like *man* and the genitive suffix was something like *-s*. Thus English and German belong to the same language family, which is the same as saying that they share a common ancestor. We can readily add other languages to this family, since a word like *man* and a genitive suffix like *-s* are also found in Dutch, Frisian, and the Scandinavian languages. The family to which these languages belong has been given the name Germanic, and the ancestor language is Proto-Germanic. It should be emphasised that the proto-language is not an attested language — although if written records had gone back far enough, we might well have had attestations of this language — but its postulation is the most plausible hypothesis explaining the remarkable similarities among the various Germanic languages.

Although not so obvious, similarities can be found among the Germanic languages and a number of other languages spoken in Europe and spreading across northern India as far as Bangladesh. These other languages share fewer similarities with the Germanic languages than individual Germanic languages do with one another, so that they are more remotely related. The overall language family to which all these languages belong is the Indo-European family, with its reconstructed ancestor language Proto-Indo-European. The Indo-European family contains a number of branches (i.e. smaller language families, or subfamilies), such as Slavonic (including Russian and Polish), Iranian (including Persian and Pashto), and Celtic (including Irish and Welsh). The overall structure is therefore hierarchical: the most distant ancestor is Proto-Indo-European. At an intermediate point in the family tree, and therefore at a later period of history, we have such languages as Proto-Germanic and Proto-Celtic, which are descendants of Proto-Indo-European but ancestors of languages spoken today. Still later in history, we find the individual languages as they are spoken today or attested in recent history, such as English or German as descendants of Proto-Germanic and Irish and Welsh as descendants of Proto-Celtic. One typical property of language change that is represented accurately by this family-tree model is that, as time goes by, languages descending from a common ancestor tend to become less and less similar. For instance, Old English and Old High German (the ancestor of Modern German) were much closer to one another than are the modern languages — they may even have been mutually intelligible, at least to a large extent.

Although the family-tree model of language relatedness is an important foundation of all current work in historical and comparative linguistics, it is not without its problems, both in practice and in principle. Some of these will now be discussed.

We noted above that with the passage of time, genetically related languages will grow less and less similar. This follows from the fact that, once two languages have split off as separate languages from a common ancestor, each will innovate its own changes, different from changes that take place in the other language, so that the cumulative effect will be increasing divergence. With the passage of enough time, the divergence may come to be so great that it is no longer possible to tell, other than by directly examining the history, that the two languages do in fact come from a common ancestor. The best established language families, such as Indo-European or Sino-Tibetan, are those where the passage of time has not been long enough to erase the obvious traces of genetic relatedness. (For language families that have a long written tradition, one can of course make use of earlier stages of the language, which contain more evidence of genetic relatedness). In addition, there are many hypothesised language families for which the evidence is not sufficient to convince all, or even the majority, of scholars. For instance, the Turkic language family is a well-established language family, as is each of the Uralic, Mongolian and Tungusic families. What is controversial, however, is whether or not these individual families are related as members of an even larger family. The possibility of an Altaic family, comprising Turkic, Mongolian, and Tungusic, is rather widely accepted, and some scholars would advocate increasing the size of this family by adding some or all of Uralic, Korean and Japanese.

The attitudes of different linguists to problems of this kind have been characterised as an opposition between 'splitters' (who require the firmest evidence before they are prepared to acknowledge genetic relatedness) and 'clumpers' (who are ready to assign languages to the same family on the basis of quite restricted similarities). I should, incidentally, declare my own splitter bias, lest any of my own views that creep in be interpreted as generally accepted dogma. The most extreme clumper position would, of course, be to maintain that all languages of the world are genetically related, although there are less radical positions that are somewhat more widely accepted, such as the following list of sixteen stocks, where a stock is simply the highest hierarchical level of genetic relatedness (just as a language family has branches, so families would group together to form stocks): Dravidian, Eurasiatic (including, inter alia, Uralic and Altaic), Indo-European, Nilo-Saharan, Niger-Kordofanian, Afroasiatic, Khoisan, Amerind (all indigenous languages of the Americas except Eskimo-Aleut and Na-Dene), Na-Dene, Austric (including Austro-Asiatic, Tai and Austronesian), Indo-Pacific (including all Papuan languages and Tasmanian), Australian, Sino-Tibetan, Ibero-Caucasian (including Basque and Causcasian), Ket, Burushaski — this schema still operates, incidentally, with two language isolates (Ket and Burushaski), i.e. languages not related to any other language, and retains a number of established language families as distinct (Dravidian, Indo-European, Nilo-Saharan, Niger-Kordofanian, Afroasiatic, Khoisan, Australian, and Sino-Tibetan).

While no linguist would doubt that some similarities among languages are due to genetic relatedness, there are several other possibilities for the explanation of any particular similarity, and before assuming genetic relatedness one must be able to exclude, at least with some degree of plausibility, these other possibilities. Unfortunately, in a great many cases it is not possible to reach a firm and convincing decision. Let us now examine some of the explanations other than genetic relatedness.

First, two languages may happen purely by chance to have some feature in common. For instance, the word for 'dog' in Mbabaram, an Australian Aboriginal language, happens to be *dog*. This Mbabaram word is not, incidentally, a borrowing from English, but is the regular development in Mbabaram of a Proto-Australian form something like **gudaga* (it is usual to prefix reconstructed forms with an asterisk). If anyone were tempted to assume on this basis, however, that English and Mbabaram are genetically related, examination of the rest of Mbabaram vocabulary and grammar would soon quash the genetic relatedness hypothesis, since there is otherwise minimal similarity between the two languages. In comparing English and German, by contrast, there are many similarities at all levels of linguistic analysis. Even sticking to vocabulary, the correspondence *man* : *Mann* can be matched by *wife* : *Weib*, *father* : *Vater*, *mother* : *Mutter*, *son* : *Sohn*, *daughter* : *Tochter*, etc. Given that other languages have radically different words for these concepts (e.g. Japanese *titi* 'father', *haha* 'mother', *musuko* 'son', *musume* 'daughter'), it clearly can not be merely the result of chance that English and German have so many similar items. But if the number of similar items in two languages is small, it may be difficult or impossible to distinguish between chance similarity and distant genetic relatedness.

Certain features shared by two languages might turn out to be manifestations of language universals, i.e. of features that are common to all languages or are inherently likely to occur in any language. Most discussions of language universals require a fair amount of theoretical linguistic background, but for present purposes I will take a simple, if not particularly profound, example. In many languages across the world, the syllable *ma* or its reduplicated form *mama* or some other similar form is the word for 'mother'. The initial syllable *ma* enters into the Proto-Indo-European word for 'mother' which has given English *mother*, Spanish *madre*, Russian *mat´*, Sanskrit *mātā*. In Mandarin Chinese, the equivalent word is *mā*, while in Wiyaw (Papua New Guinea) it is *mam*. Once again, examination of other features of Indo-European languages, Chinese and Wiyaw would soon dispel any possibility of assigning Chinese or Wiyaw to the Indo-European language family. Presumably the frequency across languages of the syllable *ma* in the word for 'mother' simply reflects the fact that this is typically one of the first syllables that babies articulate clearly, and is therefore interpreted by adults as the word for 'mother'. (In the South Caucasian language Georgian, incidentally, *mama* means 'father' — and 'mother' is *deda* — so that there are other ways of interpreting baby's first utterance.)

Somewhat similar to universals are patterns whereby certain linguistic features frequently cooccur in the same language, i.e. where the presence of one feature seems to require or at least to foster the presence of some other feature. For instance, the study of word order universals by Greenberg (1963) showed that if a language has verb-final word order (i.e. if 'the man saw the woman' is expressed literally as 'the man the woman saw'), then it is highly probatle that it will also have postpositions rather than prepositions (i.e. 'in the house' will be expressed as 'the house in') and that it will have genitives before the noun (i.e. the pattern 'cat's house' rather than 'house of cat'). Thus, if we find two languages that happen to share the features: verb-final word order, postpositions, prenominal genitives, then the cooccurrence of these features is not evidence for genetic relatedness. Many earlier attempts at establishing wide-ranging genetic relationships suffer precisely from failure to take this property of typological patterns into account. Thus the fact that Turkic languages, Mongolian languages, Tungusic languages, Korean and Japanese share all of these features is not evidence for their genetic relatedness (although there may, of course, be other similarities, not connected with recurrent typological patterns, that do establish genetic relatedness). If one were to accept just these features as evidence for an Altaic language family, then the family would have to be extended to include a variety of other languages with the same word order properties, such as the Dravidian languages of southern India and Quechua, spoken in South America.

Finally, two languages might share some feature in common because one of them has borrowed it from the other (or because they have both borrowed it from some third language). English, for instance, borrowed a huge number of words from French during the Middle Ages, to such an extent that an uncritical examination of English vocabulary might well lead to the conclusion that English is a Romance language, rather than a Germanic language. The term 'borrow', as used here, is the accepted linguistic term, although the terminology is rather strange, since 'borrow' suggests a relatively superficial acquisition, one which is moreover temporary. Linguistic borrowings may run quite deep, and there is of course no implication that they will ever be repaid. Among English loans from French, for instance, there are many basic vocabulary items, such as *very* (replacing the native Germanic *sore*, as in the biblical *sore afraid*). Examples from other languages show even more deep-seated loans: the Semitic language Amharic — the dominant and official language of Ethiopia — for instance, has lost the typical Semitic word order patterns, in which the verb precedes its object and adjectives and genitives follow their noun, in favour of the order where the verb follows its object and adjectives and genitives precede their noun; Amharic is in close contact with Cushitic languages, and Cushitic languages typically have the order object-verb, adjective/genitive-noun, so that Amharic has in fact borrowed these word orders from neighbouring Cushitic languages.

It seems that whenever two languages come into close contact, they will borrow features from one another. In some cases the contact can be so intense among the languages in a given area that they come to share a significant number of common features, setting this area off from adjacent languages, even languages that may happen to be more closely related genetically to languages within the area. The languages in an area of this kind are often said to belong to a sprachbund (German for 'language league'), and perhaps the most famous example of a sprachbund is the Balkan sprachbund, whose members (Modern Greek, Albanian, Bulgarian (with Macedonian), Rumanian) share a number of striking features not shared by closely related languages like Ancient Greek, other Slavonic languages (Bulgarian is Slavonic), or other Romance languages (Rumanian is Romance). The most striking of these features is loss of the infinitive, so that instead of 'give me to drink' one says 'give me that I drink' (Modern Greek *ðos mu na pjo*, Albanian *a-më të pi*, Bulgarian *daj mi da pija*, Rumanian *dă-mi să beau*; in all four languages the subject of the subordinate clause is encoded in the inflection of the verb).

Since we happen to know a lot about the history of the Balkan languages, linguists were not deceived by these similarities into assigning a closer genetic relatedness to the Balkan languages than in fact holds (all are ultimately members of the Indo-European family, though from different branches). In other parts of the world, however, there is the danger of mistaking areal phenomena for evidence of genetic relatedness. In South-East Asia, for instance, many languages share very similar phonological and morphological patterns: in Chinese, Thai and Vietnamese words are typically monosyllabic, there is effectively no morphology (i.e. words do not change after the manner of English *dog, dogs* or *love, loves, loved*), syllable structure is very simple (only a few single consonants are permitted word-finally, while syllable-initially consonant clusters are either disallowed or highly restricted), and there is a phonemic tone (thus Mandarin Chinese *mā*, with a high level tone, means 'mother', while *mǎ*, with a falling-rising tone, means 'horse'), and moreover there are a number of shared lexical items. For these reasons, it was for a long time believed that Thai and Vietnamese were related genetically to Chinese, as members of the Sino-Tibetan family. More recently, however, it has been established that these similarities are not the result of common ancestry, and Thai and Vietnamese are now generally acknowledged not to be genetically related to Chinese. The similarities are the results of areal contact. The shared vocabulary items are primarily the result of intensive Chinese cultural influence, especially on Vietnamese. The tones and simple syllable structures can often be shown to be the result of relatively recent developments, and indeed in one language that is incontrovertibly related to Chinese, namely Classical Tibetan, one finds complex consonant clusters but no phonemic tone, i.e. the similarities noted above are neither necessary nor sufficient conditions for genetic relatedness.

In practice, the most difficult task in establishing genetic relatedness is to distinguish between genuine cognates (i.e. forms going back to a common ancestor) and those that are the result of borrowing. It would therefore be helpful if one could distinguish between those features of a language that are borrowable and those that are not. Unfortunately, it seems that there is no feature that can absolutely be excluded from borrowing. Basic vocabulary can be borrowed, so that for instance Japanese has borrowed the whole set of numerals from Chinese, and even English borrowed its current set of third person plural pronouns (*they, them, their*) from Scandinavian. Bound morphemes can be borrowed: a good example is the agent suffix *-er* in English, with close cognates in other Germanic languages; this is ultimately a loan from the Latin agentive suffix *-ārius*, which has however become so entrenched in English that it is a productive morphological device applicable in principle to any verb to derive a corresponding agentive noun.

At one period in the recent history of comparative linguistics, it was believed that a certain basic vocabulary list could be isolated, constant across languages and cultures, such that the words on this list would be replaced at a constant rate. Thus, if one assumes that the retention rate is around 86 per cent per millennium, this means that if a single language splits into two descendant languages, then after 1,000 years each language would retain about 86 per cent of the words in the list from the ancestor language, i.e. the two descendants would then share just over 70 per cent of the words in the list. In some parts of the world, groupings based on this 'glottochronological' method still form the basis of the only available detailed and comprehensive attempt at establishing genetic relations. It must be emphasised that the number of clear counter-examples to the glottochronological method, i.e. instances where independent evidence contradicts the predictions of this approach, is so great that no reliance can be placed on its results.

It is, however, true that there are significant differences in the ease with which different features of a language can be borrowed. The thing that seems most easily borrowable is cultural vocabulary, and indeed it is quite normal for a community borrowing some concept (or artifact) from another community to borrow the foreign name along with the object. Another set of features that seem rather easily borrowable are general typological features, such as word order: in addition to the Amharic example cited above, one might note the fact that many Austronesian languages spoken in New Guinea have adopted the word order where the object is placed before the verb, whereas almost all other Austronesian languages place the object after the verb; this change occurred under the influence of Papuan languages, almost all of which are verb-final. Basic vocabulary comes next. And last of all one finds bound morphology. But even though it is difficult to borrow bound morphology, it is not impossible, so in arguments over genetic relatedness one cannot exclude *a priori* the possibility that even affixes may have been borrowed.

2   Languages of East and South-East Asia

While the genetic relations among the languages of East and South-East Asia are much clearer today than even a few years ago, in particular now that there is a better understanding of which similarities are due to areal contact rather than genetic relatedness, a number of controversial areas nonetheless remain. In mainland South-East Asia, there are three main families: Austro-Asiatic, Tai and Sino-Tibetan. While a number of Austro-Asiatic languages are scattered from central India eastwards to Vietnam, the languages of this family with most speakers are spoken in South-East Asia: Vietnamese in Vietnam and Khmer (Cambodian) in Cambodia, these being the only languages of the family to have the status of official languages. The assignment of some languages to Austro-Asiatic is controversial, and it is only recently that the assignment of Vietnamese to this family has gained widespread acceptance. The Tai family, or more accurately the Kadai family (comprising Tai and some other smaller languages), which includes Thai (Siamese) and Lao, was earlier often considered a branch of Sino-Tibetan, but this view has now been largely rejected; the languages are spoken in Thailand, Laos, southern China and also in parts of Burma and Vietnam. Sino-Tibetan contains the language with the largest number of speakers in the world today, Chinese (and this remains true even if one divides Chinese into several different languages, in which case Mandarin occupies first position). The other Sino-Tibetan languages form the Tibeto-Burman branch, which includes Tibetan and Burmese, in addition to a vast number of languages spoken predominantly in southern China, Burma, northern India and Nepal. Whether the Miao-Yao languages, spoken in southern China and adjacent areas, are to be assigned to the Sino-Tibetan family remains controversial.

In East Asia there are also two language isolates, Korean and Japanese, whose genetic affiliations to each other or to other languages (such as Altaic) remain the subject of at times heated debate.

The Austronesian family (formerly called Malayo-Polynesian), though including some languages spoken on the Asian mainland, such as Malay of the Malay peninsula and Cham spoken in Cambodia and Vietnam, comprises predominantly languages of the islands stretching eastwards from the South-East Asian mainland: even Malay-Indonesian has more speakers in insular South-East Asia than on the Malay peninsula.

Austronesian languages are dominant on most of the islands from Sumatra in the west to Easter Island in the east, including the Philippines, but excluding New Guinea (where Austronesian languages are, however, spoken in many coastal areas); Malagasy, the language of Madagascar, is a western outlier of the family; Austronesian languages are also indigenous to Taiwan, though now very much in the minority relative to Chinese.

3 The Social Interaction of Languages

As was indicated in the Preface, the notion of 'major language' is defined in social terms, so it is now time to look somewhat more consistently at some notions relating to the social side of language, in particular the social interaction of languages. Whether a language is a major language or not has nothing to do with its structure or with its genetic affiliation, and the fact that so many of the world's major languages are Indo-European is a mere accident of history.

First, we may look in more detail at the criteria that serve to define a language as being major. One of the most obvious criteria is the number of speakers, and certainly in making my choice of languages to be given individual chapters number of speakers was one of my main criteria. However, number of speakers is equally clearly not the sole criterion.

An interesting comparison to make here is between Chinese (or even more specifically, Mandarin) and English. Mandarin has far more native speakers than English, yet still English is generally considered a more useful language in the world at large than is Mandarin, as seen in the much larger number of people studying English as a second language than studying Mandarin as a second language. One of the reasons for this is that English is an international language, understood by a large number of people in many different parts of the world; Mandarin, by contrast, is by and large confined to China, and even taking all Chinese dialects (or languages) together, the extension of Chinese goes little beyond China and overseas Chinese communities. English is not only the native language of sizable populations in different parts of the world (especially the British Isles, North America, Australia and New Zealand) but it is also spoken as a second language in even more countries. English happens also to be the language of some of the technologically most advanced countries (in particular of the USA), so that English is the basic medium for access to current technological developments. Thus factors other than mere number of speakers are relevant in determining the social importance of a language.

Indeed, some of the languages given individual chapters in this volume have relatively few native speakers. Some of them are important not so much by virtue of the number of native speakers but rather because of the extent to which they are used as a lingua franca, as a second language among people who do not share a common first language. Good examples here are Swahili and Malay. Swahili is the native language of a relatively small population, primarily on the coast of East Africa, but its use as a lingua franca has spread through much of East Africa (especially Kenya and Tanzania), and even stretches into parts of Zaire. Malay too is the native language of relatively few people in western Malaysia and an even smaller number in Indonesia, but its adoption as the lingua franca and official language of both countries has raised the combined first and second language speakers to well over a hundred million. In many instances, in my choice of languages I have been guided by this factor rather than by raw statistics. Among the Philippine languages, for instance, Cebuano has more native speakers than Tagalog, but I selected Tagalog because it is both the national language of the Philippines and used as a lingua franca across much of the country. Among the Indonesian languages, Javanese has more native speakers than Malay and is also the bearer of an old culture, but in terms of the current social situation Malay is clearly the dominant language of this branch of Austronesian. A number of other Indo-Aryan languages would surely have qualified for inclusion in terms of number of speakers, such as Marathi, Rajasthani, Panjabi, Gujarati, but they have not been assigned individual chapters because in social terms the major languages of the northern part of South Asia are clearly Hindi-Urdu and Bengali.

Another important criterion is the cultural importance of a language, in terms of the age and influence of its cultural heritage. An example in point is provided by the Dravidian languages, where Telugu actually has more speakers than Tamil; Tamil, however, is the more ancient literary language, and for this reason my choice rested with Tamil. I am aware that many of these decisions are in part subjective, and in part dangerous: as I emphasised in the Preface, the thing furthest from my mind is to intend any slight to speakers of languages that are not considered major in the contents of this volume.

Certain languages are major even despite the absence of native speakers, as with Latin and Sanskrit. Latin has provided a major contribution to all European languages, as can be seen most superficially in the extent to which words of Latin origin are used in European languages. Even those languages that have tried to avoid the appearance of Latinity by creating their own vocabulary have often fallen back on Latin models: German *Gewissen* 'conscience', for instance, contains the prefix *ge-*, meaning 'with', the stem *wiss-*, meaning 'know', and the suffix *-en* to form an abstract noun — an exact copy of the Latin *con-sci-entia*; borrowings that follow the structure rather than the form in this way are known as calques or loan translations. Sanskrit has played a similar role in relation to the languages of India, including Hindi. Hebrew is included not because of the number of its speakers — this has never been large — but because of the contribution of Hebrew and its culture to European and Middle Eastern society.

A language can thus have influence beyond the areas where it is the native or second language. A good example to illustrate this is Arabic. Arabic loans form a large part of the vocabulary of many languages spoken by Islamic peoples, even of languages that are genetically only distantly related to Arabic (e.g. Hausa) or that are genetically totally unrelated (e.g. Turkish, Persian and Urdu). The influence of Arabic can also be seen in the adoption of the Arabic writing system by many Islamic peoples. Similarly, Chinese loan words form an important part of the vocabulary of some East Asian languages, in particular Vietnamese, Japanese and Korean; the use of written Chinese characters has also spread to Japan and Korea, and in earlier times also to Vietnam.

It is important to note also that the status of a language as a major language is far from immutable. Indeed, as we go back into history we find many significant changes. For instance, the possibility of characterising English as the world's major language is an innovation of the twentieth century. One of the most important shifts in the distribution of major languages resulted from the expansion of European languages, especially English, Spanish, Portuguese, and to a lesser extent French as a result of the colonisation of the Americas: English, Spanish and Portuguese all now have far more native speakers in the New World than in Britain, Spain or Portugal. Indeed, in the Middle Ages one would hardly have imagined that English, confined to an island off the coast of Europe, would have become a major international language.

In medieval Europe, Latin was clearly the major language, since, despite the lack of native speakers, it was the lingua franca of those who needed to communicate across linguistic boundaries. Yet the rise of Latin to such preeminence — which includes the fact that Latin and its descendants have ousted virtually all other languages from southwestern Europe — could hardly have been foreseen from its inauspicious beginnings confined to the area around Rome. Equally spectacular has been the spread of Arabic, in the wake of Islamic religious zeal, from being confined to the Arabian peninsula to being the dominant language of the Middle East and North Africa.

In addition to languages that have become major languages, there are equally languages that have lost this status. The earliest records from Mesopotamia, often considered the cradle of civilisation, are in two languages: Sumerian and Akkadian (the latter the language of the Assyrian and Babylonian empires); Akkadian belongs to the Semitic branch of Afroasiatic, while Sumerian is as far as we can tell unrelated to any other known language. Even at the time of attested Sumerian inscriptions, the language was probably already approaching extinction, and it continued to be used in deference to tradition (as with Latin in medieval Europe). The dominant language of the period was to become Akkadian, but in the intervening period this too has died out, leaving no direct descendants. Gone too is Ancient Egyptian, the language of the Pharaohs. The linguistic picture of the Mediterranean and Middle East in the year nought was very different from that which we observe today.

Social factors and social attitudes can even bring about apparent reversals in the family-tree model of language relatedness. At the time of the earliest texts from Germany, two distinct Germanic languages are recognised: Old Saxon and Old High German. Old Saxon is the ancestor of the modern Low German (Plattdeutsch) dialects, while Old High German is the ancestor of the modern High German dialects and of the standard language. Because of social changes — such as the decline of the Hanseatic league, the economic mainstay of northern Germany — High German gained social ascendancy over Low German. Since the standard language, based on High German, is now recognised as the standard in both northern and southern Germany, both Low and High German dialects are now considered dialects of a single German language, and the social relations between a given Low German dialect and standard German are in practice no different from those between any High German dialect and standard German.

One of the most interesting developments to have arisen from language contact is the development of pidgin and creole languages. A pidgin language arises from a very practical situation: speakers of different languages need to communicate with one another to carry out some practical task, but do not speak any language in common and moreover do not have the opportunity to learn each other's languages properly. What arises in such a situation is, initially, an unstable pidgin, or jargon, with highly variable structure — considerably simplified relative to the native languages of the people involved in its creation — and just enough vocabulary to permit practical tasks to be carried out reasonably successfully. The clearest examples of the development of such pidgins arose from European colonisation, in particular from the Atlantic slave trade and from indenturing labourers in the South Pacific. These pidgins take most of their vocabulary from the colonising language, although their structures are often very different from those of the colonising language.

At a later stage, the jargon may expand, particularly when its usefulness as a lingua franca is recognised among the speakers of non-European origin, leading to a stabilised pidgin, such as Tok Pisin, the major lingua franca of Papua New Guinea. This expansion is on several planes: the range of functions is expanded, since the pidgin is no longer restricted to uses of language essential to practical tasks; the vocabulary is expanded as a result of this greater range of functions, new words often being created internally to the pidgin rather than borrowed from some other language (as with Tok Pisin *maus gras* 'moustache', literally 'mouth grass'); the structure becomes stabilised, i.e. the language has a well defined grammar.

Throughout all of this development, the pidgin has no native speakers. The next possible stage (or this may take place even before stabilisation) is for the pidgin to 'acquire native speakers'. For instance, if native speakers of different languages marry and have the pidgin as their only common language, then this will be the language of their household and will become the first language of their children. Once a pidgin has acquired native speakers, it is referred to as a creole. The native languages of many inhabitants of the Caribbean islands are creoles, for instance the English-based creole of Jamaica, the French-based creole of Haiti, and the Spanish- and/or Portuguese-based creole Papiamentu (Papiamento) of the Netherlands Antilles (Aruba, Bonaire and Curaçao). At an even later stage, social improvements and education may bring the creole back into close contact with the European language that originally contributed much of its vocabulary. In this situation, the two languages may interact and the creole, or some of its varieties, may start approaching the standard language. This gives rise to the so-called post-creole continuum, in which one finds a continuous scale of varieties of speech from forms close to the original creole (basilect) through intermediate forms (mesolect) up to a slightly regionally coloured version of the standard language. Jamaican English is a good example of a post-creole continuum.

No pidgin or creole language has succeeded in gaining sufficient status or number of speakers to become one of the world's major languages, but pidgin and creole languages provide important insights into the processes that arise from natural language contact. And while it would probably be an exaggeration to consider any of the world's major languages a creole, it is not unlikely that some of the processes that go to create a pidgin or a creole have been active in the history of some of these languages — witness, for instance, the morphological simplification that has attended the development from Old English to Modern English, or from Latin to the modern Romance languages.

A few centuries ago, as we saw above, it would have been difficult to predict the present-day distribution of major languages in the world. It is equally impossible to predict the future. In terms of number of native speakers, it is clear that a major shift is underway in favour of non-European languages: the rate of population increase is much higher outside Europe than in Europe, and while some European languages draw some benefit from this (such as Spanish and Portuguese in Latin America), the main beneficiaries are the indigenous languages of southern Asia and Africa. It might well be that a later version of this series would include fewer of the European languages that are restricted to a single country, and devote more space to non-European languages. Another factor is the increase in the range of functions of many non-European languages: during the colonial period European languages (primarily English and French) were used for most official purposes and also for education in much of Asia and Africa, but the winning of independence has meant that many countries have turned more to their own languages, using these as official language and medium of education. The extent to which this will lead to increase in their status as major languages is difficult to predict — at present, access to the frontiers of scholarship and technology is still primarily through European languages, especially English; but one should not forget that the use of English, French and German as vehicles for science was gained only through a prolonged struggle against what then seemed the obvious language for such writing: Latin. (The process may go back indefinitely: Cicero was criticised for writing philosophical treatises in Latin by those who thought he should have used Greek.) But at least I hope to have shown the reader that the social interaction of languages is a dynamic process, one that is moreover exciting to follow.

Bibliography

The most comprehensive and up-to-date index of the world's languages, with genetic classification, is Grimes (1988), which supersedes Voegelin and Voegelin (1977). A recent valuable work on genetic classification of the world's languages is Ruhlen (1987).

References

Greenberg, J.H. 1963. 'Some Universals of Grammar with Particular Reference to the Order of Meaningful Elements', in J.H. Greenberg (ed.), *Universals of Language* (MIT Press, Cambridge, Mass.), pp. 73–112.

Grimes, B.F. (ed.). 1988. *Ethnologue: Languages of the World* (11th edition) (Summer Institute of Linguistics, Dallas).

Ruhlen, M. 1987. *A Guide to the World's Languages, Volume 1: Classification* (Stanford University Press, Stanford).

Voegelin, C.F. and F.M. 1977. *Classification and Index of the World's Languages* (Elsevier, New York).

1 TAI LANGUAGES

David Strecker

Tai is the most widespread and best known subgroup of the Kadai or Kam-Tai family. Figure 1.1 shows the distribution of the Kadai languages and figure 1.2 shows, in an approximate and oversimplified way, the distribution of the Tai languages (the actual linguistic geography of Tai is very complex, with much overlapping and interpenetration of languages). The Tai group comprises the following branches:

Southwestern, including Ahom (extinct), Khamti, Tai Nuea (Chinese Shan, Dehong Dai), Tai Long (Shan), Khuen, Tai Lue (Xishuangbanna Dai), Kam Muang (Tai Yuan, Northern Thai), Thai (Siamese, Central Thai), Southern Thai, Lao (Lao dialects in Thailand are also called 'Northeastern Thai'), White Tai, Tai Dam (Black Tai), Red Tai and several other languages which could not be shown in figure 1.2 for lack of space.

Central, an extraordinarily diverse group of dialects known by such names as Tay, Nung and Tho.

Northern, including the languages officially known in China as Bouyei (Buyi) and Zhuang (these actually appear to constitute a dialect continuum, and the name *Zhuang* is also, confusingly, applied to certain Central dialects) and the Yay language in Vietnam.

Saek, generally treated as a Northern Tai language, but showing certain phonological peculiarities that set it apart from all other Tai languages, including Northern.

The total number of native speakers of Tai languages is probably somewhere in the neighbourhood of 60 or 70 million. The largest number of speakers live in Thailand, perhaps somewhere in the neighbourhood of 45 million or more (including speakers both of Thai and of other Tai languages) and the next largest number live in China, about 15 million. Smaller numbers of Tai speakers live in the other countries shown in figure 1.2, perhaps something like five or six million altogether. To this we should add maybe a million or more Tai speakers living in the USA, France and other Western countries, including both many refugees from the Indochinese War and many who emigrated under peaceful circumstances.

Map 1.1: The Kadai Language Family

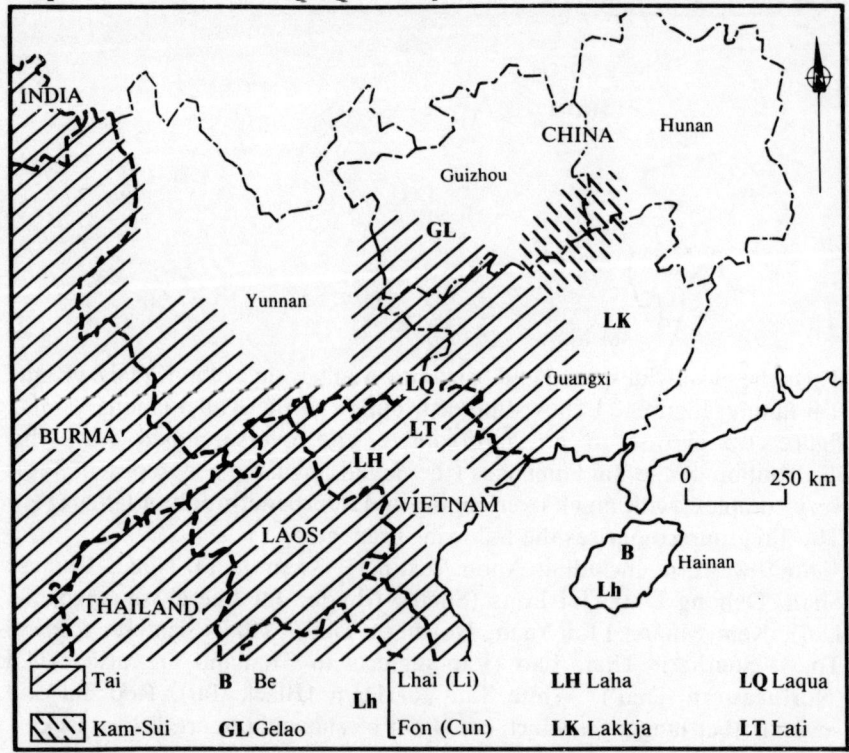

The name *Tai* or *Thai* is the name by which speakers of many, though not all, Southwestern and Central Tai languages call themselves. In accordance with regular rules of sound correspondence, the name is pronounced with either an unaspirated or aspirated *t*, depending on the particular language. Earlier writers on comparative Tai usually called the family *Thai*, but most Tai specialists nowadays call it *Tai*. The form *Thai* nowadays usually refers to one particular Tai language, the national language of Thailand. Some writers, notably A.-G. Haudricourt, restrict the term *Tai* to the Southwestern and Central branches of Tai, but I will follow the usage of F.-K. Li, W. Gedney and others and use *Tai* for the whole group, including the Northern branch.

In phonology and syntax the Tai languages differ from one another about as much as do the Romance languages. The same applies to much of their basic lexicon; for more abstract and technical vocabulary the languages of Vietnam, Guangxi and Guizhou tend to borrow from Chinese whereas those further to the west tend to borrow from Sanskrit and Pali. There is also surprising diversity in grammatical morphemes (e.g. prepositions and aspect and mood particles) and in certain common words such as 'to speak' and 'delicious', which contributes greatly to mutual unintelligibility among Tai

Map 1.2: Approximate General Location of Some Tai Languages

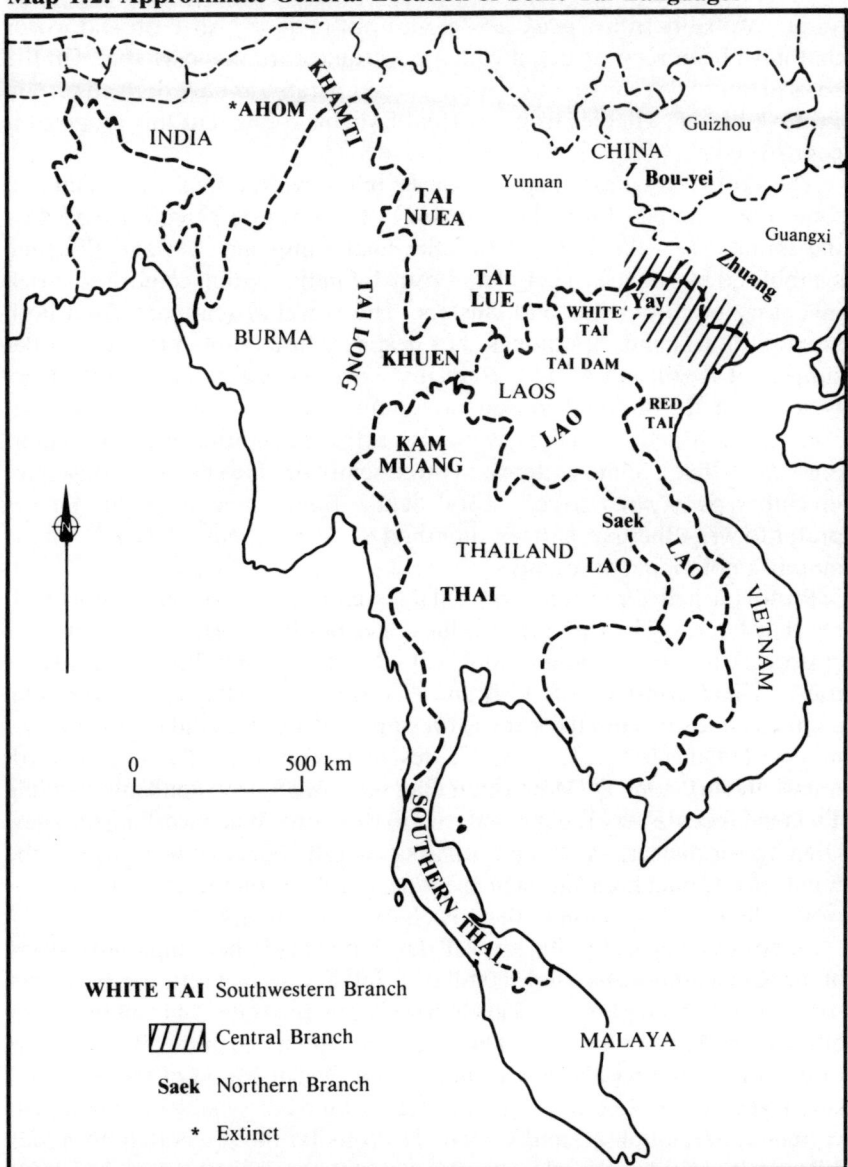

languages that in most respects are very close. Certain words serve to identify the different branches of the Tai family. For example *kuk* or *kuuk* is a characteristic Northern Tai word for 'tiger'; Southwestern and Central Tai use a different word, represented by Thai *sǐa* and its cognates.

In Tai languages, as in many other South-East Asian languages, most words are monosyllabic. All the exceptions to this rule in Tai languages seem to be either loanwords or reduced compounds, such as Kam Muang *pàtŭu* 'door', probably from **pàak tŭu* 'mouth of the door'. All Proto-Tai words that have been reconstructed with any certainty are monosyllabic. On the basis of internal reconstruction some Tai comparativists have derived certain Proto-Tai monosyllables from pre-Tai bisyllabic forms, but this proposal is controversial.

The Proto-Tai syllable had four parts: initial, vowel, final consonant and tone. For example, Proto-Tai **thraam^A*, 'two or more persons carry', had the initial **thr-*, the vowel **-aa-*, the final consonant **-m* and the tone symbolised by superscript A. The Proto-Tai initial system comprised a rich inventory of consonants and clusters. The vowel system comprised both monophthongs and diphthongs, but despite considerable research on the subject, it is still not at all certain just how many different vowel nuclei Proto-Tai had. The final consonant system was very simple: **-p*, **-t*, **-k*, **-m*, **-n*, **-ŋ* and **-l*. There were also syllables with no final consonant, e.g. **haa^C* 'five'. Some writers add three semi-vowels to the final consonant inventory, as in **pay^A* 'to go', **ʔbay^A* 'leaf', **ʔbaw^A* 'light in weight'. Others prefer to write these as parts of diphthongs: **pai^A*, **ʔbai^A*, **ʔbau^A*. This is merely a notational difference.

Proto-Tai had three tones on syllables ending in a vowel, semi-vowel, nasal or lateral. Their phonetic values have not been determined, and it is customary to refer to them simply as A, B and C. (A few Tai comparativists use 0, 1 and 2 instead of A, B and C.) Stop-final syllables had no tonal contrasts but since tonal contrasts on stop-final syllables did develop in the modern languages it is convenient to designate stop-final syllables as a fourth tonal category, tone D. More often than not, tonal correspondences among Tai languages are very regular and easy to work out. When working on a new language or dialect, Tai comparativists generally begin by working out the tonal correspondences and then use tone as a check on the accuracy of their work when they move on to the vowels and consonants.

Although comparative Tai is a well developed field, the comparative study of the Kadai family as a whole is still in its infancy, so that little can be said at the moment about phonological changes which separate Tai from the other branches of Kadai. One thing which has been discussed in the literature has to do with initial nasals. For example, Sui, which is one of the Kam-Sui languages, has no less than three different kinds of syllable-initial nasals: voiceless, preglottalised and voiced. In Proto-Tai the preglottalised nasals fell together with the voiceless nasals, so that Proto-Tai had only two types of syllable-initial nasals, voiceless and voiced, for example:

	Sui	*Proto-Tai*
'dog'	m̥a^1	**m̥aa^A
'mark'	ʔme^1	**m̥aay^A
'yam'	man^2	**man^A

We may now move on to changes specifically within the Tai group. In the development from Proto-Tai to the modern Tai languages, one change which occurs in all languages is the Great Tone Split. What happened was that in each Tai language, tones developed different allotones conditioned by the manner of articulation of the initial consonant of the syllable. Then certain consonants fell together so that these originally allophonic tonal distinctions became contrastive, as for example in the words for 'face' and 'mother's younger sibling' in Thai:

	Proto-Tai	Thai
'face'	*n̥aa^C	nâa (falling tone)
'mother's younger sibling'	*naa^C	náa (high tone)

Notice that in Proto-Tai, 'face' and 'mother's younger sibling' had the same tone but different initials whereas in modern Thai they have the same initial but different tones. Thus the overall effect of the Great Tone Split has been to cause modern Tai languages to have fewer initials and more tones than Proto-Tai did. The Great Tone Split was a South-East Asian areal change, affecting not only Tai but also most other Kadai languages, most Hmong-Mien languages, Chinese, many Tibeto-Burman languages, Vietnamese and so forth. Some Southwestern Tai languages are written in orthographies that were developed before the Great Tone Split took place, so that in Thai, for example, 'face' and 'mother's younger sibling' are spelled หน้า {hn̥aa} and น้า {n̥aa} respectively, with the same tonal diacritic, ʼ, but different initials: {hn} versus {n}.

The major phonological differences among the different branches of the Tai family include:

(1) differences in tone reflecting an earlier difference between a voiced initial in one group of dialects versus a voiceless initial in others,
(2) differences in vowels.

The examples in the chart given here illustrate the tonal differences.

	Thai (SW)	Longzhou (Central)	Yay (Northern)	Proto-Tai
'to plough'	thǎy (rising)	thay^1 (mid level)	say^1 (mid-low level)	*thlay^A
'to reach, arrive'	thǐŋ (rising)	thəŋ^1 (mid level)	taŋ^4 (high rising-falling)	---
'to smear, paint'	thaa (mid)	taa^2 (mid falling)	taa^4 (high rising-falling)	*daa^A

All three words appear to have had tone A in Proto-Tai. After voiceless aspirated stops, tone A became Thai rising tone, Longzhou mid level tone and Yay mid-low level tone, as in 'to plough'. After voiced stops it became Thai mid, Longzhou mid falling and Yay high rising-falling, as in 'to smear'. The problem is determining the initial of 'to reach': in Southwestern and Central Tai this word has the tone which developed after voiceless aspirated stops, as if from Proto-Tai *thiŋ^A, whereas in Northern Tai it has the tone which developed after voiced stops, as if from Proto-Tai *diŋ^A. One possibility is that the Proto-Tai form was *dɦiŋ^A, with a murmured stop which subsequently fell together with *d in the Northern branch but with *th in Southwestern and Central.

The problem with vowels is analogous to the problem with tones. Consider the examples 'year', 'fire' and 'to plough' in the chart.

	Thai (SW)	Longzhou (Central)	Yay (Northern)	Proto-Tai
'year'	pii	pii¹	pi¹	*pii^A
'fire'	fay	fay²	fi⁴	---
'to plough'	thǎy	thay¹	say¹	*thlay^A

It is reasonably certain that 'year' had Proto-Tai *ii and that 'to plough' had Proto-Tai *ay, but what about 'fire'? In Southwestern and Central Tai 'fire' regularly rhymes with 'to plough', whereas in Northern Tai it regularly rhymes with 'year'. Some Tai comparativists have proposed a special diphthong in 'fire' and other words showing the same pattern. This diphthong subsequently merged with *ay in Southwestern and Central Tai and with *ii in Northern Tai. Others have suggested that such words as 'fire' were originally bisyllabic. Thus 'fire' might have been something like Proto-Tai *avii^A. In Northern Tai the weak pretonic syllable *a* was simply lost, giving *vii^A, whereas in Southwestern and Central Tai it interacted with the vowel of the tonic syllable, giving *vay^A. Both suggestions are plausible but difficult to prove. The reconstruction of Proto-Tai vowels is perhaps the most controversial and vexing area in comparative Tai.

Since the Tai languages are uninflected, Tai comparativists have not been able to draw upon comparative morphology in the way that Indo-Europeanists have. This has not been a handicap, since the purely phonological comparisons have been extremely fruitful. Almost no research has been done on comparative Tai syntax. One difference which has been noted involves the order of noun, numeral and classifier. In Tai languages of Vietnam, Guangxi and Guizhou the order is usually numeral + classifier + noun, e.g. Tai Dam

sɔŋ¹ fin¹ faa³
two (classifier) cloth
'two pieces of cloth'

It is possible that this is a result of the influence of Chinese, which has the same order. In languages further to the west the order is usually noun + numeral + classifier, e.g. Thai

phâa   sɔ̌ɔŋ   phǐin
cloth   two   (classifier)
'two pieces of cloth'

Amost all Tai languages have subject–verb–object word order, but in Khamti and other Tai languages of northeastern India the order is subject–object–verb, possibly as a result of influence from Tibeto-Burman or Indo-Aryan languages.

Finally, I will say a few words about Tai writing systems. Some Tai languages are not written. Speakers of Saek, for example, are literate in Thai or Lao but do not write their own language. But a good many Tai languages do have written forms. Central Tai languages, and Northern Tai languages in Guangxi and Guizhou, are generally written with Chinese characters. The details are complex: some characters represent a Tai word similar in *meaning* to the Chinese word, others represent a Tai word similar in *sound* to the Chinese word and in still other cases Tai-speakers have coined new characters which are not used in Chinese. Southwestern Tai languages are generally written in alphabetic scripts derived from those of India, usually not directly from Indian scripts but rather via other South-East Asian scripts such as that of Cambodian. A great many such Tai alphabets exist; they are often quite different from one another superficially, but systematic study reveals similar patterns in, for example, the representation of vowels and diphthongs and similarities in the shapes of many letters.

Bibliography

The standard handbook is Li (1977). For the relationship of Tai to Kam-Sui, reference may be made to Li (1965). Tai phonology is treated in Harris and Noss (1972) and Haudricourt (1972). Three valuable collections of articles are Harris and Chamberlain (1975), Gething et al. (1976) and Bickner et al. (Forthcoming).

References

Bickner, R.J., J.F. Hartmann, T.J. Hudak and P. Peyasantiwong (eds.) Forthcoming. *Selected Writings in Tai Linguistics by William J. Gedney* (Center for South and Southeast Asian Studies, Ann Arbor)

Gething, T. W., J.G. Harris and P. Kullavanijaya (eds.) 1976. *Tai Linguistics in Honor of Fang-Kuei Li* (Chulalongkorn University Press, Bangkok)

Harris, J.G. and J.R. Chamberlain (eds.) 1975. *Studies in Tai Linguistics in Honor of William J. Gedney* (Central Institute of English Language, Bangkok)

Harris, J.G. and R.B. Noss (eds.) 1972. *Tai Phonetics and Phonology* (Central Institute of English Language, Bangkok)
Haudricourt, A.G. 1972. *Problèmes de phonologie diachronique* (Société pour l'Étude des Langues Africaines, Paris)
Li, F.-K. 1965. 'The Tai and Kam-Sui Languages', *Lingua*, vol. 14, pp. 148–79.
────── 1977. *A Handbook of Comparative Tai* (University Press of Hawaii, Honolulu)

2 Thai

Thomas John Hudak

1 Historical Background

Thai (Siamese, Central Thai) belongs to the Tai language family, a subgroup of the Kadai or Kam-Tai family. A number of linguists now regard Kam-Tai, along with Austronesian, as a branch of Austro-Tai, although this hypothesis remains controversial. All members of the Tai family derive from a single proto-parent designated as Proto-Tai. Linguistic research has shown the area near the border of northern Vietman and southeastern China as the probable place of origin for the Tai languages. Today the Tai family includes languages spoken in Assam, northern Burma, all of Thailand including the peninsula, Laos, northern Vietnam and the Chinese provinces of Yunnan, Guizhou (Kweichow) and Guangxi (Kwangsi). Linguists, notably Fang Kuei Li, divide these languages into a Northern, a Central, and a Southwestern branch. Others, in particular William J. Gedney and A.-G. Haudricourt, view the Central and Southwestern branch as a single group. In the tripartite division, Thai falls into the Southwestern branch.

Sukhothai, established in central Thailand in the early and mid-thirteenth century, represents the first major kingdom of the Thai. Current theories state that the language spoken in Sukhothai resembled Proto-Tai in tonal structure. This early system consisted of three tones on syllables ending in a long vowel, a semi-vowel or a nasal (*kham pen* 'live syllable' in traditional Thai grammatical terms). On syllables ending in *p*, *t*, *k* or in a glottal stop after a short vowel a fourth tone existed, although these syllables showed no tonal differentiation at all (*kham taay* 'dead syllable' in traditional Thai grammatical terms). While the presence of some type of suprasegmental contrasts is considered conclusive at this early stage of the language, the phonetic nature of these contrasts still remains a matter of speculation. This system prevailed at the time of the creation of the writing system by King Ramkhamhaeng (1275–1317) in the latter part of the thirteenth century.

In 1350 the centre of power shifted from Sukhothai to Ayutthaya. Recent theories, which will not be discussed here for lack of space, claim that the Sukhothai and Ayutthaya dialects underwent different sound changes. These theories, furthermore, claim that Southern Thai evolved from the

Sukhothai dialect and Central Thai or Thai from the Ayutthaya dialect (see Brown 1965). The generally accepted theory, however, holds that Thai descended from the Sukhothai dialect with the following sound changes.

The first of the changes, the sound changes known as the tonal splits, affected all of the languages in the Tai family (see the chapter on Tai languages). Because of the splits, sound systems with three contrasting tones, for example, became systems typically with six tones, two different tones from each of the three earlier tones. In some dialects, however, special characteristics of the dialect created more or fewer tones. Thai, for example, now has five tones. In brief, these shifts resulted when the phonetic nature of the initial consonant of each syllable conditioned an allophonic pitch difference. Subsequent changes in the initial consonant, then, caused these allophonic non-contrastive pitches to become contrastive (see section 2 for details of the early tones and the tone split in Thai). Linguists frequently set a date as early as AD 1000 for these sound changes. For the Thai spoken in Ayutthaya, however, the splits seem to have occurred much later.

Several factors suggest a later date for the splits in Thai. First, late thirteenth-century and early fourteenth-century Ayutthayan poetic compositions appear in the three tone language. Second, Khmer loanwords, which probably entered the language after the Thai conquest of Angkor in 1431, also predate the split. In addition, seventeenth-century descriptions of the Thai alphabet demonstrate that the consonant changes involved with the tonal splits had already taken place by that date. Citing this evidence, Gedney proposes a date sometime between the mid-fifteenth and the mid-seventeeth centuries for the tone splits in Thai.

The Ayutthaya period (1350–1767) also saw large numbers of Sanskrit and Pali words borrowed, although this phenomenon was not strictly limited to this period. These Indic loanwords comprise a large portion of the technical vocabularies for science, government, education, religion and literature. Gedney (1947:1) states that these loanwords are as common in spoken Thai as Latin and Greek forms are in spoken English. Sanskrit and, to a much lesser extent, Pali assume the same cultural importance for Thai as Latin does for English. Many of these loanwords exist in both a short and a long form. The shorter form represents the usual Thai pronunciation: *rát* 'state', *thêep* 'god'. The longer alternant usually, but not always, functions as a combining form: *rátthàbaan* 'government' (latter constituent *baan* 'protector, protection'); *thêepphábùt* 'angel' (latter constituent *bùt* 'son'). Most of these compounds seem to have been formed in modern Thai since they do not appear in either Sanskrit or Pali.

During the Ayutthaya period, Thai began to acquire other characteristics that have led the Thai to regard their language as highly complex and stratified, difficult to acquire even for the very educated. In part, this impression grew because of the Indic loanwords. But far more central to the creation of this image was the proliferation of titles, ranks, pronouns, royal vocabulary and royal kin terminology that reflected the growing stratification and complexity of the society. Although much of the complexity applied only to the court, Thai speakers nevertheless interpreted these changes as changes in their own language.

Many of these new terms had their origin in Sanskrit and Pali. Still others came from Khmer. Khmer institutions had always had an influence on the Thai court and this influence increased when the Thai imported Khmer intelligentsia into Thailand after the fall of Angkor. Royal titles provide a good example of this increasing complexity. Originally, during the Sukhothai period, the Khmer title *khŭn* referred to the king. By the Ayutthaya period, this title applied only to officials and the king had acquired far more elaborate ones. Other changes affected the titles for the king's offspring. Newly created titles included those for children by a royal queen, for children by a non-royal queen and for grandchildren. In the nineteenth century titles for great-grandchildren and great-great-grandchildren were also added.

Royalty who assisted the king in the performance of his duties received another set of titles, the *krom* titles, another Khmer institution. Introduced in the seventeenth century, these titles probably first indicated private administrative units, then ministries and finally departments within the ministries. Non-royalty working in the expanding civil service received a different set of titles, also from the Khmer.

This terminology and the emphasis upon its correct use began to be standardised during the reign of King Mongkut (1851–68). Valuing adherence to ancient patterns that produced a 'correctness' in the language, Mongkut issued decrees and proclamations that formalised place names and titles. In addition to these terms, he directed his attention to function words such as prepositions and adverbs. In a letter to Norodom of Cambodia, he listed the rules for correct pronoun usage. Both King Chulalongkorn (1868–1910) and King Vajiravudh (1910–26) added to the regulating of this system. Among other things, Chulalongkorn wrote a lengthy essay explaining the Thai system of royal titles in his reign and Vajiravudh created titles for the ministries and regulated titles for women. In 1932, the revolution abandoned the nobility and granting of titles, other than to the royal offspring. The Thai perceptions of their language, however, were not altered, and Thai is still regarded as a highly complex and difficult language.

In Thailand, Thai serves as the official national language. It is the language taught and used in the schools, the one used by the media and the one used for all government affairs. According to the 1980 census, 47 million people live in Thailand. An estimated 80 per cent of this total or 37,600,000 people speak Thai. Outside of Bangkok and the central plains, other dialects and languages of the Tai family coexist with the standard: Northern Thai (Kam Muang or Yuan) in the north, Southern Thai in the south and Lao or Northeastern Thai in the north-east. Still other Tai languages such as Lue,

Phuthai and Phuan are spoken as small speech islands in various parts of the country. In addition, Thailand has many minority groups who speak languages that do not belong to the Tai family.

2 Phonology

Spoken Thai divides into clearly marked syllables bounded on either side by juncture. Each syllable consists of a vocalic nucleus and a tone. In addition, an initial consonant, a final consonant or an initial and final consonant may or may not occur. Possible syllable shapes include V, VV, VC, VVC, CV, CVV, CCV, CCVV, CVC, CVVC, CCVC and CCVVC, where VV represents a long vowel.

2.1 Consonants

Table 2.1 lists the twenty segmental consonant phonemes in Thai.

Table 2.1: Thai Consonants

	Bilabial	Labio-dental	Alveolar	Palatal	Velar	Glottal
Stops						
Vls. unaspirated	p		t	c	k	
Vls. aspirated	ph		th	ch	kh	
Voiced	b		d			
Fricatives		f	s			h
Sonorants						
Nasals	m		n		ŋ	
Lateral			l			
Trill/Tap			r			
Semi-vowels	w			y		

All twenty consonants may appear in initial position. Permitted initial consonant clusters include labials — *pr*, *pl*, *phr*, *phl*; alveolars — *tr*, *thr*; and velars — *kr*, *kl*, *kw*, *khr*, *khl*, *khw*. Only *p t k m n ŋ w y* occur in final position. No consonant clusters exist in final position.

At this point, some elaboration will help to clarify the status of the glottal stop in this description and the general status of /l/ and /r/ in Thai. Because of its predictability, the glottal stop is not listed as a separate phoneme. It appears initially before a vowel that lacks a syllable-initial consonant or consonant cluster: *ʔaahǎan* 'food'. Finally, it appears with the cessation of a short vowel nucleus followed by no final consonant: *tóʔ* 'table'. Internally, in words of more than one syllable, the glottal stop is frequently omitted, particularly at rapid, conversational speed: *pràʔwàt* → *pràwàt* 'history'.

The phonemic status of /l/ and /r/ in Thai appears to be in a state of flux; however, all phonemic descriptions of Thai still list the two sounds as separate phonemes. The writing system, moreover, has separate symbols for each of them. Most Thai, especially the educated, claim to distinguish between the two. This seems to be the case for slow and highly conscious speech. In fast speech, however, /r/ freely alternates with /l/, although certain forms occur more often with /l/ than with /r/. Many speakers regard these alternating forms as indicative of 'less correct' or 'substandard' speech. Linguistic hypotheses suggest that this lack of stable contrast may signal a sound change in process.

2.2 Vowels
Table 2.2 lists the nine vowel phonemes.

Table 2.2: Thai Vowels

	Front	Back unrounded	Back rounded
High	i	ɨ	u
Mid	e	ə	o
Low	ɛ	a	ɔ

Each vowel may occur phonemically short or long. When long, the nuclei may be interpreted as two instances of the corresponding short vowel: *ii, ɨɨ, uu, ee, əə, oo, ɛɛ, aa, ɔɔ*. Phonetically, the long vowels average in duration about twice as long as the short vowels. All 18 vocalic nuclei may occur alone, with an initial consonant, with a final consonant or with an initial and final consonant.

2.3 Diphthongs
Each of the three short and long high vowels may be followed by a centring off-glide *a*. The rare short combinations occupy about as much time as the single short vowels and the long combinations about as much time as the long vowels.

Transcriptions of these diphthongs differ. Some studies make no distinction between the long and the short. Others transcribe the short diphthongs as *ia, ɨa, ua* and the long as *iia, ɨɨa, uua*. Still another interprets the short combination as a single short vowel plus *ə*. Because of the relative rarity of the short diphthongs, this description designates both the short and long forms as a sequence of VV.

Gedney notes (1947:14, 20, 21) that for the short diphthongs only *p, t, c, k, ph, th, ch, kh* seem to appear as initials and only *p, t, k*, as finals. The long diphthongs seem to have no restrictions on the permitted initials and finals.

2.4 Tones
Each syllable in Thai carries one of five phonemic tones. These tones, with

the symbols used in this transcription placed over the first vowel, include: a mid tone (unmarked, *khaa* 'to be lodged in'); a low tone (*khàa* 'a kind of aromatic root'); a falling tone (*khâa* 'servant, slave'); a high tone (*kháa* 'to do business in'); and a rising tone (*khǎa* 'leg'). Tones in Thai may be described in terms of pitch contour, pitch height and glottalised or non-glottalised voice quality.

Table 2.3: Tones in Thai

Tone	Pitch contour	Pitch height	Voice quality
Mid	Level	Medium	Non-glottalised
Low	Level	Low	Non-glottalised
Falling	Falling	High to low	Glottalised
High	Level	High	Glottalised
Rising	Rising	Low to high	Non-glottalised

Based on tonal occurences, syllables can be divided into three types:

(1) Syllables ending in a long vowel, a semi-vowel or a nasal. All five tones occur on these syllables (see above examples).

(2) Syllables ending with a short vowel and a stop or no final. These syllables have either a low or high tone: *phèt* 'to be peppery, spicy'; *kè* 'sheep'; *rák* 'to love'. Occasionally a falling tone occurs: *kɔ̂* 'then, consequently'. The mid and rising tones do not occur on syllables with this structure.

(3) Syllables with a long vowel followed by a stop. These syllables usually have low and falling tones: *pàak* 'mouth', *châat* 'nation'. Occasionally a high tone appears: *nóot* 'note'; *khwɔ́ɔt* 'quart' (both English borrowings). Mid and rising tones never occur on syllables with this structure.

In addition to these five tones, some linguists analyse a variant of the high tone as a sixth tone. Occurring in emphatic exclamations, this tone, higher in pitch and longer than the normal high tone, may replace any one of the five tones: *dīidii* 'very good' (see section 4, page 38).

The historical development of the Thai tonal system has long been of great interest. Early Thai (pre-fifteenth century) had a system of three tones, A, B, C, on syllables ending in a long vowel, a semi-vowel or a nasal. Syllables with no tone mark had the A tone. Syllables with the *máy èek* (') tone mark had the B tone and those with the *máy thoo* (ゞ) tone mark had the C tone. Checked syllables, i.e. those terminating in *p, t, k* or in a glottal after a short vowel, had a fourth tone D, although these syllables actually showed no tonal differentiation at all. It should be noted that these designated tones and tone markers reveal nothing about the phonetic nature of the ancient tones. Although various theories about the tonal phonetics have been offered, the question remains controversial.

Probably between the fifteenth and seventeenth centuries, the tones in each of the categories split, conditioned by the phonetic nature of the initial consonant of each syllable. In some cases, the presence or absence of friction or aspiration caused the split. In others, the conditioning factor was the presence or absence of voicing. For the checked syllables, both the phonetic nature of the initial and the quantity of the nuclear vowel conditioned the split. Table 2.4 summarises these splits.

Table 2.4: Tone Splits in Thai

Initials at time of split	A	B (่)	C (้)	D Short vowel nucleus	D Long vowel nucleus
Voiceless friction: h, ph, hm, etc.	Rising tone	Low tone	Falling tone	Low tone	Low tone
Voiceless unaspirated and glottal	Mid tone				
Voiced		Falling tone	High tone	High tone	Falling tone

Note: This chart does not account for words with *máy trii* (๊) or *máy càttàwaa* (+) tone marks. Words with these tones must have resulted from other changes in the language after the tone splits. Borrowings from other dialects or languages represent other possible sources for these words. The tone marks were created after the words entered the language.

Following the split, some initial consonants also changed, for example voiced consonants to voiceless ones:

*gaa^B → gâa → khâa 'fee, cost'

Originally, both in sound and in spelling, the initial consonant and tone distinguished **gaa^B* from **khaa^C* 'slave, servant'. However as a consequence of the tone split and subsequent changes **gaa^B* changed to *khâa* while *khaa^C* changed to *khâa*. Thus the two forms came to be pronounced exactly alike, but spelled differently. Much of the complication of the spelling system results from these types of sound changes.

2.5 Stress

The question of stress in Thai remains a much debated issue with no consensus whether stress is conditioned by rhythm or rhythm by stress or whether both are phonemic. Most studies agree, however, that the syllable in final position has the greatest prominence or stress. In disyllabic and polysyllabic words, the remaining vowels are reduced, although the reduced vowel may not be as short as a phonemically short vowel. Tone neutralisation may also occur with the vowel reduction.

3 Writing System

The Thai writing system uses as a base an Indic alphabet originally designed to represent the sounds of Sanskrit. King Ramkhamhaeng (1275–1317) of Sukhothai generally receives credit for creating the new alphabet some time prior to AD 1283, the date of the earliest extant inscription written in the alphabet. Borrowing the alphabet then in use by the Khmers, Ramkhamhaeng kept the symbols for the Sanskrit sounds not found in Thai and used them in Indic loanwords to reflect the origin of their pronunciation. For Thai sounds not accommodated by the alphabet, he created new symbols, including those for tones. Because of the redesigning of the

Table 2.5: Consonants (Adapted from Brown vol. 3, 1967: 211)

Mid	Mid	High	High	Low	Low	Low	Low	Low	High	
ก	ข	ฃ	ค	ฅ	ฆ	ง				
k	kh	kh	kh	kh	kh	ŋ				High
										ห
										h
	จ	ฉ	ช	ซ	ฌ	ญ	ย	ศ		
	c	ch	ch	s	ch	y	y	s		Low
										ฬ
										l
ฎ	ฏ	ฐ	ฑ		ฒ	ณ	ร	ษ		
d	t	th	th		th	n	r	s		Mid
										อ
										ʔ
ด	ต	ถ	ท		ธ	น	ล	ส		
d	t	th	th		th	n	l	s		Low
										ฮ
										h
บ	ป	ผ	ฝ	พ	ฟ	ภ	ม	ว		
b	p	ph	f	ph	f	ph	m	w		

symbols to fit Khmer first and then to fit Thai, the eventual system created by Ramkhamhaeng had little resemblance to the Sanskrit originals.

The two types of symbols in the alphabet resulted in a system characterised by several symbols for the same sound. The division of the consonants into three groups (high, mid, low) to indicate tone in spelling further complicated the system. High class consonants represent the original voiceless aspirated sounds, the mid class represent the original voiceless non-aspirated and the preglottalised voiced sounds and the low class represent the original voiced sounds.

Table 2.5 lists the 44 consonants in their alphabetic arrangement and in their consonant classes. To read the chart, proceed from left to right until the solid line, then move to the next line. At the completion of the first section (ม), move up to the beginning of the next section (ย) and continue as before. Table 2.6 lists the symbols for the 18 vowels and the six diphthongs. A ค indicates an initial consonant and a น a non-specific final.

Table 2.6: Vowels (Adapted from Brown vol. 3, 1967: 212)

	Long			Short					
	With final		Without	With final				Without final	
	y	Other	final	y	w	m	Other		
a		คา		ไค	ใค	เคา	คำ	คัน	คะ	ค
ə	เคย	เคิน	เคอ					เคอะ	
e		เค			เค็น			เคะ	
o		โค			คน			โคะ	
ua	ควน		คัว		*			คัวะ	
ia		เคีย			*			เคียะ	
ɨa		เคือ			*			เคือะ	
ɛ		แค			แค็น			แคะ	
ɔ		คอ			คอน			เคาะ	
ɨ	คืน		คือ		คึ				
i		คี			คิ				
u		คู			คุ				

*Note: This chart does not include the symbols for the rare short diphthongs plus final consonant.

Table 2.7 shows the five tones as they appear on each of the syllable types in each of the three consonant groups.

Table 2.7: Syllable Types, Consonant Classes and Their Respective Tones (Adapted from Brown vol. 3, 1967: 213)

Syllables with final long vowel, m, n, ŋ, w, y

Consonant class	Tone mark: No mark	◌̀ Low tone mark	◌̂ Falling tone mark	◌́ High tone mark	◌̌ Rising tone mark
High	Rising tone	Low tone	Falling tone		
Mid	Mid tone	Low tone	Falling tone	Low tone	Rising tone
Low	Mid tone	Falling tone	High tone		

Syllables ending with final p, t, k or syllables ending with short vowel and no final

	Short vowel*	Long vowel**
High		
Mid	Low tone	
Low	High tone	Falling tone

Notes: *In rare instances, a falling tone will appear on a syllable with a short vowel ending in a *p*, *t* or *k*. **In rare instances, a high tone will appear on a syllable with a long vowel ending in *p*, *t* or *k*.

4 Morphology

Thai has no inflections for case, gender, tense or number. Affixing, compounding and reduplicating represent the major derivational processes.

4.1 Affixing

Derivatives may be formed with a few prefixes and suffixes. The more common affixes include:

1. *kaan-* 'the act of, affairs of, matter of' forms abstract nouns from verbs and some nouns: e.g. *lên* 'to play', *kaanlên* 'playing'; *miaŋ* 'city', *kaanmiaŋ* 'politics'.

2. *khwaam-* 'the condition of' forms abstract nouns that express a quality or state: e.g. *rúusìk* 'to feel'; *khwaamrúusìk* 'feeling'.
3. *khîi-* 'characterised by': e.g. *bòn* 'to complain'; *khîibòn* 'given to complaining'.
4. *khrîaŋ-* 'a collection, equipment': e.g. *khǐan* 'to write'; *khrîaŋkhǐan* 'stationery'.
5. *nâa-* 'worthy of': e.g. *rák* 'to love'; *nâarák* 'cute, lovable'.
6. *nák-* 'expert, authority': e.g. *rian* 'to study'; *nákrian* 'student'.
7. *-sàat* 'branch, field of knowledge': e.g. *daaraa* 'star'; *daaraasàat* 'astronomy'.

4.2 Compounding
Compounds in Thai are endocentric constructions in which the first constituent generally determines the syntactic word class. Compounds may be coordinate or attributive. Coordinate nouns include *phɔ̂ɔmɛ̂ɛ* 'parents' (*phɔ̂ɔ* 'father' + *mɛ̂ɛ* 'mother'); *phîinɔ́ɔŋ* 'brothers and sisters' (*phîi* 'older sibling' + *nɔ́ɔŋ* 'younger sibling'). Coordinate verbs include *hǔŋtôm* 'to cook' (*hǔŋ* 'to cook rice' + *tôm* 'to boil food'); *ráprúu* 'to acknowledge, take responsibility' (*ráp* 'to take, accept' + *rúu* 'to know'). Attributive compounds include *námkhɛ̌ŋ* 'ice' (*nám* 'water' + *khɛ̌ŋ* 'to be hard'); *rótfay* 'train' (*rót* 'vehicle, car' + *fay* 'fire').

4.3 Reduplication
Three general types of reduplication occur in Thai: reduplication of a base form with no changes, ablauting reduplication and reduplication with an accompanying change in tone.

Reduplication of the base conveys several different meanings: softens the base, *dii* 'good' → *diidii* 'rather good'; indicates plurality, *dèk* 'child' → *dèkdèk* 'children'; forms imitatives, *khɛ́k* 'to knock' → *khɛ́kkhɛ́k* 'rapping sound'; intensifies meaning, *ciŋ* 'to be true' → *ciŋciŋ* 'really'.

Examples of ablauting reduplication include: (1) the alternation of a back vowel with its corresponding front vowel, *yûŋ* 'to be confused' → *yûŋyîŋ*; *soosee* 'to stagger'; and (2) the alternation of any vowel with *a*, *chaŋ* 'to hate' → *chiŋchaŋ* 'to hate, detest, loathe'.

Reduplication with an accompanying change in tone generally signifies emphasis in speech. Used more often by women than men, the intensified form consists of the base word with any of the five tones preceded by the reduplication which carries a high tone higher in pitch and longer than the normal high tone: *dii* 'good' → *dīidii* 'really good'.

4.4 Elaborate Expressions
Elaborate expressions, a common South-East Asian areal feature, represent a special type of compounding achieved through the reduplication of part of a compound and the addition of a new part. Usually the expression consists

of four syllables, with the repeated elements the first and third syllable or the second and fourth.

    tɨ̀ɨn   taa tɨ̀ɨn   cay
    to wake eye to wake heart
    'to be full of wonder and excitement'

Frequently rhyme occurs as part of the expression, in which case the second and third syllables rhyme.

    hǔu pàa   taa thìan
    ear forest eye forest
    'to be ignorant of what is going on'

The new syllable may be added solely for rhyme and/or it may have some semantic relationship to the original part.

For the Thai, the ability to use elaborate expressions is an essential quality of speaking well and fluently (*phayrɔ́*). Attempts to classify the expressions according to the structure and semantics of the components have largely been unsuccessful.

5 Syntax

Subject–verb–object, in that order, constitutes the most favoured word order in Thai:

    khǎw sɨ́ɨ   aahǎan
    he   buy food
    'He buys food.'

Both subject and object may be filled with: (1) a noun phrase consisting of a noun, a pronoun, a demonstrative pronoun or an interrogative-indefinite pronoun; or (2) a noun phrase consisting of noun + attribute in which case the head noun always precedes the attribute. Noun + attribute constructions may be simple or complex. Predicates may be nominal or verbal, simple or complex.

5.1 Noun Phrases

5.1.1 Nouns
Nouns form one of the largest classes of words in the vocabulary, the other being the verbs. Single nouns may occupy the subject or object position (see above example). Typically nouns occur as the head of noun expressions (see noun + attribute).

5.1.2 Pronouns

Like many other South-East Asian languages, Thai exhibits a complex pronoun system. The choice of pronoun used in any one situation depends upon factors such as sex, age, social position and the attitude of the speaker toward the addressee. In those contexts in which the referent is understood, the pronoun is frequently omitted. Common first and second person singular pronouns include those given in table 2.8.

Table 2.8: First and Second Person Singular Pronouns

Situation	First Person	Second Person
1. Polite conversation with strangers and acquaintances	phǒm (used by male) dìchǎn (used by female)	khun
2. Speaking to a superior, showing deference	phǒm (used by male) dìchǎn (used by female)	thân
3. Informal conversation with close friends and family	chǎn	thəə
4. Conversation between intimates of the same sex	kan	kɛɛ
5. Adult to a child	chǎn or kinship term	nǔu or kinship term
6. Child to adult	nǔu	kinship term
7. Child to older sibling	nǔu	phîi

Fewer choices exist for third person singular pronouns. In general, *man* is used for inferiors, for non-humans and for expressing anger. *khǎw* is the general polite form and *thân* the form for superiors. Additional forms not discussed here are employed for the royalty.

raw, which may be inclusive or exclusive, expresses first person plural. It may also be used to mean 'I' when addressing inferiors or oneself.

Second and third person plural forms are generally expressed by the singular forms.

Kinship terms and other nouns referring to relationships may also be used as pronouns. For example, *mɛ̂ɛ* 'mother' may mean 'you, she' when speaking to or about one's mother or 'I, mother' when the mother speaks to her child. Other terms following this pattern include *phɔ̂ɔ* 'father', *lûuk* 'child', *phîi* 'older sibling', *nɔ́ɔŋ* 'younger sibling', *phîan* 'friend'.

5.1.3 Demonstrative Pronouns

Demonstrative pronouns may occupy positions available to nouns, although they never occur with attributes. These pronouns include *nîi* 'this one', *nân* 'that one', and *nôon* 'that one over there'.

nîi sǔay mâak
this one beautiful much, many
'This one is very beautiful.'

For some speakers, the demonstrative adjectives, *níi* 'this', *nán* 'that', *nóon* 'that over there', also function as demonstrative pronouns.

5.1.4 Interrogative-indefinite Pronouns

In Thai, the interrogatives and indefinite pronouns have the same form. Occurring in the same positions as nouns, these words make a question or an indefinite statement:

khray rian   phaasăa thay
who   study language Thai
'Who's studying Thai?'
mây   mii   khray rian   phaasăa thay
negative have anyone study language Thai
'No one's studying Thai.'

Besides *khray* 'who?, anyone', this group includes *àray* 'what?, anything', *năy* 'which?' *thîi năy* 'where?, anywhere', *day* 'which?, what?, any'.

5.1.5 Noun + Attribute: Simple

Simple attributes consist of single constituents. These constituents may be another noun, a pronoun, a demonstrative adjective or a verb. A noun following the head noun may function as the possessor and the head noun the possessed: *năŋsŭ dèk* ('book child') 'child's book'. A complex noun phrase with the preposition *khɔ̌ɔŋ* 'of' frequently replaces this construction: *năŋsŭ khɔ̌ɔŋ dèk* 'child's book'. *dèk* may also modify the head noun in which case the expression means 'a book for children'. When a pronoun, the attribute functions as a possessive adjective: *mɛ̂ɛ phŏm* ('mother I') 'my mother'. The three demonstrative adjectives, *níi* 'this, these', *nán* 'that, those', and *nóon* 'that, those over there', may also fill the attribute position.

Words considered to be adjectives in English (*sŭay* 'beautiful', *dii* 'good', *yaaw* 'long') may function as nominal attributes, verbal attributes or as predicates. Because these words behave syntactically as verbs without a copula, they are treated here as verbs. Thus, *bâan sŭay* may be translated as 'the house is beautiful' or 'a beautiful house'.

5.1.6 Noun + Attribute: Complex

Complex attributes consist of more than one constituent. The use of classifiers, one of the most characteristic features of Thai syntax, serves to illustrate a typical complex attribute. With quantifiers, classifiers are obligatory, and the usual word order is noun + quantifier + classifier:

dèk   săam khon
child three classifier
'three children'

This regular order changes in two situations. First, when the numeral 'one' is used, the numeral and classifier rearrange to indicate an indefinite meaning: *dèk khon nìŋ* 'a child'. To specify the number of objects, the original order remains: *dèk nìŋ khon* 'one child'. Second, with the verb *hây* 'to give' and an indirect object, the word order following *hây* becomes thing given, person given to, and amount given:

```
khruu    hây   sàmùt      nákrian  săam   lêm
teacher  give  notebook   student  three  classifier
'The teacher gave the student three notebooks.'
```

In each noun + classifier construction, the head noun determines the choice of classifier. Examples include *khon* for human beings, *tua* for animals, tables, chairs, clothes, *lêm* for books, carts, sharp pointed instruments and *muan* for cigars and cigarettes. Although unsuccessful, various attempts have been made to link the nouns semantically with their respective classifiers. When referring to a group, more general classifiers such as *fŭuŋ* 'flock, herd' may be used.

Expanding the attribute forms more complex noun phrases:

```
Noun  Attribute
dèk   săam khon              'three boys'
dèk   lɔɔ săam khon          'three handsome boys'
dèk   lɔɔ săam khon níi      'these three handsome boys'
```

In more precise and particularised speech, a classifier is used between the noun and the following verbal attribute or demonstrative adjective: *dèk khon lɔɔ* 'the handsome boy'; *dèk khon níi* 'this very boy'; *dèk khon lɔɔ săam khon níi* 'these three handsome boys'.

5.2 Predicates

Normal word order places the predicate immediately after the subject. Thai verbs have no inflection for tense or number. Context, added time expressions or preverbs generally specify the tense:

```
khăw  àan   năŋsɨ̈  dĭawníi
he    read  book   now
'He is reading a book now.'
```

mây 'not' negates the verb:

```
khăw mây àan năŋsɨ̈ dĭawníi
'He isn't reading a book now.'
```

Predicates may be nominal or verbal, simple or complex.

5.2.1 Nominal Predicate
In predicates of this type, no verb appears, only a noun phrase.

nîi   rooŋrian   phŏm
this one school   I
'This is my school.'

Far more frequent are verbal predicates.

5.2.2 Verbal Predicate: Simple
Main verbs, the semantics of which roughly correspond to English verbs, form the nucleus of simple predicates.

5.2.3 Verbal Predicate: Complex
Complex verbal predicates consist of a collocation of verbs generally referred to as serial verbs. In complex collocations, the meaning of the main verb is modified by two classes of secondary verbs, one which precedes the main verb and one which follows. The first class of secondary verbs, those that precede the main verb and follow the subject, often translate as English modals or adverbs:

khăw tôŋ   klàp   bâan
he   must   return home
'He must return home.'
khăw yaŋ rian   wíchaa nán
he   still study subject that
'He's still studying that subject.'

Other examples of these verbs include *cà* 'shall, will', *mây* 'not', *khuan* 'should, ought to', *khəəy* 'ever, to have experienced', *àat* 'capable of', *yàak* 'to want to, wish for'. Verbs in this class may occur together in which case their order is fixed.

phŏm mây yàak   cà   rian   wíchaa nán
I   not want to will study   subject that
'I don't want to study that subject.'

The preverb *dây* frequently indicates the past tense: *mây dây pay* 'did not go'.

The second class of secondary verbs follows both transitive and intransitive main verbs.

khăw yók   nâatàaŋ khîn
he   raise window   up   (transitive)
'He raised the window up.'
diŋ   tàbuu   ɔ̀ɔk
pull nail   out   (transitive)
'Pull the nail out'

khǎw	nâŋ	loŋ	
he	sit	down	(intransitive)

'He sat down'

As a class, these verbs have a general meaning of having successfully completed the action begun by the main verb. Other representative examples of this large class include *dâyˆ* 'to be able', *pen* 'to know how to, to do from habit', *wǎy* 'to be physically capable of', *pay* 'action away from the speaker', *maa* 'action toward the speaker', *lɛ́ɛw* 'completed action', *yùu* 'ongoing action'. Many of the secondary verbs may also function as main verbs. As a main verb, *khîn* in the above example, means 'to rise, grow, board, climb'.

Frequently, the collocation may consist of all three types of verbs:

khun cà thon	yùu kàp chaawbâan	wǎy		rɨ́ɨ
you will endure	live with villagers	to be physically capable of		question particle

'Can you stand living with villagers?'

5.2.4 Particles

Thai has a large class of particles that end an utterance. These particles can be divided into three broad groups: question particles, polite particles and mood particles.

Question particles form questions that require a yes-no answer. These questions result when the particle is placed at the end of a statement. Two main particles, alone and in combinations with other words, occur: *máy* and *rɨ́ɨ*.

(a) khun cà pay hǎa phîan máy
   you will go see friend Q-particle
   'Are you going to see a friend?'

In this situation, the speaker has no particular expectation as to what the answer will be.

(b) khun cà pay hǎa phîan rɨ́ɨ
   'Are you going to see a friend?'

With *rɨ́ɨ*, the speaker has reason to believe his assumption is correct, and the addressee will confirm it.

(c) khun cà pay hǎa phîan rɨ́ɨ plàaw
   'Are you going to see a friend or not?'

This question is similar to the first question, with no particular expectation for an answer. Literally, *plàaw* means 'to be empty'. In a question, it means 'or not so'.

(d) khun cà pay hăa phîan chây máy
'You're going to see a friend, aren't you?'

With *châymáy* 'isn't that so', the speaker is quite certain of his statement and expects agreement. This particle is similar to English tag questions.

Polite particles show respect or deference toward the addressee. Marked for gender, these particles include: *khâ* — marks statements by women; *khá* — marks questions by women; *khráp* — marks statements and questions by men.

Mood particles form the third general group of particles. These particles signal the attitude or emotion of the speaker toward the situation at the time of speaking. Representative examples include *nâ* — indicates urging, persuading; *rɔ̀ɔk* — used with negative statements, usually makes a statement milder or corrects a misapprehension; *ləəy* — encourages the addressee to do something; *sí* — softens requests or commands.

All of these particles may be used in clusters in which case their order is fixed.

5.3 Complements
Three examples serve to illustrate complements in Thai.

5.3.1 Relative Clauses
The word *thîi* introduces relative clauses. In literary contexts, *sîŋ* replaces *thîi*, although the exact distribution of these two relative pronouns remains unclear.

dèk thîi rian phaasăa thay maa lɛ́ɛw
child relative study language Thai come already
   pronoun
'The child who is studying Thai has come already.'

5.3.2 Causatives
The verb *hây* 'to give' forms causatives with the result following *hây*.

phŏm cà àthíbaay hây khun khâwcay
I will explain make, give you understand
'I'll explain so you understand.'

5.3.3 Comparative-superlative
kwàa 'more' and *thîisùt* 'most' inserted after the verb form the comparative, (a), and the superlative, (b):

(a) năŋsɨɨ níi yâak kwàa năŋsɨɨ nán
    book this hard more book that
    'This book is harder than that one.'
(b) năŋsɨɨ níi yâak thîisùt
    book this hard most
    'This book is the hardest.'

Bibliography

Brown (1965) presents a theory of sound change in Tai dialects; this is a difficult, but worthwhile work. Noss (1964) is an excellent descriptive grammar, while Brown (1967) is a standard course book in spoken Thai, including separate volumes for reading (1979) and writing (1979). On individual problems, Cooke (1968) is probably the most comprehensive examination of pronouns in Thai available; Haas (1942) is a basic work on classifiers. Warotamasikkhadit (1972) is a generative approach to Thai syntax. Gedney (1961) is a discussion of royal vocabulary.

References

Brown, J.M. 1965. *From Ancient Thai to Modern Dialects* (Social Science Association Press of Thailand, Bangkok)
────── 1967-79. *A.U.A. Center Thai Course*, 5 vols. (A.U.A. Language Center, Bangkok)
Cooke, J.R. 1968. *Pronominal Reference in Thai, Burmese, and Vietnamese* (University of Calfornia Press, Berkeley)
Gedney, W.J. 1947. 'Indic Loanwords in Spoken Thai', Ph.D. dissertation, Yale University
────── 1961. 'Special Vocabularies in Thai', *Georgetown University Institute of Languages Monograph Series on Languages and Linguistics*, vol. 14, pp. 109-14.
Haas, M.R. 1942. 'The Use of Numeral Classifiers in Thai', *Language*, vol. 18, pp. 201-5
Noss, R.B. 1964. *Thai Reference Grammar* (Foreign Service Institute, Washington, DC)
Warotamasikkhadit, U. 1972. *Thai Syntax* (Mouton, The Hague)

3 VIETNAMESE

Đình-Hoà Nguyễn

1 Background

The language described here, known to its native speakers as *tiếng Việt-nam* or simply *tiếng Việt* (literary appellations: *Việt-ngữ* or *Việt-văn*) is used in daily communication over the whole territory of Vietnam, formerly known as Annam (whence the older name for the language, Annamese or Annamite). It is the mother tongue of the ethnic majority called *người Việt* or *người Kinh* — some 57 million inhabitants who live in the delta lowlands of Vietnam, plus over one million overseas Vietnamese, in France, the USA, Canada, Australia etc. The other ethnic groups (Chinese, Cambodians, Indians and the highlanders called 'Montagnards') know Vietnamese and can use it in their contacts with the Vietnamese.

Although Chinese characters were used in literary texts, in which Chinese loanwords also abound (on account of ten centuries of Chinese political domination), Vietnamese is not at all genetically related to Chinese. It belongs rather to the Mon-Khmer stock, within the Austro-Asiatic family, which comprises several major language groups spoken in a wide area running from Chota Nagpur eastward to Indochina.

In comparing Vietnamese and Mường, a language spoken in the highlands of northern and central Vietnam and considered an archaic form of Vietnamese, the French scholar Jean Przyluski maintained that ancient Vietnamese was at least closely related to the Mon-Khmer group of languages, which have no tones but several prefixes and infixes. Another French linguist, Henri Maspéro, was more inclined to include Vietnamese in the Tai family, whose members are all tonal languages. According to Maspéro, modern Vietnamese seems to result from a mixture of many elements, precisely because it has been successively, at different times in its history, at the northern limit of the Mon-Khmer languages, the eastern limit of the Tai languages and the southern boundary of Chinese. More recently, however, the French botanist-linguist A.-G. Haudricourt pointed out the origin of Vietnamese tones, arguing lucidly in his 1954 article that Vietnamese, a member of the Mon-Khmer phylum, had, as a non-tonal language at the beginning of the Christian era, developed three tones by the sixth century, and that by the twelfth century it had acquired all six tones which characterise it today. This explanation of Vietnamese tonogenesis has thus helped us to point conclusively to the true genetic relationship of Vietnamese: its kinship to Mường, the sister language, with which it forms the Vietnamese-Mường group within the Mon-Khmer phylum.

Up to the late nineteenth century, traditional Vietnamese society comprised the four classes of scholars, farmers, craftsmen and merchants. The French colonial administration, which lasted until 1945, created a small bourgeoisie of functionaries, merchants, physicians, lawyers, importers and exporters, etc. within and around the major urban centres. The language of the class of rural workers retains dialect peculiarities, both in grammar and vocabulary, whereas the language of the city dwellers accepts a large number of loanwords from Chinese and from French, the latter having been the official language for more than eighty years. Since 1945, Vietnamese has replaced French as the medium of instruction in all schools of the land.

The history of Vietnamese has been sketched by Maspéro as follows:

(1) Pre-Vietnamese, common to Vietnamese and Mường before their separation;

(2) Proto-Vietnamese, before the formation of Sino-Vietnamese;

(3) Archaic Vietnamese, characterised by the individualisation of Sino-Vietnamese (towards the tenth century);

(4) Ancient Vietnamese, represented by the Chinese-Vietnamese glossary *Hua-yi Yi-yu* (sixteenth century);

(5) Middle Vietnamese of the Vietnamese-Portuguese-Latin dictionary of Alexandre de Rhodes (seventeenth century); and

(6) Modern Vietnamese, beginning in the nineteenth century.

There are three distinct writing systems: (1) Chinese characters, referred to as *chữ nho* 'scholars' script' or *chữ hán* 'Han script'; (2) the demotic characters called *chữ nôm* (from *nam* 'south') 'southern script'; and finally (3) the Roman script called *chữ quốc-ngữ* 'national script'.

Written Chinese characters, shared by Japanese and Korean, the other two Asian cultures that were also under Chinese influence, for a long time served as the medium of education and official communication, at least among the educated classes of scholars and officials. Indeed, from the early days of Chinese rule (111 BC–AD 939) the Chinese rulers taught the natives not only Chinese calligraphy, but also the texts of Chinese history, philosophy and literature.

The so-called Sino-Vietnamese pronunciation is based on the pronunciation of Ancient Chinese, learned first through the spoken language of the rulers, then later through the scholarly writings of Chinese philosophers and poets. The latter constituted the curriculum of an educational system sanctioned by gruelling literary examinations which were designed to recruit a local scholar-gentry class, thus denying education to the vast majority of illiterate peasants.

While continuing to use Chinese to compose regulated verse as well as prose pieces, some of which were real gems of Vietnamese literature in classical *wen-yen*, Buddhist monks and Confucian scholars, starting in the thirteenth century, proudly used their own language for eight-line stanzas or long narratives in native verse blockprinted in the 'southern characters'. The *chữ nôm* system, whose invention definitely dated from the days when Sino-Vietnamese, or the pronunciation of Chinese graphs *à la vietnamienne*, had been stabilised, i.e. around the eleventh century, was already widely used under the Trần dynasty. Samples of these characters, often undecipherable to the Chinese, have been found on temple bells, on stone inscriptions and in Buddhist-inspired poems and rhymed prose pieces. A fairly extensive number of *nôm* characters appeared in Nguyễn Trãi's *Quốc-âm Thi-tập (Collected Poems in the National Language)*, as the seventh volume in the posthumous works of this scholar-poet-strategist involved in the anti-Ming campaign by his emperor Lê Lợi. The charming 254 poems, long thought lost, yield the earliest evidence of Vietnamese phonology, since many characters, roughly including a semantic element and a phonetic element, shed light on fifteenth-century Vietnamese pronunciation, some features of which were later corroborated in the *Dictionarium Annamiticum-Lusitanum-et-Latinum* and a *Catechism for Eight Days* authored by the gifted Jesuit missionary Alexandre de Rhodes and published in Rome in 1651.

Vietnam owes its Roman script to Catholic missionaries, who at first needed some transcription to help them learn the language of their new converts to Christianity, and some of whom succeeded in learning the tonal language well enough to preach in it in the middle of the seventeenth century. The French colonialists saw in this Romanisation an effective tool for the assimilation of their subjects, who, they thought, would through the intermediary transliteration of Vietnamese in Latin letters make a smooth transition to the process of learning the language of the *métropole*. *Quốc-ngữ* proved to be indeed an adequate system of writing, enabling

Table 3.1: Some Examples of Chữ Nôm

Chữ nôm	Modern Vietnamese	Gloss	Comments
才	tài	talent	Chinese character for Sino-Vietnamese *tài* 'talent'.
符	bùa	written charm	Chinese character for Sino-Vietnamese *phù* 'charm'; the reading *bùa* is earlier than the learned *phù*.
爫	làm	do, make	Part of the Chinese character for Sino-Vietnamese *vi* 'act': 爲
没	một	one	Cf. the homophonous Sino-Vietnamese *một* 'die', for which this is the Chinese character.
別	biét	know	Cf. the nearly homophonous Sino-Vietnamese *biệt* 'separate', for which this is the Chinese character.
買〈	mới	new	Cf. the nearly homophonous Sino-Vietnamese *mãi* 'buy'; the chữ nôm is the Chinese character for this Sino-Vietnamese syllable with the addition of the diacritic: 〈.
巴賴	trái	fruit	A compound of the two Chinese characters, with Sino-Vietnamese readings *ba* and *lại*, respectively, to give a pronunciation with initial *bl-*, as recorded in the 1651 dictionary: 巴賴
坙	trời	sky	A semantic compound, using the Chinese characters for, respectively, 'sky' and 'high': 天上
找	quơ	reach for	A combination of, respectively, the Chinese radical for 'hand' (semantic component) and the character with the Sino-Vietnamese reading *qua* (phonetic component): 扌戈
𦰟	cỏ	grass	A combination of, respectively, the Chinese character for 'grass' (semantic component) and the character with the Sino-Vietnamese reading *cổ*: 草古

Vietnamese speakers to learn how to read and write their own language in the space of several weeks. Not only did the novel script assist in the literacy campaign, it also helped the spread of education and the dissemination of knowledge, including information about political and social revolutionary movements in Europe and elsewhere in Asia. Nowadays, *quốc-ngữ*, often called *chữ phổ-thông* 'standard script', serves as the medium of instruction at all three levels of education and has been successfully groomed as the official orthography; both before and after reunification in 1976 conferences and seminars have been held to discuss its inconsistencies and to recommend spelling reforms, to be carried out gradually in the future.

Maspéro divided Vietnamese dialects into two main groups: the Upper Annam group, which comprises many local dialects found in villages from the north of Nghệ-an Province to the south of Thừa-thiên Province, and the Tonkin-Cochinchina dialect which covers the remainder.

Phonological structure diverges from the dialect of Hanoi (Hà-Nội), for a long time the political and cultural capital of the Empire of Annam, as one moves towards the south. The second vowel of the three diphthongs *iê*, *uô* and *ươ*, for example, tends towards *â* in the groups written *iêc* [iʌk], *iêng* [iʌŋ], *uôc* [uʌk] and *uông* [uʌŋ]. The Vinh dialect, which should belong to the Upper Annam group, has three retroflexes: affricate *tr* [tʂ], voiceless fricative *s* [ʂ], and voiced fricative *r* [ʐ]. The Hué dialect, considered archaic and difficult, has only five tones, with the hỏi and ngã tones pronounced in the same way with a long rising contour. The initial *z-* is replaced by a semi-vowel *y-*, and the palatal finals *-ch* and *-nh* are replaced by *-t* and *-n*.

In the dialect of Saigon (Sài-Gòn, now renamed Ho Chi Minh City) the phonemes generally are not arranged as shown in the orthography. However, the consonants of the Saigon dialect present the distinction between ordinary and retroflex initials. Also, the groups *iêp*, *iêm*, *uôm*, *ươp* and *ươm* are pronounced *ip*, *im*, *um*, *ưp* and *ưm*, respectively.

Most dialects form part of a continuum from north to south, each of them different to some extent from the neighbouring dialect on either side. Such major urban centres as Hanoi, Hue and Saigon represent rather special dialects marked by the influence of educated speakers and of more frequent contacts with the other regions.

The language described below is typified by the Hanoi dialect, which has served as the basis for the elaboration of the literary language. The spoken style keeps its natural charm in each locality although efforts have been made from the elementary grades up to nationwide conferences and meetings 'to preserve the purity and the clarity' of the standard language, whether spoken or written. The spoken tongue is used for all oral communications except public speeches, whereas the written medium, which one can qualify as literary style, is uniformly used in the press and over the radio and television.

While noting the inconsistencies of the Roman script, French administrators tried several times to recommend spelling reforms. However, efforts at standardisation, begun as early as 1945, started to move ahead only in 1954, when the governments in both zones established spelling norms, a task now facilitated by the spread of literacy to thousands of peasants and workers between 1954 and 1975. There is a very clear tendency to standardise the transliterations of place names and personal names from foreign languages, as well as the transliteration and/or translation of technical terms more and more required by progress in Vietnamese science and technology. Committees responsible for terminological work, i.e. the invention, elaboration and codification of terms in exact sciences as well as in human and social sciences, have contributed considerably to the enrichment of the national lexicon.

Members of the generations that grew up under French rule are bilingual, but later on have added English. The generation of 1945, for whom French ceased to be the medium of instruction, speaks Vietnamese and English. Because of the influence of socialist countries, Chinese, i.e. Mandarin, as well as Russian have become familiar to classes of professors, researchers, cadres and students exposed to various currents of Marxist thought, chiefly in the northern half of the country. In the south, English gained the upper hand over French as a foreign language taught in schools, while French remained and will remain the official language in diplomatic and political contacts. Chinese characters continue to be taught as a classical language needed for studies in Eastern humanities.

2 Phonology and Orthography

The *quốc-ngữ* writing system has the advantage of being close to a phonemic script, to which Portuguese, French and Italian, undoubtedly assisted by Vietnamese priests, contributed. It is fairly consistent, and below Vietnamese orthography is used to represent the phonology, with comments on the few areas of discrepancy.

A syllable has a vocalic nucleus, with a single vowel or two vowels, optionally preceded by an initial consonant and/or followed by a final consonant; this final consonant can only be a voiceless stop or a nasal. There may be an intercalary semi-vowel /w/ (spelled *o* before *a, ă, e*, otherwise *u*). These possibilities can be summarised by the formula $(C_1)(w) V_1 (V_2)(C_2)$. The syllable carries an obligatory toneme.

The vowels are presented in table 3.2.

Table 3.2: Vietnamese Vowels

Front	Central	Back Unrounded	Rounded
i, y		ư	u
ê		ơ	ô
e	ă	â	o
a			

There are some discrepancies between the phonology and orthography of vowels: (1) the letters *i* and *y* are purely orthographic variants representing the phoneme /i/, while *o* and *u* are orthographic variants in representing intercalary /w/ or V_2 (but not V_1). (2) The orthography does not represent the predictable V_2 after a high or high mid vowel not followed by some other V_2, i.e. we find [iị] in *đi* 'go', [êị] in *đê* 'dike', [ưụ] in *dứ dừ* 'exhausted', [oụ] in tơ 'silk', [uṵ] in mù 'blind', and [oṵ] in đổ 'pour'. (3) Phonemically, there are only four possible V₂s: *i, u, ư, â*, though there are phonetic and orthographic complications in addition to those already noted: (a) /â/ as V₂ is written *a* in open syllables (e.g. *mía* 'sugar cane', *mưa* 'to rain', *mua* 'buy'), but in closed syllables the orthographic representation depends on the V₁: *iê, ươ, uô*, and the pronunciation is with *â* before *ng* (e.g. *miếng* 'morsel', *mương* 'canal', *muống* 'bindweed'), but *ê, ơ* or *ô* (depending on the V₁) before *n* (e.g. *miền* 'region', *vườn* 'garden', *muôn* 'ten thousand'); (b) the spellings *uc, ung, oc, ong, ôc, ông* represent [uṵkᵖ], [uṵngᵐ], [ăṵkᵖ], [ăṵngᵐ], [âṵkᵖ], [âṵngᵐ] respectively, with final labio-velar coarticulation, as in *cúc* 'chrysanthemum', *cốc* 'glass', *cọc* 'stake', *cung* 'arc', *công* 'effort', *cong* 'curve'; (c) syllable-final *ch* and *nh* are orthographic representations of [ḭk] and [ḭng] respectively, e.g. *anh* [ăḭng] 'elder brother'. (4) /ă/ is spelled *a* before *ch, nh, u* and *y*, e.g. *bạch* 'white', *tranh* 'picture', *tàu* 'ship', *vay* 'borrow' (/a/ does not occur before *ch* and *nh*, while /ai/ is written *ai*, e.g. *vai* 'shoulder' and /au/ is written *ao*, e.g. *cao* 'high'). (5) /â/ is spelled *ê* before *ch* and *nh*, e.g. *bênh* 'protect'.

The six tonemes that affect the vocalic nucleus of each syllable are noted by means of diacritics as in table 3.3; when C₂ is a final stop, only tones 2 and 6 are possible.

Table 3.3: Vietnamese Tones

Name	Symbol	Pitch-level	Contour	Other features
1. bằng/ngang	(no mark)	high mid	drawn out, falling	
2. sắc	/´/	high	rising	tense
3. huyền	/`/	low	drawn out	lax
4. hỏi	/ˀ/	mid low	dipping-rising	tense
5. ngã	/˜/	high	rising	glottalised
6. nặng	/./	low	falling	glottalised or tense

Table 3.4: Vietnamese Consonants

	Labial	Labio-dental	Alveolar	Retroflex	Palatal	Velar	Laryngeal
Voiceless stop	p		t	tr	ch	c	
Aspirated stop			th				
Voiced stop	b		đ				
Voiceless fricative		ph	x	s		kh	h
Voiced fricative	v		d	r	gi	g	
Nasal	m		n		nh	ng	
Lateral			l				

The consonant inventory is given in table 3.4. Syllable-finally, the voiceless stops are unexploded. The voiced stops *b, d* are preglottalised and often implosive; note that *b*, occurring only syllable-initially, is in fact in complementary distribution with *p*, which occurs only syllable-finally. Word-final *k, ng* after *u* have labio-velar articulation (see the examples for point (3b) under vowels). /g/ is a voiced stop after a syllable ending in *ng*, otherwise a voiced fricative, e.g. *gác* 'upper floor' (fricative), but *thang gác* 'staircase' (stop). Word-finally, *ch* is pronounced /ịk/ and *nh* is pronounced [ịng], as already noted in the discussion of vowels.

The voiceless velar plosive is spelled *q* before /w/ (i.e. *qu*), *k* before *i/y, e, ê* and *c* elsewhere. Following the Italian convention, /g/ is spelled *gh* (and /ng/ *ngh*) before *i, e, ê*. The voiced palatal fricative is spelled *g* before *i* (and *iê*), e.g. *gì* 'what', but *gi* elsewhere, e.g. *giời* 'sky'.

In the Hanoi dialect, *tr* merges in pronunciation with *ch* (palatal), *s* with *x* (alveolar), while all three of *d, gi, r* merge as a voiced alveolar fricative.

3 Syntax

The noun phrase consists of a head noun, which may be followed by other words (noun, pronoun, place-noun, numeral, classifier, verb, demonstrative or even a relative clause). Examples of different constituents following the head noun follow:

(1) Noun–noun: no function word occurs between the head noun and the second noun; this construction can express (a) measure: *tạ gạo* 'quintal₁ of rice₂', *lít nước* 'litre₁ of water₂', *bát cơm* 'bowl₁ of rice₂', *cốc nước* 'glass₁ of water₂'; (b) space: *bao thuốc lá* 'pack₁ of cigarettes₂₋₃', *phòng khách* 'guest₂ room₁', *chuồng lợn* 'pig₂ sty₁'; (c) groups: *đàn bò* 'herd₁ of cows₂', *đoàn sinh-viên* 'group₁ of students₂', *nải chuối* 'hand₁ of bananas₂'; (d) images: *tóc mây* 'soft hair' (lit. 'hair cloud'), *cổ cò* 'crane₂ neck₁', *ngón tay búp măng* 'tapered fingers' (lit. 'bamboo₄ shoot₃ finger₁₋₂'), *tóc rễ tre* 'hair₁ stiff as bamboo₃ roots₂'; (e) characteristics: *gà mẹ* 'mother₂ hen₁', *máy bay cánh quạt* 'propeller₃₋₄-driven aeroplane₁₋₂'; (f) identity: *làng Khê-hồi* 'the village₁ of Khe-hoi₂', *sông Hương* 'the Perfume₂ River₁', *tuổi Hợi* 'the sign₁ of the Pig₂'.

(2) Noun–preposition–noun: *vấn-đề của tôi* 'my₃ problem₁' (note that the second noun may be replaced by a pronoun), *kỳ thi ở Huế* 'the examination₁₋₂ in₃ Hue₄', *cấu-trúc về chi-tiết* 'detailed₃ structure₁', *bổn-phận đối với cha mẹ* 'duty₁ towards₂₋₃ one's parents₄₋₅'. The preposition may be absent when the idea of kinship, ownership, origin, or utility is obvious: *nhà mày* 'your₂ house₁', *cha (của) Nguyễn Trãi* 'Nguyen₃ Trai's₄ father₁', *nhà (bằng) gạch* 'brick₃ house₁', *vải (ở) Tó* 'lychees₁ from₂ To₃', *sách (cho) lớp tám* 'textbook₁ for₂ the eighth₄ grade₃'.

(3) Noun–place-noun: *nhà trên* 'main₂ building₁', *nhà dưới* 'annex₂ building₁', *ngón giữa* 'middle₂ finger₁'.

(4) Noun–numeral: *hàng sáu* 'row₁ six₂, six abreast', *lớp nhất* 'top₂ grade₁', *tháng ba* 'March' (lit. 'month three'). In cardinal numeral constructions, however, a classifier must be used with the numeral; the usual order is numeral–classifier–noun, though noun–numeral–classifier is also possible: *hai cây nến* 'two₁ candles₃', *ba quyển sách* 'three₁ rolls₂ books₃', *bốn tờ giấy* 'four₁ sheets₂ of paper₃', *vài chú tiều* 'a few₁ woodcutters₃', or *tiều vài chú*. Nouns denoting concrete time units do not require a classifier, e.g. *hai năm* 'two years', *ba tuần* 'three weeks'. The choice of classifier is dependent on such features as the animateness, humanness (and social position for humans), and shape (for inanimates) of the noun; e.g. *cây* is used for stick-shaped objects, *quyển* for scrolls and volumes, *tấm* for sheet-like objects, *con* for animals, and *cái* for miscellaneous inanimates.

(5) Noun–verb/adjective (in Vietnamese, there is little reason for setting up distinct classes of verb and adjective — see section 4): *thịt kho* 'meat₁ stewed in fish sauce₂', *thịt nướng* 'broiled₂ meat₁', *thịt sống* 'raw₂ meat₁', *đường về* 'the way₁ back₂', *con người khổ sở* 'miserable₃₋₄ person₁₋₂'.

(6) Noun–demonstrative: *cô này* 'this₂ young lady₁', *ông nọ* 'the other₂ gentleman₁', *bà kia* 'the other₂ lady₁'. In such phrases with a demonstrative, a classifier is often used, the order then being classifier–noun–demonstrative: *cái bàn này* 'this₃ table₂', *con bò ấy* 'that₃ cow₂'.

(7) Noun–relative clause: *ngôi nhà mà chú tôi vừa tậu năm ngoái* 'the house₁₋₂ that₃ my₅ uncle₄ just₆ bought₇ last₉ year₈', *voi làm ở Việt-nam* 'the (ceramic) elephants₁ made₂ in₃ Vietnam₄'.

The verb phrase consists of a head verb followed by one or two noun phrases, a place-noun, a numeral, another verb, or an adjective (i.e. a stative verb). Likewise, when the head verb is stative ('adjectival'), several different configurations are possible:

(1) Verb–noun (direct object): *xây nhà* 'build₁ a house₂', *yêu nước* 'love₁ one's country₂', *ăn đũa* 'eat₁ with chopsticks₂', *cúi đầu* 'bow₁ one's head₂', *hết tiền* 'lack₁ money₂', *nghỉ hè* 'take a summer vacation' (lit. 'rest summer'), *trở nên người hữu-dụng* 'become₁₋₂ a useful₄ person₃'.

(2) Verb–noun–noun (the basic order is for direct object to precede indirect object, but the direct object may also follow if it consists of more than one syllable): *gửi tiền cho bố* 'send₁ money₂ to₃ his father₄', *gửi cho bố nhiều tiền* 'send₁ to₂ his father₃ a lot₄ of money₅', *lấy của ông Giáp hai bộ quần áo* 'steal₁ two₅ suits₆₋₇ from₂ Mr₃ Giap₄', *thọc tay vào túi* 'thrust₁ his hand₂ into₃ his pocket₄'.

(3) Verb–noun–verb: *mời sinh-viên ăn tiệc* 'invite₁ the students₂ to eat₃ dinner₄', *dạy tôi chữ Hán* 'teach₁ me₂ Chinese₄ characters₃'.

(4) Verb–place-noun: *ngồi trên* 'sit₁ at a higher position₂'.

(5) Verb–numeral: *về nhất* 'finish₁ first₂', *lên tám* 'be eight years old' (lit. 'reach eight').

(6) Verb–verb(–verb): *lo thi* 'worry about examinations' (lit 'worry take-examination'), *liều chết* 'risk death' (lit. 'risk die'), *đi học* 'go to school' (lit. 'go study'), *ngủ ngồi* 'fall asleep in one's chair' (lit. 'sleep sit'), *chôn sống* 'bury alive' (lit. 'bury live'), *ngủ dậy* 'wake up, get up' (lit. 'sleep wake'), *đi học về* 'come back from school' (lit. 'go study return').

(7) Verb–adjective (there is no separate class of adverbs of manner): *ăn nhanh* 'eat₁ fast₂', *bôi bẩn* 'smear' (lit. 'spread dirty'), *đối-đãi tử-tế* 'treat₁ nicely₂'.

(8) Adjective–noun: *mù mắt* 'blind₁ in the eyes₂', *mỏi tay* 'tired₁ in the arms₂', *đông người* 'crowded₁ with people₂', *giống bố* 'resemble₁ one's father₂', *thạo tiếng Nhật* 'good₁ at Japanese₃ language₂'.

(9) Adjective–verb: *khó nói* 'difficult₁ to say₂'.

(10) Adjective–adjective: *mừng thầm* 'inwardly₂ happy₁'.

A normal message consists of two parts, the subject and the predicate; these two parts are separated by a pause, e.g. *ông ấy / đến rồi* 'he₁₋₂ has already₄ arrived₃', *bà ấy / là người Hành-thiện* 'she₁₋₂ is₃ a native₄ of Hanh-thien₅'. However, the subject can be ellipted, i.e. one can say simply *đến rồi, là người Hành-thiện*.

In addition to the subject and predicate, a sentence may optionally contain supplementary terms; these other phrases manifest complements of time, location, cause, goal, condition, concession etc.: *đêm qua ra đứng bờ ao* 'last₂ night₁ I went₃ to stand₄ on the edge₅ of the pond₆', *ở Việt-nam, chúng tôi học theo lục-cá-nguyệt* 'in₁ Vietnam₂, we₃₋₄ study₅ following₆ the semester₇ system', *tại vợ nó, nó mới chết* 'because of₁ his₃ wife₂, he₄ died₆', *vì tổ-quốc, chúng ta phải hi-sinh tất cả* 'we₃₋₄ must₅ sacrifice₆ everything₇₋₈ for₁ the fatherland₂', *nếu anh bận thì tôi sẽ đi một mình* 'if₁ you₂ are busy₃, then₄ I₅ will₆ go₇ by myself₈₋₉', *tuy nghèo, nhưng anh thích giúp bạn* 'though₁ poor₂, yet₃ he₄ likes₅ to help₆ his friends₇'.

Word order is important, especially given the virtual absence of other overt indicators of grammatical relations, for instance the subject normally precedes its verb while the direct object normally follows. The adverbial of time *bao giờ* or *khi nào* 'when' is placed at the beginning of the sentence to indicate future time reference and at the end to indicate past time reference, e.g. *khi nào cô thư-ký đến?* 'when₁₋₂ will the secretary₃₋₄ arrive₅?', *cô thư-ký đến khi nào?* 'when did the secretary arrive?'.

A noun phrase can be highlighted by placing it at the beginning of the sentence: it then announces a topic ('as for...'), and we have a specific reference to a certain person, a certain thing, a certain concept, an exact location, a given time, a precise quantity or a determined manner, e.g. *chúng tôi thì chúng tôi học theo lục-cá-nguyệt* 'as for us, we follow the semester system', *nước mắm, anh ấy ăn được* 'fish₂ sauce₁ he₃₋₄ can₆ eat₅'.

In the first example, the subject is repeated as topic with the particle *thì*; in the second, the direct object is simply preposed (cf. *anh ấy ăn được nước mắm* 'he can eat fish sauce'). With the particle *cũng* 'even', such preposing can indicate the extent of the scope of the particle: compare *ông ấy mời sinh-viên ăn cơm* 'he invites the students to eat dinner', with *sinh-viên, ông ấy cũng mời ăn cơm* 'he invites even the students to eat dinner' and *ăn cơm, ông ấy cũng mời sinh-viên* 'he invites the students even to eat dinner'. Other examples of topicalisation are *ông ấy tên là Bảng* 'he is named Bang' (lit. 'he$_{1-2}$ name$_3$ is$_4$ Bang$_5$') (cf. *tên ông ấy là Bảng* 'his$_{2-3}$ name$_1$ is$_4$ Bang$_5$'), *bà cụ mắt kém* 'the old lady has poor eyesight' (cf. *mắt bà cụ kém* 'the old$_3$ lady's$_2$ eyes$_1$ are weak$_4$').

A number of verbs denoting existence, appearance or disappearance may have the object whose existence etc. is expressed either before or after the verb; in the latter case, the verb may be preceded by a noun phrase expressing the experiencer of the existence etc., e.g. *đê vỡ* 'the dike$_1$ broke$_2$' or *vỡ đê; tiền mất, tật mang* 'the money$_1$ has gone$_2$, the sickness$_3$ remains$_4$', *(tôi) mất tiền* 'I lost some money'. In such sentences, the noun phrase before the verb is best analysed as a topic.

Passive sentences are found in Vietnamese, e.g. the active *Tám yêu Hiền* 'Tam$_1$ loves$_2$ Hien$_3$' may also appear as *Hiền được Tám yêu* 'Hien is loved by Tam'. However, such passives are best analysed as a subordinate clause *Tám yêu (Hiền)*, dependent on the main verb *được* 'get, enjoy'. If, instead of obtaining a happy result, the party involved suffers from a disadvantage or unpleasant experience, then the main verb *bị* 'suffer' will be used, e.g. *Liên bị Tám ghét* 'Lien is hated by Tam' (cf. *Tám ghét Liên* 'Tam$_1$ hates$_2$ Lien$_3$'). Such passives are not to be confused with instances of topicalisation discussed above, even though the latter are sometimes translatable into English as passives (e.g. *cơm thổi rồi* as 'the rice$_1$ has already$_3$ been cooked$_2$', but cf. *cơm, mẹ thổi rồi* 'the rice$_1$, mother$_2$ has already$_4$ cooked$_3$').

Negation is expressed by means of the negative marker *không*, which literally means 'null, not to be, not to exist', and whose emphatic equivalents are *chẳng* and *chả*, e.g. *ông ấy không/chẳng/chả đến* 'he$_{1-2}$ is not$_3$ coming$_4$'. Either *chưa* or *chửa* means 'not yet', e.g. *ông ấy chưa/chửa đến* 'he hasn't arrived yet'. Before the copula *là*, negation is expressed by *không phải*, literally '(it) is not correct (that) it is...', e.g. *bà ấy không phải là người Hành-thiện* 'she's not a native of Hanh-thien'. Stronger denial may be achieved by means of an interrogative pronoun used as an indefinite pronoun (see page 60), e.g. *ông ấy có đến đâu!* (lit. 'he$_{1-2}$ indeed$_3$ arrive$_4$ where$_5$'), *ông ấy đâu có đến!* 'no, he did *not* show up!', or even *ông ấy không đến đâu!* 'he's not coming, I tell you!*, *bà ấy có phải là người Hành-thiện đâu!* or *bà ấy đâu có phải là người Hành-thiện!* 'she's not at all a native of Hanh-thien!'.

Interrogative sentences have three basic structures. The first is used for alternative questions, i.e. the interlocutor has to choose between two terms separated by the conjunction *hay* 'or', e.g. *cô ấy đi hay ông đi?* 'is she$_{1-2}$ going$_3$ or$_4$ are you$_5$ going$_6$?', *nó đi học hay không đi học?* 'is he$_1$ going$_2$ to school$_3$ or$_4$ isn't$_5$ he going$_6$ to school$_7$?'. With the latter example, where the choice is between affirmative and negative alternants, the second clause may be reduced right down to the particle *không*, i.e. *nó có đi học hay không đi học?*, *nó có đi học hay không?*, *nó có đi học không?*, *nó đi học không?* In such examples where the predicate is nominal, the confirmative particle *có* is obligatory in the first clause: *bà ấy có phải là người Hành-thiện không?* 'is she a native of Hanh-thien?'. When the question is about the realisation of an action or process ('yet'), the group *có không* is replaced by *đã chưa*, e.g. *ông ấy (đã) đến chưa?* 'has he$_{1-2}$ arrived$_4$ yet$_{3-5}$?', cf. the fuller version *ông ấy đã đến hay chưa (đến)?* Such questions (lacking an interrogative pronoun) normally have sostenuto intonation, in which the pitch level of each toneme is somewhat higher than in a normal sentence, rather than the more normal diminuendo intonation (in, for instance, statements), in which the intensity gradually diminishes from the beginning of the syllable.

The basic answers to such questions are *có* 'yes' and *không* 'no', e.g. *có, nó có đi học* 'yes, he is going to school', *không, nó không đi học* 'no, he isn't going to school'. But different answers are required with a nominal predicate: *phải, bà ấy là người Hành-thiện* 'yes, she is a native of Hanh-thien', *không phải, bà ấy không phải là người Hành-thiện* 'no, she isn't a native of Hanh-thien', and with 'yet' questions: *rồi, ông ấy đến rồi* 'yes, he has already arrived', *chưa, ông ấy chưa đến* 'no, he hasn't arrived yet'.

The second type of interrogative structure is the content question (*wh*-question), with an interrogative substantive: *ai?* 'who?', *gì?* 'what?', *nào?* 'which?', *đâu?* 'where?', *bao giờ?* 'when?', *bao nhiêu?* 'how much?', *bao lâu?* 'how long?', *sao?* 'why?'. The interrogative substantive normally occurs in the same position in the sentence as would an equivalent ordinary noun phrase, as can be seen in the following question and answer pairs: *ai đến? ông Nam đến?* 'who$_1$ has arrived$_2$? Mr$_3$ Nam$_4$ has arrived$_5$'; *nó bảo ai? nó bảo tôi* 'who$_3$ did he$_1$ tell$_2$? he$_4$ told$_5$ me$_6$'; *người nào đi với anh? ông Nam đi với tôi* 'which$_2$ person$_1$ is going$_3$ with$_4$ you$_5$? Mr$_6$ Nam$_7$ is going$_8$ with$_9$ me$_{10}$'; *anh đi với người nào? tôi đi với sinh-viên* 'which$_5$ people$_4$ are you$_1$ going$_2$ with$_3$? I'm$_6$ going$_7$ with$_8$ the students$_9$'; *nó ăn gì? nó ăn cá* 'what$_3$ does he$_1$ eat$_2$? he$_4$ eats$_5$ fish$_6$'; *ông ấy ở đâu? ông ấy ở Cần-thơ* 'where$_4$ does he$_{1-2}$ live$_3$? he$_{5-6}$ lives in$_7$ Can-tho$_8$'. Content questions usually have crescendo intonation, with the main stress on the interrogative substantive. Incidentally, these same interrogative substantives can also have the function of indefinite pronouns, e.g. *không ai nói* 'no one spoke' (lit. 'not who spoke'); especially in women's speech, they can even have negative indefinite function, provided the interrogative substantive receives very heavy stress, e.g. *ai nói*, with very heavy stress on *ai*, 'no one spoke'.

The confirmation-seeking tag is *phải không*, often reduced to *phỏng*, e.g. *không ăn, phải không? không ăn, phỏng?* 'you're not$_1$ eating$_2$, are you?' A number of final particles serve to mark various nuances of interrogation. Thus *a*, *à* and *ư* are used to express astonishment or to seek confirmation of what is supposed or has been discovered, e.g. *anh chịu à?* 'you₁ gave up₂? I'm surprised!', *ông không mệt à?'* 'aren't₂ you₁ tired₃?'. In the sentence *sao con lại làm thế hử?* 'how₁ did you₂ dare₃ do₄ that₅ my dear?', the particle *hử* expresses a mild reproach while pressing the culprit for a reply. The particle *nhỉ* is used to elicit the confirmation of something just noticed, e.g. *ông Chân có cái nhà to nhỉ?* 'Mr₁ Chan₂ has₃ a big₆ house₄₋₅, hasn't he?'. The dubitative sentence, which expresses doubt or uncertainty, contains the particle *chăng*: *trời sắp sửa mưa chăng?* 'could it be that it's going to rain?' (lit. 'sky about-to rain'), *có lẽ họ không đến chăng?* 'maybe₁₋₂ they₃ are not₄ coming₅'.

Other particles occur at the end of a sentence to lend more movement or force to it: in order to show politeness, the particle *ạ* is used in a social context where the speaker assumes an inferior attitude, expected of children, students, domestic help etc., e.g. *mời Bố xơi cơm ạ* 'please₁ eat₃ the meal₄, Daddy₂', *thưa Thày, hôm nay thứ năm ạ* 'report₁ Teacher₂ today₃₋₄ Thursday₅₋₆', *ông đưa tiền cho tôi rồi ạ* 'you₁ already₆ handed₂ the money₃ to₄ me₅, sir'.

In order to remind someone of something, the final particle *nghe* or *nhé* is used, e.g. *em đứng đây chờ anh nhé!* 'you₁ stand₂ wait for₄ me₅ here₃, O.K.?'.

The particle *chứ* is used to seek confirmation, e.g. *ông uống cà-phê rồi chứ!* 'you₁ already₄ had₂ your coffee₃, I presume', *ông uống cà-phê chứ!* 'you will have some coffee, won't you?'.

Exhortation is expressed by means of *đi*, which marks the imperative or injunctive, e.g. *anh đi ăn đi!* '(you₁) go₂ and eat₃!', *chúng ta đi ăn đi!* 'let us₁₋₂ go₃ and eat₄!', *lấy vợ đi chứ* 'get married₁₋₂! what are you waiting for?'.

The particle *mà*, occurring at the end of a statement, connotes insistence: *tôi biết mà!* 'I₁ know₂ it all', *tôi không biết mà!* 'I told you I₁ didn't₂ know₃ it at all!'.

In addition to the injunctive particle *đi*, which indicates a mild order, a curt intonation makes a statement into a command, e.g. *đứng lại!* 'halt!', *im* 'quiet! shut up!', *nín!* 'shut up! stop crying!', *thôi!* 'enough!'. When inviting or exhorting someone to do something, one uses the particle *hãy* placed before the verb, with or without an expressed subject: *anh hãy ngồi đây* '(you₁) sit₃ here₄', *hãy ăn cơm đi đã* 'go₄ ahead and eat₂₋₃ first₅'. To express prohibition or dissuasion, the particle *đừng* or *chớ* is put before the verb of action: *anh đừng hút thuốc lá nữa* '(you₁) don't₂ smoke₃ cigarettes₄₋₅ any more₆', *chớ nói nhảm* 'don't₁ talk₂ nonsense₃'.

A complex sentence may contain as many clauses as there are action verbs or stative verbs, and under this general heading we may examine both subordination and coordination. The main kinds of subordinate clauses are noun clauses, relative clauses and adverbial clauses.

A noun clause, always placed after the main clause, functions as object of the main clause. It is linked to the main clause either directly, or through the intermediary of the particles *rằng* or *là* 'that', e.g. *đừng cho nó biết (là) tôi trượt* 'don't₁ let₂ him₃ know₄ (that₅) I₆ flunked₇', *tôi hi-vọng (rằng) họ sẽ giúp tôi* 'I₁ hope₂ (that₃) they₄ will₅ help₆ me₇'.

A relative clause functions as an attribute modifying a noun phrase in the main clause, and is often, though optionally, introduced by the particle *mà*, e.g. *quyển sách (mà) tôi nói hôm nọ bị mất rồi* 'the book₁₋₂ (that₃) I₄ told₅ you about the other₇ day₆ has already₁₀ been₈ lost₉', where the relative clause *(mà) tôi nói hôm nọ* helps specify which book is being spoken of; in *thím tôi đã bán ngôi nhà (mà) chú tôi vừa tậu năm ngoái* 'my₂ aunt₁ has already₃ sold₄ the house₅₋₆ (that₇) my₉ uncle₈ just₁₀ bought₁₁ last₁₃ year₁₂', the clause *(mà) chú tôi vừa tậu năm ngoái* describes further the house that is being discussed. Relative clauses follow their antecedent.

Adverbial clauses serve the same functions as adverbs in the main clause, and express such ideas as purpose, cause, condition, concession etc. Adverbial clauses are introduced by conjunctions, such as *để (cho)* 'so that', *(bởi) vì* 'because', *nếu* 'if', *giá* 'suppose', *dù* 'though'. Examples follow; note that the adverbial clause may either precede or follow the main clause: *tôi xin nói để quí-vị biết* 'I₁ beg₂ to speak up₃ so that₄ you₅ may know₆', *vì anh ấy không có tiền, cho nên chúng tôi cho miễn học-phí* 'because₁ he₂₋₃ has₅ no₄ money₆, so₇₋₈ we₉₋₁₀ gave₁₁ him a tuition₁₃ waiver₁₂', *nếu tôi có tiền, tôi đã mua quyển sách ấy* 'if₁ I₂ had had₃ money₄, I₅ would already₆ have bought₇ that₁₀ book₈₋₉', *giá anh nghe tôi thì việc đó không hỏng* 'suppose₁ you₂ had listened₃ to me₄, then₅ that₇ thing₆ would not₈ have failed₉', *dù phải khó nhọc, nhưng/song họ không nản* 'although₁ it was indeed₂ tough going₃₋₄, yet₅ they₆ did not₇ get discouraged₈'.

As for coordination, several independent clauses may either be juxtaposed without any connective, or may be conjoined by means of such conjunctions as *và* 'and', *mà* 'but, yet', *nhưng* 'however', *song* 'nevertheless', e.g. *tôi rửa mặt, chải đầu, đánh răng, ăn sáng* 'I₁ washed₂ my face₃, combed₄ my hair₅, brushed₆ my teeth₇ and ate₈ breakfast₉', *tôi cho hắn vay tiền và giúp hắn tìm con* 'I₁ lent₂₋₄ him₃ money₅ and₆ helped₇ him₈ find₉ his child₁₀', *ông dùng cơm hay dùng bánh mì ạ?* 'would you₁ like to eat₂ rice₃ or₄ eat₅ bread₆₋₇?', *no bụng mà vẫn đói con mắt* 'his belly₂ is full₁, yet₃ he's still₄ hungry₅ in his eyes₆₋₇', *cái bút này rẻ nhưng tốt* 'this₃ pen₁₋₂ is cheap₄, but₅ good₆'.

4 Word Classes and Grammatical Categories

In the absence of purely morphological criteria, lexico-syntactic criteria are used to distinguish word classes, i.e. the environment of a word and its possible combinations in the spoken chain are examined together with its meaning(s).

A large number of nouns can be identified by means of such prefixed elements as *cái* 'thing, object', *sự* 'fact', *việc* 'action', *niềm* 'sentiment', *chủ-nghĩa* 'ideology, -ism'. The classifier *cái* serves to create a noun from an adjective (*cái đẹp* 'beauty') or from a verb (*cái tát* 'a slap'). Likewise, with the classifier *cuộc* 'action, process, game' one can construct such nouns as *cuộc đình-công* 'a strike (industrial)' (from the verb *đình-công* 'be on strike'), *cuộc vui* 'party' (from the adjective *vui* 'merry, fun').

In the southern dialect, such kinship terms as *ông* 'grandfather', *bà* 'grandmother', *cô* 'paternal aunt', *anh* 'elder brother', *chị* 'elder sister' followed by the demonstrative *ấy* 'that' take the dipping-rising *hỏi* tone to function as third person pronouns, e.g. *ổng* 'he', *bả* 'she', *cỏ* 'she', *ảnh* 'he', *chỉ* 'she'. The words indicating a given point or position in space or time also display this morphophonemic trait, e.g. *trong ấy* becomes *trỏng* 'in there', *ngoài ấy* becomes *ngoải* 'out there', *trên ấy* becomes *trển* 'up there'. The words designating portions of space have other characteristics of the noun class. This is why it is preferable to put them among nouns instead of considering them prepositions. Predicatives consist of verbs and adjectives. The latter, which are actually stative verbs, or verbs of quality, can be preceded by *rất* 'very', *khá* 'rather', but cannot occur with the exhortative particle *hãy!*: contrast *hãy chăm-chỉ học-hành!* 'study₃ hard₂!' with **hãy đúng!* 'be accurate!'. Moreover, only verbs of action can be followed by a verb of direction ('coverb') (*ra* 'exit', *vào* 'enter', *lên* 'ascend', *xuống* 'descend'), or be used in the frame ...*đi*...*lai* to mark repetition of an action, e.g. *chạy ra* 'run out(side)', *chạy xuống* 'run down', *chạy đi chạy lại* 'run back and forth' (but not, with *mặn* 'salty', **mặn ra*, **mặn xuống*, **mặn đi mặn lại*).

A noun, often defined as a word which denotes a being or thing, can function as predicate only if it is preceded by the copula *là* or its negative *không phải là*. It cannot follow the injunctive particle *hãy* or the prohibitive particles *đừng, chớ*. It can constitute a nominal phrase when it is combined with a numeral or plural particle (*những, các*) and a classifier, or with a demonstrative (*này* 'this', *ấy* 'that'). Likewise, certain particles can be used to establish the class of verbs, which can be preceded by aspect markers such as *sẽ* 'future', *đã* 'completion', *đều* 'togetherness'. On the other hand, by considering the position of a word in a syntactic group within a sentence, we can confirm its word class: in the noun phrase *khó-khăn của người công-chức* 'the difficulties₁ of₂ an official₃₋₄', the possessive element *của người công-chức* helps us to establish the noun status of *khó-khăn* even when it does not follow a classifier like *nỗi* or a pluraliser like *những*.

Such tests suggest that lexical items in Vietnamese fall into eight broad classes, as follows: nouns, verbs, quantifiers, substitutes, particles, connectors, modals, interjections. The first four classes consist of 'full (content) words', whereas the remaining four represent 'empty (function) words'.

The language does not have paradigms in the classical sense. There are, however, categories, some of which are non-existent in Indo-European languages. Within the class of nouns, it is necessary to mention, besides number, the various features that determine the choice of classifier (see page 57), such as animateness, humanness, shape and social status. Verbs, or more generally predicatives, manifest such categories as tense, result, direction, voice, intensity, orientation. Thus, in addition to the simple sentence *ông ấy đi*, one can specify time reference by means of particles: *ông ấy sẽ đi* 'he will go', *ông ấy sắp đi* 'he is about to go', *ông ấy đã đi rồi* 'he has already gone', *ông ấy vừa/mới đi* 'he has just gone', *ông ấy đang đi* 'he is on his way'. Other categories are illustrated by the following: *tìm thấy* 'find' (lit. 'search find'), *chịu được* 'endure' (lit. 'endure gain'), *bỏ đi* 'abandon' (lit. 'drop go'), *đóng vào* 'close' (lit. 'close enter'), *nhận ra* 'recognise' (lit. 'notice exit'), *phải phạt* 'be punished' (lit. 'suffer punish'), *bị thua* 'be defeated' (lit. 'undergo lose'), *được thưởng* 'be rewarded' (lit. 'gain reward'). Intensity is expressed by repeating the verb, with main stress on the first occurrence, e.g. '*đau đau đau là!* 'oh how it hurts!'.

In the family, kinship terms are used in place of personal pronouns, e.g. *bố cho con tiền ạ!* 'please give me some money, Dad' (lit. 'father give child money please'), *bố không muốn cho con tiền* 'I (lit. 'father') don't want to give you (lit. 'child') money'. Each individual must use appropriate terms of address and reference which place him where he belongs in the clan, and the terms are dictated by the relationship shown in a very precise nomenclature. The term *ông* 'grandfather' is used in formal conversation with a stranger one meets for the first time. The correct first person pronoun is *tôi* 'servant'. Between friends, the term *anh* 'elder brother' is applied to the hearer. Some arrogant pronouns (*tao* 'I', *mày* 'you', etc.) are used only in a familiar or vulgar context. Normally, etiquette recommends an attitude of humility before others, who are addressed in honorific terms (e.g. *cụ* 'great-grandfather', *ngài* 'your excellency', *thày* 'master'), which show respect for the hearer's age, knowledge and social rank.

5 Lexicon

Although the great majority of words have only one syllable (e.g. *nhà* 'house', *có* 'have', *ma* 'ghost', *ăn* 'eat', *cơm* 'rice', *ngon* 'delicious'), one cannot help noticing in modern Vietnamese numerous forms that have two or more syllables. These disyllabic or polysyllabic forms are either native compounds or compounds borrowed from Chinese.

Reduplication, a very frequent derivational process, can be total or partial: *ba-ba* 'river turtle', *chuồn-chuồn* 'dragonfly', *cào-cào* 'grasshopper', *đa-đa* 'partridge', *tùng-tùng* (representation of the sound of a drum); *châu-châu* 'grasshopper', *đom-đóm* 'firebug', *đu-đủ* 'pawpaw, papaya', *đo-đỏ* 'reddish', *trăng-trắng* 'whitish' (note the tonal modifications in this group and the next); *ngấm-ngầm* 'secret(ly)' (cf. *ngầm*), *ngoan-ngoãn* 'well-behaved' (cf. *ngoan*); *mạnh-mẽ* 'strong(ly)' (cf. *mạnh*), *xấu-xa* 'hideously' (cf. *xấu*), *nhẹ-nhàng* 'gently' (cf. *nhẹ*), *sẵn-sàng* 'all ready' (cf. *sẵn*); *tỉ-mỉ* 'meticulous', *lang-thang* 'wander', *bồi-hồi* 'anxious, nervous', *lầm-bầm* 'mumble'; *học-hiệc* 'to study and the like' (cf. *học*), *xe-xiệc* 'cars and the like' (cf. *xe*); *lơ-tơ-mơ* 'vague, obscure', *sạch-sành-sanh* 'completely (empty)'; *líu-lo líu-lường* 'twitter, jabber', *đủng-đa đủng-đỉnh* 'slowly taking one's time'.

Composition consists in combining two or more lexical bases. Sometimes, the relation among the components is one of coordination, e.g. *nhà cửa* 'house, home' (lit. 'house door'), *bàn ghế* 'furniture' (lit. 'table chair'), *giàu sang* 'rich₁ and noble₂', *ăn uống* 'eating₁ and drinking₂', *được thua* 'win₁ or lose₂', *bờ cõi* 'limits, border' (lit. 'edge region'), *đường sá* 'roads' (lit. 'road street'). In other instances there is a relation of dependency between the two components, e.g. *nước mắt* 'tears' (lit. 'water eye'), *bánh ngọt* 'cake' (lit. 'pastry sweet'), *tháng hai* 'February' (lit. 'month two'), *nhà tắm* 'bathroom' (lit. 'house bathe'), *tàu bò* 'tank' (lit. 'ship crawl'), *đỏ ối* 'scarlet' (lit. 'red dark-red'), *đánh mất* 'lose' (lit. 'hit lose'); *trắng nõn* 'pure white (of skin)' (lit. 'white bud'); *bao-giờ* 'when' (lit. 'what time'), *bây-giờ* 'now' (lit. 'this time'), *bấy-giờ* 'then' (lit. 'that time'). A special case of this dependent relationship is complementation, as in *vâng lời* 'obey' (lit. 'obey words'), *qua đời* 'pass away' (lit. 'pass life'), *khó tính* 'difficult to please' (lit. 'difficult character'); *buồn ngủ* 'sleepy' (lit. 'desire sleep'), *dễ bảo* 'docile' (lit. 'easy tell'). The numerals, which are based on the decimal system, combine dependence and coordination, e.g. *bốn mươi chín* 'forty-nine', literally 'four ten nine', i.e. (4 × 10) + 9.

Within native Vietnamese compounds, the usual order is modified–modifier. Among the numerous Chinese loans, this order applies in cases of complementation (e.g. verb-object), such as *thu-ngân* 'cashier' (lit. 'collect money'), *vệ-sinh* 'hygiene, sanitary' (lit. 'guard life'), but the order is modifier-modified if the head component is a noun, e.g. *giáo-sư* 'teacher' (lit. 'teach master'), *đại-học* 'university' (lit. 'great study'), *ngữ-pháp* 'grammar' (lit. 'language rules'), *Pháp-ngữ* 'French language', *quan-sát-viên* 'observer' (lit. 'observe person'). This parallels the fact that modifiers normally follow the head noun in noun phrases in Vietnamese, but precede in Chinese.

One can even speak of prefixes and suffixes in the Sino-Vietnamese compounds, such as *bất-* (e.g. *bất-hợp-pháp* 'illegal'), *vô-* (e.g. *vô-ích* 'useless'), *khả-* (e.g. *khả-ố* 'loathsome'), *phản-* (e.g. *phản-cách-mạng* 'counter-revolutionary'), *thân-* (e.g. *thân-chính-phủ* 'pro-government'), *đệ-* (ordinal prefix, e.g. *đệ-nhất* 'first'); *-giả* (e.g. *tác-giả* 'author'), *-gia* (e.g. *khoa-học-gia* 'scientist'), *-sư* (e.g. *kiến-trúc-sư* 'architect'), *-sĩ* (e.g. *văn-sĩ* 'writer'), *-viên* (e.g. *đoàn-viên* 'member (of group)'), *-hoá* (e.g. *âu-hoá* 'Europeanise'), *-trưởng* (e.g. *viện-trưởng* 'rector').

Descriptive forms have been created to denote articles of merchandise imported from abroad, e.g. *cái bật lửa* 'cigarette lighter' (lit. 'thing switch fire'), *cái gạt tàn thuốc lá* 'ash tray' (lit. 'thing shake-off ash drug leaf'), *máy thu thanh* 'radio receiver' (lit. 'machine gather sound'), *máy quay phim* 'movie camera' (lit. 'machine turn film'), *máy bay cánh cụp cánh xòe* 'F-111' (lit. 'machine fly wing close wing spread'), *tàu há mồm* 'landing craft' (lit. 'ship open mouth').

The Chinese lexical fund being predominant in literary and scholarly language, an educated speaker often has access to two synonymous terms, a native one used in daily parlance and the other, of Chinese origin, reserved for written texts. For instance, 'train' is either *xe lửa* (lit. 'vehicle fire') or *hoả-xa*, and 'aeroplane' is either *máy bay* (lit. 'machine fly') or *phi-cơ*. Some advocates of standardisation have advocated the exclusive use of native words in place of Sino-Vietnamese loanwords, e.g. *máy bay lên thẳng* (lit. 'machine fly ascend straight') instead of *máy bay trực-thăng* 'helicopter', *Tòa Nhà Trắng* (lit. 'building house white') instead of *Tòa Bạch-ốc* 'White House', *Lầu Năm Góc* (lit. 'palace five angle') instead of *Ngũ-giác-đài* 'Pentagon', *vùng trời* (lit. 'area sky') instead of *không-phận* 'airspace'.

The use of abbreviations to replace entire appellations of administrative units or publications is very widespread, but each syllable (rather than each word) is represented by its initial, e.g. *TCPV* for *Tối-cao Pháp-viện* 'Supreme$_1$ Court$_2$', *DHVK* for *Đại-học Văn-khoa* 'Faculty$_1$ of Letters$_2$', *TCVH* for *Tạp-chí Văn-học* 'Review$_1$ of Literature$_2$'. This practice is, however, limited to the written language, and administrative titles are sometimes very long, e.g. *TGD-TTHBDHV* for *Tổng-giám-đốc Trung, Tiểu-học và Bình-dân Học-vụ* 'Director-General$_1$ of Secondary$_2$, Primary$_3$ and$_4$ Popular$_5$ Education$_6$'.

Since Vietnamese was strongly influenced by Chinese during the ten centuries of Chinese rule, the number of words of Chinese origin is inevitably very large: simple words, disyllables, as well as whole expressions make up the majority of lexical items in any written text of a technical nature. However, this invasion is limited to the large body of content words, while grammatical morphemes ('function words') retain their native identity. 'Suffixes' borrowed from Chinese are sometimes abused, and people say things like *cửa hàng trưởng* for 'store$_{1-2}$ manager$_3$', *đại-khái chủ-nghĩa* 'doctrine$_2$ of approximation$_1$'. A recent convention distinguishes the noun *chủ-nghĩa xã-hội* 'socialism' (lit. 'doctrine society/socialist') from the adjective *xã-hội-chủ-nghĩa* 'socialist'.

Loans from French are relatively less numerous: *ga* 'station', *cà-phê* 'coffee', *xà-phòng* 'soap', *cao-su* 'rubber', *bồ-tạt* 'potash', *xi-măng* 'cement', *bơm* 'pump', *xúc-xích* 'sausage', etc. The spoken language under certain circumstances tolerates such forms, with French bound morphemes, as: *qua-loa-rơ-măng* 'just so and so, not thoroughly' (cf. *qua-loa* 'rough, summary' and the French adverbial suffix *-ment*), *bét-đem* 'the bottom one' (cf. *bét* 'last' and the French ordinal suffix *-ième*), *inchêable* 'impeccable' (with the French negative prefix *in-*, Vietnamese *chê* 'denigrate', and the French adjectival suffix *-able*)!

Bibliography

For the social background to Vietnamese, reference may be made to Nguyễn Đình-Hoà (1980). For the genetic classification, see Haudricourt (1953; 1954); more specific historical topics are covered by Maspéro (1912) and Gregerson (1969), while Nguyễn Đình-Hoà (1982–4) is the state-of-the-art discussion of *chữ nôm*.

In the absence of a single comprehensive and authoritative grammar of Vietnamese, the reader will need to refer to a range of sources, such as Cadière (1958), Emeneau (1951), Lê (1960), Nguyễn Đăng Liêm (1969), Thompson (1965), Trần et al. (1943) and Trương (1970). For special topics, Honey (1959) may be consulted for word classes, and Nguyễn Đình-Hoà (1972a; 1972b; 1979) for various facets of the verb.

A useful collection of articles is Nguyễn Khắc Viện et al. (1976).

References

Cadière, L.M. 1958. *Syntaxe de la langue vietnamienne* (=Publications de l'École Française d'Extrême-Orient, vol. XLII) (Paris)

Emeneau, M.B. 1951. *Studies in Vietnamese (Annamese) Grammar* (University of California Press, Berkeley and Los Angeles)

Gregerson, K.J. 1969. 'A Study of Middle Vietnamese Phonology', *Bulletin de la Société des Études Indochinoises*, vol. 44, no. 2, pp. 131–93

Haudricourt, A.-G. 1953. 'La place du vietnamien dans les langues austroasiatiques', *Bulletin de la Société Linguistique de Paris*, vol. 49, pp. 122–8

—— 1954. 'De l'origine des tons en vietnamien', *Journal Asiatique*, vol. 242, pp. 69–82

Honey, P.J. 1959. 'Word Classes in Vietnamese', *Bulletin of the School of Oriental and African Studies*, vol. 18, pp. 534–44

Lê Văn Lý. 1960. *Le Parler vietnamien: sa structure phonologique et morphologique functionnelle: esquisse d'une grammaire vietnamienne*, revised ed. (Publications de l'Institut des Recherches Historiques, Saigon)

Maspéro, H. 1912. 'Études sur la phonétique historique de la langue annamite: les initiales', *Bulletin de l'École Française d'Extrême-Orient*, vol. 12, pp. 1–127

Nguyễn Đăng Liêm. 1969. *Vietnamese Grammar: A Combined Tagmemic and Transformational Approach: A Contrastive Analysis of English and Vietnamese*, vol. 2 (Research School of Pacific Studies, Canberra)

Nguyễn Đình-Hoà. 1972a. 'Passivization in Vietnamese', in L. Bernot and J.M.C. Thomas (eds.), *Langues et techniques, nature et société* (Klincksieck, Paris), pp. 179–87

—— 1972b. 'Vietnamese Categories of Result, Direction and Orientation', in M.E. Smith (ed.), *Studies in Linguistics: Essays in Honor of George L. Trager* (Mouton, The Hague), pp. 395–412

—— 1979. *201 Vietnamese Verbs* (Barron's Educational Series, Woodbury, NY)

—— 1980. *Language in Vietnamese Society* (Asia Books, Carbondale, Ill.)

—— 1982–4. 'Studies in Nôm Characters: The State of the Art'. *Vietnam Culture Journal*, vol. 1, no. 1, pp. 25–36, vol. 2, nos. 1–2 and vol. 3, no. 1, pp. 107–113

Nguyễn Khắc Viện et al. 1976. *Linguistic Essays* (Xunhasaba, Hanoi)
Thompson, L.C. 1965. *A Vietnamese Grammar* (University of Washington Press, Seattle)
Trần Trọng Kim, Phạm Duy Khiêm and Bùi Kỷ. 1943. *Grammaire annamite*, 2nd ed. (Lê Thăng, Hanoi)
Trương Văn Chình. 1970. *Structure de la langue vietnamienne* (Librairie Orientaliste Paul Geuthner, Paris)

4 SINO-TIBETAN LANGUAGES

Scott DeLancey

1 Introduction

The Sino-Tibetan family consists of two branches: Sinitic, consisting of the Chinese languages and possibly the aberrant Bai or Minjia language of Yunnan (although Bai may also be a heavily Sinicised Tibeto-Burman language), and Tibeto-Burman, which includes several hundred languages spoken from the Tibetan plateau in the north to the Malay peninsula in the south and from northern Pakistan in the west to northeastern Vietnam in the east. Earlier classification schemes included Miao-Yao, Tai and Vietnamese in the Sino-Tibetan family on the basis of their remarkable typological resemblance to Chinese, but it is now clear that the structural resemblances and shared vocabulary among these languages are areal features rather than shared inheritance from a common ancestor.

Comparative Tibeto-Burman is a relatively unexplored field and there is not yet a complete and reliable schema for the genetic relationships among the various sub-branches of the family. (Indeed, we cannot say for certain how many Tibeto-Burman languages there are or even whether there may not still be a few — possibly in western Nepal, very probably in northern Burma and southeastern Tibet — that are yet to be discovered.) With the exception of the problematic Rung group, there is general agreement that the groupings listed below constitute genetic units at some level. (Note that many languages are known in the literature by several names, usually including one or more Chinese, Burmese or Indic ethnonyms which sometimes label groups speaking rather diverse languages. A very useful list of language names is given in Hale (1982).)

Bodish: Includes Tibetan; Kanauri, Bunan and other poorly documented languages of the Himalayan frontier of India; Gurung, Tamang, Thakali; probably Newari, the old state language of Nepal; and some (but not all) other Tibeto-Burman languages of Nepal.

East Himalayan: Includes the Kiranti/Rai (Limbu, Thulung, Bahing, Vayu etc.) languages and probably some others in eastern Nepal. Most closely related to Bodish.

Bodo-Garo: Includes Bodo (Boro), Garo and a number of other languages spoken in Assam.

Konyak: A group of languages (Nocte, Chang, Wancho etc.) spoken by tribal peoples in Arunachal Pradesh in India and probably adjacent areas of Burma. The Indian ethnonym 'Naga' is applied to these groups as well as to those speaking 'Naga' languages (see below). The Konyak 'Naga' languages are probably most closely related to the Bodo-Garo group.

Naga: Languages (Angami, Sema, Rengma, Lotha etc.) spoken by tribal peoples in Arunachal Pradesh and adjacent areas of Burma. These 'Naga proper' languages are most closely related to the Kuki-Chin and Mikir-Meithei groups.

Kuki-Chin: Called Kuki in India, Chin in Burma; includes Lushai, Lakher and numerous other languages in western Burma and easternmost India and Bangladesh.

Mikir-Meithei: Two languages of Manipur and Assam states in India; closely related to Naga and Kuki-Chin.

Abor-Miri-Dafla: A group of little known languages of Arunachal Pradesh and adjacent areas of Tibet. Reliable documentation, which is only now beginning to become available, may permit the assignment of some or all of these languages to other groups.

Kachinic: Includes at least the conservative and historically important Jinghpo (Jinghpaw, Chinghpo, often erroneously called 'Kachin', a Burmese ethnonym which refers to speakers of the Burmish Lawng and Zaiwa languages as well as of Jinghpo) dialects of Yunnan, Assam and northern Burma and perhaps the inadequately documented Luish languages.

Lolo-Burmese: The Burmish sub-branch includes Burmese and a few minor languages of Yunnan and northern Burma (notably Lawng or Maru and Zaiwa or Atsi). The Loloish languages are spoken by hill tribes in northern Burma and Thailand, Laos, Yunnan and Vietnam. Important members of Loloish include Yi (Lolo), Lahu, Lisu and Hani (Akha). The Naxi or Moso language of Yunnan is generally considered to be closely linked to Lolo-Burmese and by some scholars to fit in or near the Loloish sub-branch.

Rung: A cover term for several morphologically conservative languages of western China and northern Burma, including the Nung languages (Rawang and Trung), Gyarong, the Qiang languages (Qiang and Primi) and the extinct Tangut. (This corresponds roughly to a grouping called 'Sifan' in early work on Tibeto-Burman.) The relationships of these languages to one another and to the rest of the family are controversial; Nung and Qiang-Tangut show evidence of close relationship to Naxi and Lolo-Burmese, while Nung shows lexical links to Jinghpo, and Gyarong to Tibetan (although this is apparently a result of borrowing) and Kamarupan.

Karen: Several closely related dialects spoken in eastern Burma and adjacent parts of Thailand. Karen is typologically quite divergent from the rest of the family, manifesting fairly consistent SVO syntactic patterns where other Tibeto-Burman languages are resolutely SOV. Largely on this basis there remains some doubt as to whether Karen represents another branch of Tibeto-Burman, coordinate with the others, or one branch of a higher-order Tibeto-Karen family, the other branch of which is Tibeto-Burman. Currently opinion in the field is inclining toward the first alternative, but the problem is not yet settled.

The higher-order grouping of the Tibeto-Burman languages is problematic. The system proposed by Shafer (1966–73) and some tentative suggestions by Benedict (1972) are generally accepted as credible working hypotheses; although several other classification schemes have been proposed, none can be considered reliable. The best known classifications are summarised and compared in Hale (1982). Rather than repeat these readily available schemes here I have represented in figures 4.1 and 4.2 a classification which incorporates several hypotheses being considered in

Figure 4.1: Higher-order Groupings Within Tibeto-Burman

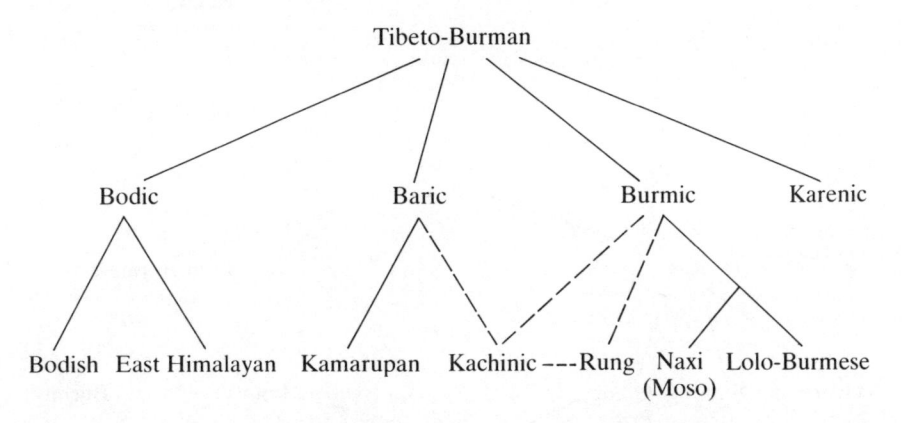

```
                        Tibeto-Burman
         ┌──────────────┬────────┬──────────────┐
       Bodic           Baric    Burmic         Karenic
       ╱  ╲            ╱ ╲      ╱╱╱ ╲
      ╱    ╲          ╱   ╲    ╱╱╱   ╲
 Bodish  East Himalayan  Kamarupan  Kachinic ---Rung  Naxi  Lolo-Burmese
                                                    (Moso)
```

Note: Dotted lines represent uncertain or controversial relationships.

current published and unpublished work by a number of scholars; this should not be taken as necessarily more correct than earlier suggestions of Shafer and Benedict.

Figure 4.2: Middle-level Relationships Within Tibeto-Burman

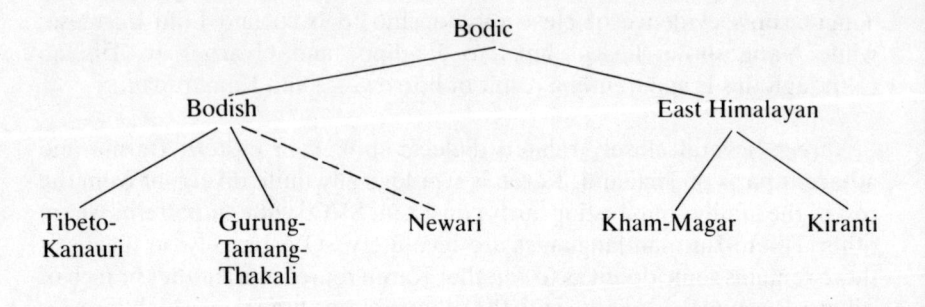

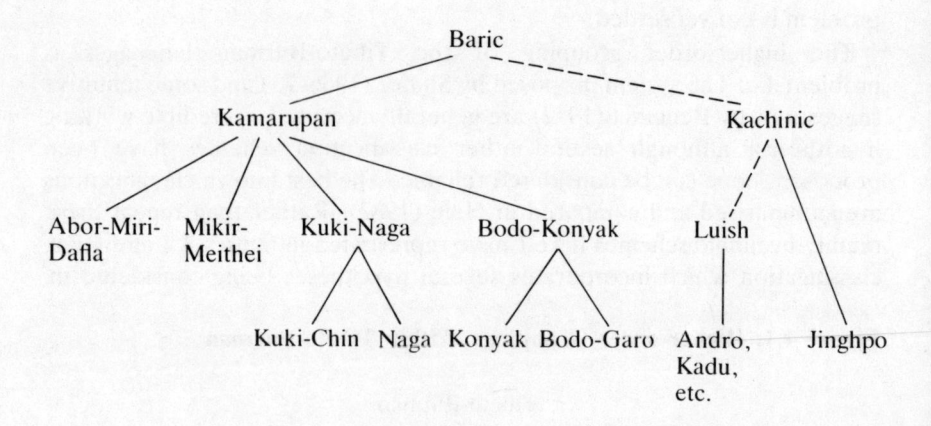

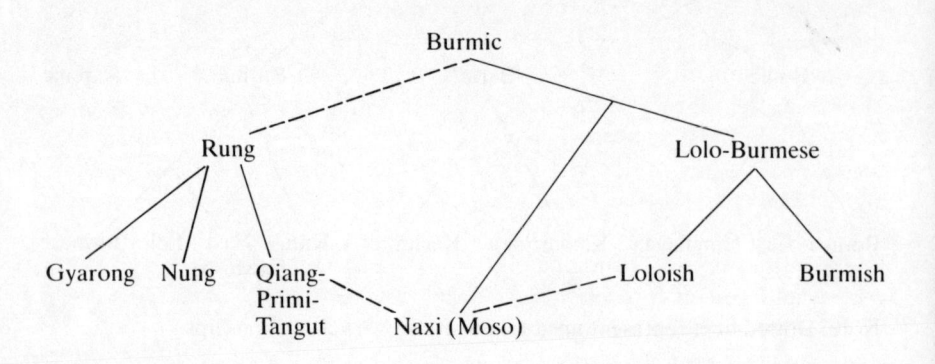

```
                          Bodic
                  ┌─────────┴─────────┐
               Bodish              East Himalayan
           ┌─────┼─ ─ ─┐           ┌─────┴─────┐
       Tibeto-  Gurung-  Newari  Kham-Magar  Kiranti
       Kanauri  Tamang-
                Thakali
```

```
                         Baric
                  ┌────────┴ ─ ─ ─ ─┐
              Kamarupan            Kachinic
        ┌────┬────┼────────┐       ┌ ─ ┴──┐
    Abor-Miri- Mikir- Kuki-Naga Bodo-Konyak Luish
    Dafla    Meithei   │          │        │
                  ┌────┴───┐  ┌───┴───┐   ┌─┴──────┐
              Kuki-Chin  Naga Konyak Bodo-Garo Andro,  Jinghpo
                                               Kadu,
                                               etc.
```

```
                         Burmic
                  ┌ ─ ─ ─ ─┴────────┐
                Rung              Lolo-Burmese
          ┌──────┼──────┐          ┌────┴────┐
       Gyarong Nung  Qiang-      Loloish   Burmish
                     Primi-
                     Tangut─ ─ Naxi (Moso)─ ─
```

The best known Tibeto-Burman languages are Tibetan and Burmese, the two which have the longest and most extensive literary traditions. Both have a primarily Buddhistic literature written in an Indic script; the Tibetan script dates to the seventh century. The earliest attestations of Burmese are in twelfth-century inscriptions; the earliest Tibetan writings extant were discovered in the caves at Tun-huang and date from the ninth century.

The vast majority of Tibeto-Burman languages are (or were until this century) non-literate, but a few have writing systems of one sort or another. In the sphere of Indian influence, Newari (spoken in Nepal), Lepcha (in Sikkim) and Meithei or Manipuri (Manipur State, India) have independently developed Devanāgarī-based alphabets (although the Lepcha, in particular, is scarcely recognisable as Indic at first glance), in which there exist historical and religious texts which have yet to be investigated linguistically. Apparently all three systems are now considered obsolete and these languages, like others in Nepal and India, are now written in Hindi or Nepali script.

Within the Chinese sphere we find two extremely interesting indigenous writing systems. The better known is that of Tangut or Xixia, the apparently extinct language used in the Tangut kingdom which existed in the north-west of China until 1227. The Tangut script consists of characters reminiscent of and obviously modelled after Chinese, but nevertheless quite distinct. Tangut and its script have been intensively studied in recent decades by scholars in Japan and the Soviet Union. The other system is a basically pictographic script, with a few syllabic phonetic elements, used by priests among the Naxi (Nakhi) or Moso of Yunnan; a very similar system was used among the neighbouring Yi (Lolo). It is generally assumed that the original stimulus for the development of this system was a vague acquaintance with Chinese writing, although there are few recognisably Chinese elements in the system.

2 Comparative Sino-Tibetan Phonology

Our current understanding of Proto-Tibeto-Burman phonology is still uncertain, although considerable progress has been made in the reconstruction of a few sub-branches, in particular Lolo-Burmese. However, the segmental inventory given in table 4.1 is generally accepted by most researchers. Proto-Tibeto-Burman is reconstructed as having two series of stops (the third series found in written Tibetan, Burmese, Jinghpo and several other languages can be shown to be secondary innovations which occurred independently in various languages, usually conditioned by the loss of earlier prefixes) and one of nasals (again, many languages have both voiced and voiceless resonants, but the voiceless series reflect an earlier voiceless prefix, most commonly *s-).

Table 4.1: The Consonants of Proto-Tibeto-Burman

p	t	k
b	d	g
m	n	ŋ
	s	
	z	
	l	r
w	y	

Proto-Tibeto-Burman certainly had no more than five phonemic vowels, and there remains some question about the Proto-Tibeto-Burman status of the mid vowels.

The relationship of this (or any alternative) Proto-Tibeto-Burman system to that of Proto-Sino-Tibetan is rather difficult to assess, given the considerable uncertainty which remains with respect to the phonological reconstruction of Early Chinese. However, recent work in that area (in particular by F.-K. Li and by N. Bodman and W. Baxter, as well as some less widely accepted proposals by E.G. Pulleyblank and A. Schuessler) present a picture which is much closer to that reconstructed for Proto-Tibeto-Burman than was the earlier and still widely cited system of B. Karlgren.

Historical developments in the Sino-Tibetan sound systems are best described in terms of syllable structure. Like modern East Asian languages, Proto-Tibeto-Burman and Proto-Chinese permitted only a subset of the consonant inventory to occur in syllable-final position; these included one series of stops (presumably voiceless), the nasals, *s, *r, *l, *w and *y. This inventory is greatly reduced in most attested languages; Tibetan orthography preserves all but the semi-vowels, but most languages preserve only the stops and nasals. Modern Central Tibetan allows only /p/ and /m/ in final position, while some Chinese, Loloish and Naga languages have no syllable-final consonants at all. The depletion of the inventory of final consonants typically correlates with a concomitant increase in the number of vowel and tone distinctions in the syllable nucleus.

In syllable-initial position clusters of obstruent or nasal plus medial *y, *w, *r and *l occurred. These are preserved in part in Tibetan and Burmese orthography and some modern languages, but in general they have simplified, typically with *Cl- merging with *Cy- or *Cr-, *Cy- giving either simple *C- or a new palatal series and *Cr- simplifying, merging with *Cy- (as in Burmese), or giving a new retroflex series (as in Central Tibetan). In addition, Benedict and most other scholars reconstruct at least some of the famous Tibetan initial clusters for Proto-Tibeto-Burman. These are probably all etymologically bimorphemic, but it is likely that fossilised, synchronically unanalysable clusters existed in Proto-Tibeto-Burman, if not Proto-Sino-Tibetan. It is, however, extremely common to find the same etymon occurring in different languages with different prefixes, as for example Written Tibetan *rna*, Balti Tibetan *sna*, Tangkhul *khana* < **g-na* 'ear', or Balti Tibetan *gwa*, Written Burmese *swa* 'go'. Some such cases may represent lexical alternants at the Proto-Tibeto-Burman level, but others reflect independent secondary compounding in the daughter languages. For example, Balti *gwa* and Burmese *swa* represent independently developed compounds of a Proto-Sino-Tibetan root **wa* 'go' with other motion verbs **ga* and **sa*.

The historical status of tone in Tibeto-Burman and Sino-Tibetan remains a topic of some controversy. Probably a majority of Tibeto-Burman languages have phonemic tone and/or voice register distinctions, as do Chinese and the unrelated Tai, Miao-Yao and Vietnamese languages. In the earliest days of Sino-Tibetan studies, lexical tone was considered a diagnostic Sino-Tibetan feature, an assumption which played a major role in the erroneous assignment of Tai and Vietnamese to the Sino-Tibetan family. It is now clear that the strikingly parallel tone systems of these languages and Chinese represent an areal feature which had diffused across genetic lines; however, the original source of the feature remains unclear.

There is now considerable evidence to suggest that the various tone systems within Sino-Tibetan may not be directly cognate, i.e. that tone systems have developed independently in various branches of the family. Research on the origin of tone systems has demonstrated that phonemic tone can develop in the course of the loss of distinctions between syllable-initial and/or -final consonants. Typically the loss of a voicing contrast in initial consonants results in a phonemic high/low tone distinction, with earlier voiced initial syllables developing low tone and voiceless initial syllables developing high tone, while the depletion of the inventory of possible syllable-final consonants results in a distinction between open syllables and those ending in a glottal stop or constriction, with the latter eventually giving rise to rising or falling tones. Such is the origin, for example, of the secondarily developed tone systems found in the Central Tibetan dialects. Several scholars have presented evidence suggesting that the tones of Chinese may have originated in this way at a date considerably later than the separation of the Chinese and the Tibeto-Burman branches of Sino-Tibetan.

If the tone systems of the Sino-Tibetan languages represent parallel independent developments rather than common inheritance, this would explain the existence of numerous non-tonal Tibeto-Burman languages and the considerable difficulty which has been encountered in attempts to find correspondences among the tones of the various tonal Tibeto-Burman languages. Within major branches tone correspondences can sometimes be found; for example, the tones of the Lolo-Burmese languages correspond regularly and it is clear that a tone system can be reconstructed for Proto-Lolo-Burmese. However, when this system is compared with the tone system of other tone languages such as Jinghpo or Tamang, it frequently turns out that otherwise clearly cognate items do not correspond in tone class, suggesting that the tone systems developed after the separation of the languages being compared.

Nevertheless, the hypothesis of the secondary origin of Sino-Tibetan tone systems is not yet universally accepted. Benedict, in particular, has called attention to some regular correspondences which can be found between the tone classes of cognate morphemes in Chinese and certain Tibeto-Burman languages, particularly Burmese and Karen, on the basis of which he reconstructs a two-tone system for Proto-Sino-Tibetan. This hypothesis entails the wholesale loss of tone in many Tibeto-Burman languages, particularly in the Himalayan branch, subsequently followed by their reemergence in Central Tibetan and a few other Himalayan languages; this consequence has resulted in considerable resistance in the field to Benedict's proposal.

3 Tibeto-Burman Typology and Reconstruction: Morphology and Syntax

With the exception of Karen, all of the Tibeto-Burman languages are postpositional SOV languages with predominantly agglutinative morphology (Burmese, described in a separate chapter in this volume, is in most respects typical) and this must also have been true of Proto-Sino-Tibetan. Several languages retain traces of older inflectional alternations in the verb, and a few show innovative case alternations in pronouns. A number of case marking typologies occur in the family, including consistently ergative marking (Gurung), aspectually split ergative or active/stative patterns (Newari and various Tibetan dialects), split ergative marking in which third person transitive subjects take ergative case while first and second persons do not (Kiranti, Gyarong) and variations on a more-or-less nominative-accusative topic marking scheme (most Lolo-Burmese languages; see the chapter on Burmese). A detailed examination of an example of this last type can be found in Hope (1974).

Current comparative work on Tibeto-Burman morphological structure presents a picture quite different from what has historically been assumed about Tibeto-Burman languages. Proto-Tibeto-Burman is now reconstructed with a split-ergative case marking and verb agreement system of the sort exemplified by the following Gyarong examples, in which third person but not first and second person transitive subjects are case marked (in the modern languages which retain this system the ergative marker is often identical to the instrumental and/or ablative postposition), while the verb shows pronominal concord with any first or second person argument, regardless of its grammatical role:

ŋa mə nasŋo-ŋ
I s/he scold-1 sg.
'I scold him/her.'

ŋə-njɔ mə nasŋo-č
I-du. he scold-1 du.
'We two scold him/her.'

ŋə-ñiɛ mə nasŋo-i
I-pl. s/he scold-1 pl.
'We (pl.) scold him/her.'

mə-kə ŋa u-nasŋo-ŋ
s/he-erg. I dir.-scold-1 sg.
'S/he scolds me.'

mə-ñiɛ-kə ŋa u-nasŋo-ŋ
he-du.-erg. I dir.-scold.-1 sg.
'They two scold me.'

mə-kə ŋə-njɔ u-nasŋo-č
he-erg. I-du. dir.-scold-1 du.
'S/he scolds us two.'

Note the ergative postposition -kə marking third but not first person subjects and the fact that both person and number agreement are always with the first person participant, whether it is subject or object.

Both the pronominal and the verb agreement systems probably distinguished dual as well as singular and plural number, as well as an inclusive/exclusive distinction. In a number of modern languages (e.g. Gyarong, Chepang, Nocte) the verb also marks in transitive clauses whether the subject is higher or lower than the object on a 1st > 2nd > 3rd or 1st=2nd > 3rd person hierarchy, and this 'direct/inverse' marking system is probably also to be reconstructed for the Proto-Tibeto-Burman verb. While no modern language preserves this reconstructed system in its entirety, most of these categories are retained at least vestigially in a large number of languages which represent nearly every major division of the family. (The most conservative morphology is found in the East Himalayan, Rung and Jinghpo languages.) Probably the closest attested system to the Proto-

Table 4.3: Intransitive Agreement Affixes in Gyarong (Suomo Dialect)

	Sg.	Du.	Pl.
1st person	V-ŋ	V-č	V-i
2nd person	tə-V-n	tə-V-n-č	tə-V-ñ
3rd person		∅	

Note: V indicates position of the verb stem.

Tibeto-Burman system is that of Gyarong, spoken in Sichuan; the example sentences above and the paradigms in tables 4.3 and 4.4 (from the work of Jin Peng) exemplify the system.

Table 4.4: Transitive Verb Affixes in Gyarong (Suomo Dialect)

Object	1st person Singular	Dual	Plural	2nd person Singular	Dual	Plural	3rd person
Subject 1st Sg./Du./Pl.				tə-a-V-n	tə-a-V-n-č	tə-a-V-ñ	V-ŋ / V-č / V-i
2nd Sg./Du./Pl.	kə-u-V-ŋ	kə-u-V-č	kə-u-V-i				tə-V / tə-V-n-č / tə-V-ñ
3rd	u-V-ŋ	u-V-č	u-V-i	tə-u-V-n	tə-u-V-n-č	tə-u-V-ñ	V-u / u-V

Note: V indicates position of the verb stem.

The -ŋ and -n suffixes reflect the Proto-Sino-Tibetan pronouns *ŋa and *na(ŋ), while the dual and plural suffixes -č and -i are probably reconstructible for Proto-Tibeto-Burman, although their exact form is uncertain. Both series of prefixes are almost certainly reconstructible for Proto-Tibeto-Burman. The u- and a- are direct/inverse markers; the tə/kə- series may also have been part of the direct/inverse system, although their original function is quite unclear. Reflexes of one or the other occur in a great many modern languages as second person agreement indices and in Gyarong one or the other occurs in all and only those verbs with a second person participant, but in the Nung and some other languages a member of the series also occurs on transitive verbs with third person subject and first person object.

Early work on comparative Tibeto-Burman assumed that, since this verbal morphology is not found in Tibetan or Burmese, it must be a secondary innovation in those languages which manifest it; hence all such languages were lumped together in a putatively genetic group of 'pronominalised' languages. Recent research has shown, however, that while the system is apparently completely extinct in Lolo-Burmese, Bodo-Garo and Tibetan proper, it is found in near relatives of each of these and is attested in all other major Tibeto-Burman subgroups except for Karen with a consistency that makes it clear that some version of it must have been a Proto-Tibeto-Burman feature. A good description of a language of this type is Caughley (1982), which also summarises much of the available data on verb paradigms in other Tibeto-Burman languages.

Several other verbal affixes can be reconstructed for Proto-Tibeto-Burman and probably Proto-Sino-Tibetan, although the original functions of most of them remain unclear. A causative *s- prefix is clearly reconstructible for Proto-Sino-Tibetan and an intransitivising *m- definitely for Proto-Tibeto-Burman and probably for Proto-Sino-Tibetan. An *-s suffix is also reconstructed for Proto-Sino-Tibetan; there is good evidence for both perfectivising and nominalising functions for such a suffix and it is possible that these functions reflect two different etyma. There is also phonological evidence for a dental stop suffix with similar functions, which may originally have been a conditioned allomorph of *-s. We also find evidence (particularly from the complex verbal system of Classical Tibetan) for prefixed *g- (or *kV-) and *l- and/or *r- (or *lV-, *rV-) of Proto-Tibeto-Burman provenience, but their original function is not yet recoverable.

There is evidence for a considerable amount of derivational morphology in Tibeto-Burman and Sino-Tibetan, most of which originated in compounding processes. Most if not all of the modern Sino-Tibetan languages and certainly all reconstructible ancestral stages have very productive compounding processes which create bimorphemic two-syllable nouns (and sometimes verbs). In the Tibeto-Burman languages these tend diachronically to reduce one syllable (generally the first), thus eventually creating what appears synchronically and etymologically to be a derivational prefix. The process is illustrated by the following forms from the Yunnan dialect of Jinghpo (for which example I am indebted to L. Diehl): the word *lam* 'road, path' occurs both free and in compounds such as *lamsun* 'narrow path', *lamshe* 'side road', *lamta?* 'level path (along a mountainside)'. But each of these also occurs in one or more reduced forms, e.g. *lamsun~masun~nsun, lamshe~mashe, lamta?~nta?*; thus there is an identifiable set of forms in which there appears to be a prefix *ma-* or *n-* meaning 'road, path'. The prevalence of this pattern of development has considerably slowed progress in lexical comparison and phonological reconstruction both for Tibeto-Burman and between Tibeto-Burman and Chinese, since these secondary prefixes typically disappear, but before doing so can affect the phonological development of the root initial consonant, thus leaving perturbations in the pattern of regular sound correspondences between attested languages.

Bibliography

Benedict (1972), actually written in the 1940s and out-of-date in some respects, is still the closest the field has come to a handbook of comparative Sino-Tibetan. Volume 1 of Shafer (1966–73) contains his classification scheme for Sino-Tibetan (including Tai); the rest of the work is of limited use. Bibliographical sources are Shafer (1957–63) and Hale (1982), which latter updates Shafer's bibliography to the mid-1970s and includes a valuable synopsis of the various classification schemes for the family, which with the extensive language index makes it possible to deal with the considerable nomenclatural confusion in the field. Wolfenden (1929) is the classic survey of Tibeto-Burman morphology, outdated but not yet supplanted. Matisoff (1978) provides an excellent introduction to the problems of Sino-Tibetan lexical comparison.

The following grammars will give an impression of some of the range of variation found within Tibeto-Burman: Caughley (1982) is a detailed presentation of the verbal system of a conservative 'pronominalised' language and includes a synopsis of verb paradigms from other morphologically conservative languages; Hope (1974) is a detailed presentation of clause organisation in a language which has completely lost the Proto-Tibeto-Burman morphological system; Matisoff (1973) is the most complete grammatical description in existence of any Tibeto-Burman language.

References

Benedict, P.K. 1972. *Sino-Tibetan: A Conspectus* (Cambridge University Press, Cambridge)
Caughley, R. 1982. *The Syntax and Morphology of the Verb in Chepang* (Research School of Pacific Studies, Australian National University, Canberra)
Hale, A. 1982. *Research on Tibeto-Burman Languages* (Mouton, The Hague)
Hope, E. 1974. *The Deep Syntax of Lisu Sentences* (Research School of Pacific Studies, Australian National University, Canberra)
Matisoff, J. 1973. *The Grammar of Lahu* (University of California Press, Berkeley)
—— 1978. *Variational Semantics in Tibeto-Burman: The 'Organic' Approach to Linguistic Comparison* (ISHI Press, Philadelphia)
Shafer, R. 1957–63. *Bibliography of Sino-Tibetan Languages*, 2 parts.
—— 1966–73. *Introduction to Sino-Tibetan* (Otto Harrassowitz, Wiesbaden)
Wolfenden, S. 1929. *Outlines of Tibeto-Burman Linguistic Morphology* (Royal Asiatic Society, London)

5 Chinese

Charles N. Li and Sandra A. Thompson

1 Introduction: The Five Major Dialect Groups of Chinese

It is estimated that more than 1,000,000,000 people, approximately one-fourth of the earth's population, are speakers of some form of Chinese. Genetically, Chinese is an independent branch of the Sino-Tibetan family of languages (see Chapter 4). Within the Chinese branch, there are a number of dialects, which can be classified into a minimum of five groups on the basis of their structural affinities.

Mandarin. This is the major dialect group in China, both in terms of political importance and in terms of number of speakers. The native speakers of this dialect group represent approximately 70 per cent of the total Chinese population. They occupy the North China plain, the middle Yángzǐ plain, the Huái plain, the north-east plain, the Sìchuān basin and most of Guǎngxī, Guèizhōu and Yúnnán provinces. The term 'Mandarin' is an English translation of the old Běijīng expression *guān-huà* 'official language', which was for many centuries the dialect of Běijīng. In modern China, Běijīng dialect was accepted as a standard for the official language in the early part of this century. Since the 1950s, because of political and geographical boundaries, the official language of China, called *pǔtōnghuà* 'common speech', and the official language of Táiwān, called *guóyǔ* 'national language', differ from each other slightly in both vocabulary and grammar, although both are based on the Běijīng dialect. One of the four official languages of Singapore, *huáyǔ*, is also based on the Běijīng dialect. Again, it is somewhat different from both *pǔtōnghuà* and *guóyǔ*.

The other basis for considering Mandarin as the 'major' Chinese dialect group is that, in terms of both vocabulary and structure, the modern written language is closer to Mandarin than to any of the other dialects.

Wú. The Wú dialects are spoken around the lower Yángzǐ River and its tributaries: the provinces of Jiāngsū, Zhèjiāng and Ānhuī, which include the major urban centres of Shànghǎi, Sūzhōu and Wēnzhōu.

Map 5.1: Dialect Map of China

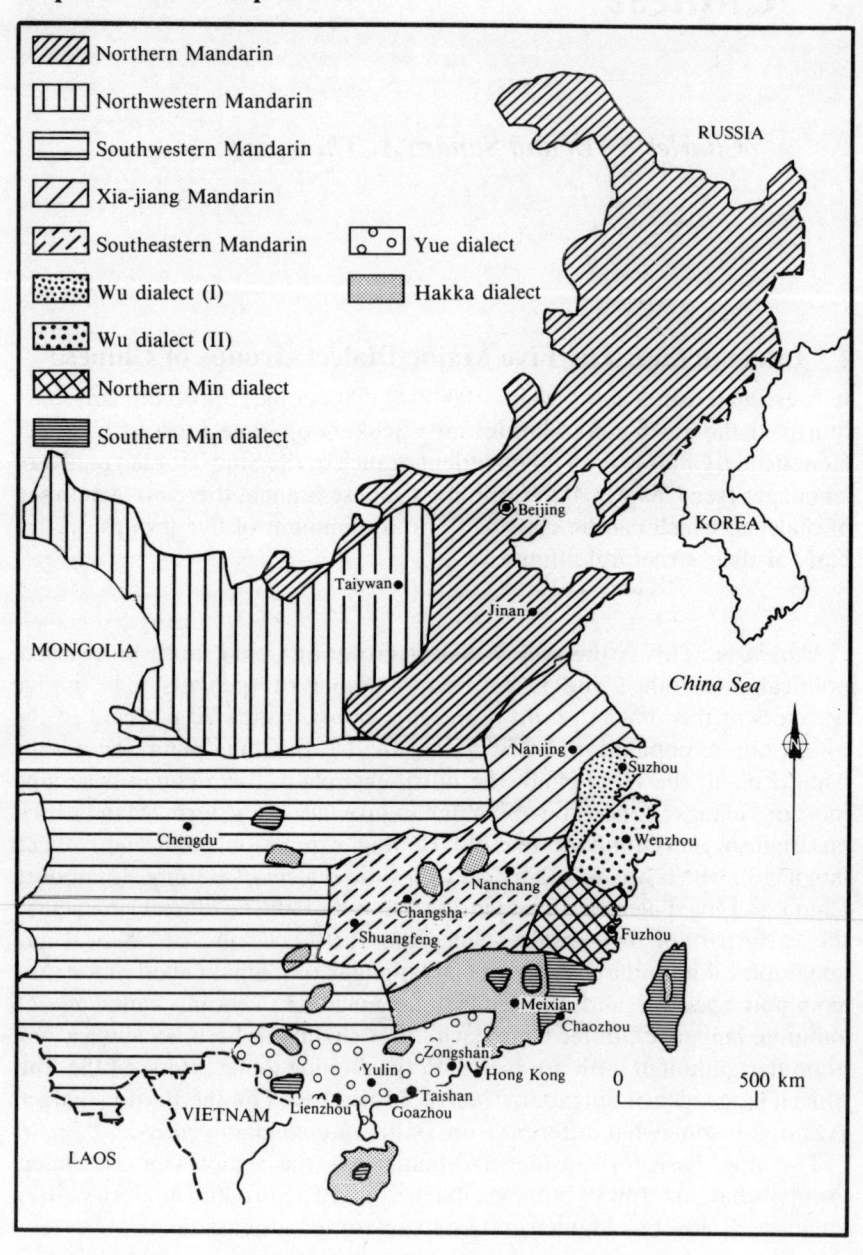

- Northern Mandarin
- Northwestern Mandarin
- Southwestern Mandarin
- Xia-jiang Mandarin
- Southeastern Mandarin
- Wu dialect (I)
- Wu dialect (II)
- Northern Min dialect
- Southern Min dialect
- Yue dialect
- Hakka dialect

Mǐn. These dialects are spoken by people living in Táiwān and Fújiàn provinces and Hǎinán Island in the Gulf of Tonkin. In English, these dialects are sometimes referred to as 'Fukkianese', 'Hokkianese', 'Amoy' and

'Taiwanese'. Most of the people of Táiwān are descendants of Mǐn speakers who emigrated from the coastal regions of Fújiàn province. For this reason, 85 per cent of the people in Táiwān still speak a Mǐn dialect as their native language. For the same reason, most of the speakers of Chinese in Singapore are also native speakers of a Mǐn dialect.

Yuè. The Yuè dialects are spoken primarily in the province of Guǎngdōng. Yuè dialects, including the well known Cantonese, the language of Guǎngzhōu (Canton), are spoken in many parts of the Chinese diaspora, particularly Hong Kong and overseas Chinese settlements such as the Chinatowns in the United States, Europe and South-East Asia. For this reason, many of the English words borrowed from Chinese have their origins in Cantonese, such as *kumquat* from Cantonese [kamkwat] and *chop suey* from Cantonese [tsap sui].

Hakka. The Hakka dialects are the least well known outside of China, because few of the Hakka people have emigrated from China. Most of the Hakka are scattered throughout southeastern China in Guǎngxī province and throughout the Mǐn and Yuè regions, as small, tightly-knit agricultural communities. Historically, the Hakka people were northerners who moved south during several waves of migration. Their name Hakka means 'guest', indicating their immigrant status in the southern areas to which they moved.

We have chosen to use the term 'dialect' for these five major groups of languages, even though the differences among them, in terms of both vocabulary and structure, are sufficient to cause mutual unintelligibility. There are two reasons for this choice. First, genetically related languages of one nation are typically considered 'dialects'. Secondly, China has always had a uniform written language which is logographic. People who cannot understand each others' speech can still read the same written language provided that they are educated. This tends to reinforce the idea of 'dialects' as opposed to separate languages.

We adopt this usage of dialect, even though it is based on political and social considerations rather than linguistic ones. In section 5, we will discuss the written language, but first, we will describe some of the structural properties common to Chinese dialects.

2 Phonology

All Chinese dialects, with rare exceptions, share two easily perceptible phonological properties: they are all tone languages, and they have a very highly constrained syllable structure. We will talk about each of these properties in turn.

2.1 Tone

When we speak of a tone language, we mean a language in which every stressed syllable has a significant contrastive pitch. This pitch may be level or contour, but it is an integral part of the pronunciation of the syllable and it serves to distinguish one syllable from another. Běijīng Mandarin serves as a good example, since it has one of the simplest tone systems of the Chinese dialects. As shown in table 5.1, it has four basic tones.

Table 5.1: Běijīng Mandarin Tones

Tone 1:	high level	˥	55
Tone 2:	high rising	˧˥	35
Tone 3:	dipping/falling	˨˩˦	214
Tone 4:	high falling	˥˩	51

The symbols in the column second from the right are known as tone letters. They provide a simplified time-pitch graph of the voice, where the vertical line on the right serves as a reference line for pitch height. The numbers at the right represent the pitch of the tone according to a scale of five levels, with 1 being the lowest and 5 the highest. Thus, tone 1 is a high level tone pronounced at the same high pitch (level 5) for its duration, while tone 4 is a falling tone which starts with the high pitch at level 5 and ends with the low pitch at level 1.

If we take the syllable [i] in Běijīng Mandarin with each of the four tones, we have four different words, as is shown in table 5.2.

Table 5.2: Four Words in Běijīng Mandarin

[i]^{55}	˥	'cloth'
[i]^{35}	˧˥	'to suspect'
[i]^{214}	˨˩˦	'chair'
[i]^{51}	˥˩	'meaning'

The Romanisation system officially adopted by the government in Běijīng, called Pīnyīn, represents the tones by means of diacritic marks above the nuclear vowel of the word. The diacritic mark for the high level tone is /ˉ/, for the rising tone, /ˊ/, for the curve tone, /ˇ/, and for the falling tone /ˋ/. For example, the four words of table 5.2 written in Pīnyīn are: yī 'cloth', yí 'to suspect', yǐ 'chair', yì 'meaning'.

Tonal variation accounts for the most common differences among the dialects of China. It is often true that the dialects in two villages, just a few miles apart, have different tone systems. As we have stated, Běijīng Mandarin has one of the simplest tone systems of all dialects: it has the

CHINESE 87

second smallest number of tones (only 4) and the rules governing the behaviour of the tones are relatively simple. In contrast, Cantonese has nine tones, six of regular length, and three for so-called 'short' syllables, as shown in table 5.3 (the short syllables are those with short vowels which end in *p, t* or *k*). (Tone 1 has a free variant 53).

Table 5.3: The Tones of Cantonese

(1)	⌐ 55	(4)	↘ 21	(7)	⌐ 5
(2)	⌐ 35	(5)	⌐ 23	(8)	⊢ 3
(3)	⊢ 33	(6)	⊥ 22	(9)	⊥ 2

In many dialects, the complexity of the tone system may be manifested not only in the number of tones, but also in the phenomenon of 'tone sandhi', that is, a change of tones when two or more syllables are pronounced together. The most complicated tone sandhi phenomena can be found in the Wú and Mǐn dialects. For example, in Cháozhōu, a southern Mǐn dialect, there are eight tones for syllables in isolation, including two short tones belonging to syllables with final stops. When a syllable is followed by another syllable, however, tone sandhi occurs: that is, each 'isolation tone' changes to a different tone, called a 'combination tone'. Table 5.4 shows the Cháozhōu isolation tones and their corresponding combination tones.

Table 5.4: Cháozhōu Tones

Isolation tones	5 ⌐	2 ⊢	33 ⊢	11 ⊥	35 ⌐	53 ↘	213 ✓	55 ⌐
Combination tones	3 ⊢	5 ⌐	33 ⊢	11 ⊥	31 ↘	35 ⌐	53 ⌐	13 ⌐

This means that for each monosyllabic word, speakers of the Cháozhōu dialect learn its isolation tone, the tone it has when it stands by itself, and the rules converting the isolation tone to the combination tone, the tone it has when it is followed by another syllable.

Let us look at an example of how tone sandhi works in Cháozhōu. In table 5.4 we can see that the high short tone in the first column becomes a mid short tone in combination. Thus, if we take the word for 'one' in isolation, we have

[tsek] ⌐ 5   'one'

but if we put it in front of the syllables meaning 'meal', it changes to

[tsek] ⊣ 3

like this:

[tsek] ⊣ 3   [tuŋ] ↘ 53   [puŋ] ⌐ 11   'one meal'

A glance at table 5.4 will reveal that the isolation tone of the second syllable [tuŋ], which is a 'classifier' (see page 95), is ↗ 213.

2.2 Syllable Structure in Chinese

The syllable structure of all the Chinese dialects is relatively simple compared with that of, say, English: no dialect, for example, allows consonant clusters and all dialects allow only a restricted set of consonants in syllable-final position. As with tone, Běijīng Mandarin has a relatively simple syllable structure:

$$(C) (V)V({}^V_N)$$

Every syllable has a nuclear vowel, which may occur with another vowel to form a diphthong or with two other vowels to form a triphthong. Initial and final consonants are optional and the only final consonants which are permitted are nasals (specifically, [n] and [ŋ]).

To take an example which differs from Mandarin, in Cantonese, a syllable may have a diphthong, but not a triphthong. Also, a Cantonese syllable may have an unreleased stop ([p], [t], [k]) or a nasal ([m], [n], [ŋ]) in the final position. The Cantonese syllable structure may be represented by the following schema:

$$(C)(V)V(C)$$

3 Morphology

Morphology concerns the internal structure of words. When a Chinese dialect is compared to a Slavonic or Romance language, for instance, one of the most obvious features to emerge is the relative simplicity of its word structure. Most Chinese words are made up of just one or two morphemes. In particular, Chinese dialects have few inflectional morphemes. Thus, while many languages, including those in the Indo-European, Semitic, Bantu, Altaic and Tibeto-Burman families, typically have inflectional morphemes indicating categories such as tense/aspect and number/person of the subject or object for verbs or categories such as gender and case for nouns, no such inflectional categories exist for Chinese dialects.

The type of morphological device found in Chinese dialects tends to involve compounds and derivational morphemes rather than inflectional ones. This type of morphological device is especially common in modern Mandarin. Because of this, the traditional characterisation of Mandarin as 'monosyllabic' is no longer accurate. A 'monosyllabic' language would be one in which each word consisted of just one syllable. While no language could be expected to be totally monosyllabic, this characterisation is certainly more applicable to the Yuè and Mǐn dialect groups than it is to Mandarin. According to one popular dictionary, roughly two-thirds of the basic everyday Běijīng Mandarin vocabulary consists of polysyllabic words. Table 5.5 provides a sample of disyllabic words in Běijīng Mandarin whose counterparts in Guǎngzhōu (Yuè) and Shàntóu (Mǐn) are monosyllabic.

Table 5.5: Mandarin Disyllabic Words and Their Corresponding Guǎngzhōu and Shàntóu Monosyllabic Words

	Běijīng Mandarin	*Guǎngzhōu (Yuè)*	*Shàntóu (Mǐn)*
'gold'	[tɕin-tsɿ]	[kɐm]	[kim]
'pond'	[tʂʰɿ-tsɿ]/[tʂʰɿ-tʰaŋ]	[tʰɔŋ]	[ti]
'ant'	[ma-i]	[ŋɐi]	[hia]
'tail'	[uei-pa]/[i-pa]	[mei]	[bue]
'clothing'	[i-ʂaŋ]	[sam]	[sā]
Negative existential verb	[mei-iou]	[mou]	[bo]
'good-looking'	[xau-kʰaŋ]	[lɛŋ]	[ɲia]
'to know'	[tʂɿ-tau]	[tɕi]	[tsai]
'contemptible'	[tʰau-iɛn]	[tsɐŋ]	[lou]

There is a historical explanation for the fact that Mandarin has the highest proportion of polysyllabic words of all the Chinese dialects. The ancestral language of the modern Chinese dialects was monosyllabic. Because of phonological changes that have taken place, more extensively in Mandarin than in the southern dialects, many formerly distinct syllables in Mandarin have become homophonous. Thus, where Guǎngzhōu, for example, still has a contrastive distinction between syllable-final [m] and [n] as shown in the words: [kɐm] 'gold' and [kɐn] 'tael', Běijīng Mandarin no longer retains that contrastive distinction. The Běijīng counterpart of the two distinct Guǎngzhōu syllables is just the one syllable, [tɕin]. If the Běijīng word for 'gold' (as listed in table 5.5) hadn't become the disyllabic form [tɕin-tsɿ], the two Běijīng words for 'gold' and 'tael' would have been homophonous in the form [tçīn]. The threat of too many homophonous words has forced the language to increase dramatically the proportion of polysyllabic words, principally by means of compounding or adding on a derivational suffix. As an example of the latter, the second syllable of the disyllabic Běijīng word, [tçīn-tsı] 'gold', was formerly a diminutive suffix. It has lost its diminutive meaning in the word [tçīn-tsı] and is now merely a part of the word for 'gold'. Let us also look at an example of a disyllabic Běijīng word obtained through compounding: [tʰău-ièn] 'contemptible'. This is a compound historically derived from two monosyllabic words, [tʰău] 'to beg' and [ièn] 'contempt'. The Guângzhōu and the Shàntóu words for 'contemptible' remain monosyllabic, as shown in table 5.5

3.1 Compounds

3.1.1 Resultative Verb Compound

One important type of verb compound is known as the 'resultative verb compound', where the second part of the compound signals some result of the action or process conveyed by the first part. Here are some examples from Běijīng Mandarin:[1] *dă-pò* 'hit-broken = hit (it) with the result that it is broken', *mà-kū* 'scold-cry = scold (someone) with the result that s/he cries'. The following sentences illustrate the use of these two sample resultative verb compounds.

```
wǒ     bǎ    píngzi   dă-pò         le
I      ba    bottle   hit-broken    crs.
```
'I broke the bottle.'

```
tā     bǎ    wǒ    mà-kū        le
s/he   ba    I     scold-cry    crs.
```
'S/he scolded me so much that I cried.'

One characteristic of all resultative verb compounds is that they may occur in what is known as the 'potential' form, which involves the insertion of *-de-* or *-bu-* between the two parts of the compound. The insertion of *-de-* has the effect of giving the compound an affirmative potential meaning, i.e. 'can', while the insertion of *-bu-* gives the compound the negative potential meaning 'cannot'. Consider one of the examples above, *dă-pò* 'hit-break'. Its two potential forms would be:

```
dă -de -pò              dă -bu     -pò
hit -can -broken        hit -cannot-broken
```

[1] Most of the examples given from here on will be from Běijīng Mandarin, which has an accepted Romanisation (Pīnyīn) familiar to some readers, rather than from other dialects for which we would have to use a phonetic notation. A table of Pīnyīn symbols and their corresponding IPA values is provided in Appendix 1.

Here they are used in sentences:

tā dǎ -de -pò nèi -ge píngzi
s/he hit -can -broken that -cl. bottle
'S/he can break that bottle.'

tā dǎ -bu -pò nèi -ge píngzi
s/he hit -cannot -broken that -cl. bottle
'S/he cannot break that bottle.'

Another type is the directional resultative verb construction. The first verb in a directional resultative verb construction implies movement and the second, which may itself be a compound, signals the direction in which the person or thing moves as a result. Here is an example and a sample sentence in which it occurs:

pǎo-húi -lái
run-return-come
'run back'

tā pǎo-húi -lái le
s/he run-return-come crs.
'S/he ran back.'

3.1.2 Parallel Verb Compounds

The two verbs that constitute a parallel verb compound are either synonymous, nearly synonymous or similar in meaning. Here are some examples:

pí-fá   'tired-tired = tired'   jiàn-zhú   'build-build = build'
fáng-shǒu   'defend-defend = defend'   bāng-zhù   'help-help = help'
fàng-qì   'loosen-abandon = to give up'   piāo-liú   'drift-flow = drift'

3.1.3 Nominal Compounds

As in English, Chinese has a wide range of nominal compound types. Here are a few examples, illustrating the different semantic relations between the nominal components of the compound.

(i) N_2 is made of N_1

máo-yī   'wool-clothing = sweater'
tiě-hézi   'iron-box = iron box'

(ii) N_2 is a container of N_1

fàn-wǎn   'rice-bowl = rice bowl'
shǔi-píngzi   'water-bottle = water bottle'

(iii) N_1 and N_2 are parallel

fù-mǔ   'father-mother = parents'
guó-jiā   'country-home = country'

(iv) N_2 denotes a product of N_1

jī-dàn   'chicken-egg = egg'
měiguó-huò   'America-product = American product'

(v) N_2 denotes a malady of N_1

xīngzàng-bìng   'heart-disease = heart disease'
fèi-yán   'lung-inflammation = inflammation of the lung'

(vi) N_2 is used for N_1

qiāng-dàn   'gun-bullet = bullet'
xié-yóu   'shoe-oil = shoe polish'

(vii) N_1 denotes the location of N_2

tián-shǔ   'field-mouse = field mouse'
tái-bù   'table-cloth = tablecloth'

3.1.4   Noun-Verb Compounds

The Chinese dialects also have several types of compounds consisting of a noun and a verb. One type might be called the 'subject-predicate' compound, where the first element historically has a 'subject' relationship to the second element. Here are two examples with sentences illustrating their usage:

dǎn-dà   'gall-big = brave'

tā   hěn   *dǎn-dà*
s/he   very   brave
'S/he is very brave.'

mìng-kǔ   'life-bitter = ill-fated'

wǒ   hěn   *mìng-kǔ*
I   very   ill-fated
'I have a hard life.'

Another type of noun-verb compound is one in which the second element historically bears a 'direct object' relationship to the first element. Here are two examples with sentences illustrating their usage:

xíng-lǐ   'perform-salutation = salute'

```
wǒ    gěi   tā    xíng-lǐ
I     to    s/he  salute
'I saluted him/her.'
```

```
zhěn-tóu    'rest-head = pillow'
```

```
wǒ   yǒu   liǎng -ge   zhěn-tóu
I    have  two   -cl.  pillow
'I have two pillows.'
```

3.2 Reduplication

As a morphological process, 'reduplication' means that a morpheme is repeated so that the original morpheme together with its repetition form a new word. One way in which reduplication is used in Chinese is to indicate that an action is being done 'a little bit'. Here is an example:

```
shuō-shuo   'speak-speak = speak a little'
```

```
nǐ    shuō-shuo        neì -jiàn   shì
you   speak a little   that -cl.   matter
'Speak a little about that matter!'
```

Adjectives can also be reduplicated, the semantic effect of which is to intensify their meaning. For example: *hóng* 'red', *hóng-hóng* 'vividly red'.

Manner adverbs can be formed from reduplicated adjectives. For example, *màn* 'slow' is an adjective but *màn-màn-de* 'slowly' is an adverb formed by reduplicating the adjective *màn* and adding on the particle *-de*. The following sentence illustrates the usage of the adverb, *màn-màn-de* 'slowly':

```
tā     màn-màn-de   pǎo
s/he   slowly       run
'S/he runs slowly.'
```

3.3 Affixation

Affixation is the morphological process whereby a bound morpheme is added to another morpheme to form a larger unit. Compared to Indo-European languages, Chinese has few affixation processes and most of them are not inflectional, but derivational.

3.3.1 Prefixes

There are very few prefixes in Chinese. *Kě-* is an example of a prefix which can be added to verbs to form adjectives; its meaning can be described as '-able', as shown in the following examples:

```
kě-ài     'lovable'      ài     'to love'
kě-xiào   'laughable'    xiào   'to laugh'
kě-kào    'dependable'   kào    'to depend'
```

Another prefix is *dì-*, which is added to numerals to form ordinals, as in:

dì-liù 'sixth'   liù 'six'

3.3.2 Suffixes

There are several categories of suffixes which are very important in Chinese grammar. Foremost among them is the category of verb suffixes serving as aspect markers. Aspect markers vary from dialect to dialect. Here, we will cite two examples from Běijīng Mandarin.

'Aspect' refers to how a situation is viewed with respect to its internal make-up. To take an example, let us first look at an English sentence:

Cheryl **was watching TV** when I **spilled the tea**.

In this English sentence, the first verb phrase, *was watching TV*, differs significantly from the second verb phrase, *spilled the tea*, because the two phrases reflect different ways in which the two situations are viewed. The second verb phrase presents the totality of the situation referred to without reference to its internal make-up: the entire situation is viewed as a single unanalysable whole. When a language has a special verb form to indicate the viewing of an event in its entirety, we say that that form signals the 'perfective' aspect. In Běijīng Mandarin, the suffix *-le* is used for the perfective aspect.

The first verb phrase, *was watching TV*, does not present the situation of Cheryl's watching TV in its entirety. Instead, it makes explicit reference to the internal make-up of 'TV watching', presenting it as ongoing, referring neither to its beginning nor its end, but to its duration. Verbal markers signalling this ongoing/durative aspect can be called 'durative' aspect markers. In Běijīng Mandarin, the durative suffix is *-zhe*, whose occurrence is restricted to certain semantic types of verbs.

Here are some examples of the perfective and the durative suffixes in Běijīng Mandarin:

tā   bǎ   chēzi   mài-*le*
s/he   *ba*   car   sell -perf.
'S/he sold the car.'

wǒ   chī-le   sān -wǎn fàn
I   eat-perf. three-bowl rice
'I ate three bowls of rice.'

tā   chuān-zhe yī -shuāng xīn xiézi
s/he wear -dur. one-pair   new shoe
'S/he is wearing a pair of new shoes.'

qiáng-shàng guà -zhe   yī -fu   huà
wall -on   hang-dur.   one-cl.   painting
'There is a painting hanging on the wall.'

Another important category of suffixes is classifiers. A classifier is a morpheme co-occurring with a noun which is individuated or specified in the discourse, that is, a noun which occurs with a numeral, a quantifier or a demonstrative. Classifiers do not occur with a noun which is non-referential or non-specific. When a noun is individuated, quantified or specified, the classifier occurs as a suffix of the numeral, the quantifier or the demonstrative. Other than the general classifier *-ge* which can occur with most nouns, a noun in Chinese can in general occur with only one classifier and the speaker must learn which classifier goes with which noun. For example, the Běijīng classifier for books is *-běn*, so that 'that book' is:

    nèi *-běn* shū
    that-cl. book

The classifier for snakes is *-tiáo*, so that 'four snakes' is:

    sì   *-tiáo* shé
    four-cl. snake

Here are a few other classifiers:

    -zhāng for tables, maps, papers etc.
    -jiàn   for garments such as shirts, coats, sweaters, and events, news etc.
    -lì   for pearls, marbles, grains of sand, wheat, rice, corn or millet etc.

Earlier we pointed out that classifiers are not used when a noun is non-referential or non-specific. The following sentence contains an example of a non-referential noun, *diànyǐng* 'movie':

    wǒ bu cháng kàn diànyǐng
    I   not often see   movie
    'I don't see movies often.'

A third important category of suffixes in Chinese is that of locative suffixes. These occur with nouns — often marked with a preposition — to specify location with respect to the referent of the noun. Here are some examples:

    tā   zài chuáng-*shàng*
    s/he at   bed   -on
    'S/he is on the bed.'

    tā   cóng fángzi-li pǎo-chū-lái   le
    s/he from house-in   run-exit-come crs.
    'S/he came running out from the house.'

Besides the three categories of grammatical suffixes mentioned above, there are the genitive morpheme *-de* and the manner adverbial marker, which also has the form *-de*. Both the genitive morpheme and the adverbial marker occur as suffixes. Examples follow:

wǒ-*de* qìchē
I -gen. car
'my car'

màn-man-*de* zǒu
slowly walk
'Walk slowly!'

Finally we will cite two derivational suffixes. Productive derivational suffixes are not numerous in Chinese, and they do not occupy a very important position in Chinese grammar. One example of a derivational suffix is *-xué* '-ology', as in:

dòngwù-xué   'animal-ology = zoology'
zhíwù -xué   'plant-ology = botany'
shéhuì -xué   'society-ology = sociology'
lìshǐ   -xué   'history-ology = history'

Another example of a derivational suffix is *-jiā* '-ist', as in:

lìshǐxué   -jiā   'history-ist = historian'
lǐlùn   -jiā   'theory-ist = theorist'
xiǎoshuō   -jiā   'novel-ist = novelist'
dòngwuxué-jiā   'zoology-ist = zoologist'

4 Syntax

4.1 Chinese as an Isolating Language

One of the first things a person familiar with Indo-European languages notices about Chinese is its lack of grammatical inflections. Although there is a morphological category of aspect in Chinese (as discussed above in section 3.3), most words in Chinese have one immutable form, which does not change according to number, case, gender, tense, mood or any of the other inflectional categories familiar from other languages. Languages with very little grammatical inflectional morphology are known as 'isolating' languages. What are some of the concomitant factors of the isolating character of Chinese?

First, there is no case morphology signalling differences between grammatical relations such as subject, direct object or indirect object, nor is there any 'agreement' or cross-indexing on the verb to indicate what is subject and what is object. In Chinese, in fact, there are few grammatical reasons for postulating grammatical relations, although there are, of course, ways of distinguishing who did what to whom, just as there are in all languages. One way to tell who did what to whom is by word order: ordinarily, the noun phrase before the verb is the agent or the experiencer and the noun phrase after the verb is the patient or affected participant, much as in English. Furthermore, in natural discourse, it is usually clear who is the agent and who or what is the patient without any special marking.

A corollary to this de-emphasis of grammatical relations is the fact that Chinese discourse makes extensive use of 'topic-comment' constructions, as shown in the following examples:

> zhèi-ge dìfang   zhòng   màizi   hǎo
> this-cl. place   plant   wheat   good
> 'At this place, it is good to plant wheat.'

> jiāzhōu   qìhou   hǎo
> California climate good
> 'California, its climate is good.'

A second factor in the lack of grammatical inflectional morphology is that gender, plurality and tense are either indicated by lexical choice or not indicated at all.

A third factor is the absence of overt markers signalling the relationship of the verbs in the 'serial verb construction'. For instance, consider the following example:

> wǒ   jiào   tā   mǎi   júzī   chī
> I   tell   s/he   buy   orange   eat
> 'I told him/her to buy oranges to eat.'

Notice that the English translation of this sentence contains the morpheme *to*, which signals that *buy* and *eat* are subordinate verbs with unspecified future tense. The Běijīng Mandarin version has no such overt signal; the relationship between the verbs must be inferred from their meanings and from the discourse context in which the combination occurs. In Chinese, there are many different types of such inferred relationships. Here are a few examples where the English translations indicate the various relationships.

> wǒ   yǒu   yí -ge   píngguǒ   hěn   hǎo   chī
> I   have   one-cl.   apple   very   good   eat
> 'I have an apple which is very delicious.'

> tā   tǎng   zài   chuáng -shang   kàn   shū
> s/he   lie   at   bed   -on   see   book
> 'S/he lay in bed reading.'

> tā   qù   zhōngguó   xué   zhōngguó   huà
> s/he   go   China   learn   China   painting
> 'S/he went to China to learn Chinese painting.'

Finally, sentences containing coverbs may be viewed as a type of serial verb construction. The class of coverbs contains words that are partly like verbs and partly like prepositions. They have this mixed status because most of them used to be verbs at earlier stages of the language and many of them still have the properties of verbs and can be used as verbs that have similar meaning. Consider, for example, the following sentences:

> tā　　zài　　jiā　-li　　gōngzuò
> s/he　at　　home -in　work
> 'S/he works at home.'

> tā　　dào　　Běijīng　qù-le
> s/he　arrive　Běijīng　go-perf.
> 'S/he went to Běijīng.'

Zài and *dào* are coverbs. Both may serve as verbs, as in the following:

> nǐ　　zài　　nǎr?
> you　at　　where
> 'Where are you?'

> wǒmen　　dào -le　Běijīng　le
> we　　　　arrive -perf. Běijīng　crs.
> 'We have arrived in Běijīng.'

The Chinese coverb phrase consisting of a coverb and a noun is equivalent to the English prepositional phrase. In English a preposition is normally distinct from a verb. In Chinese, however, the separation of a coverb and a verb is much less clear-cut, and sentences containing coverbs such as those above can be viewed as a type of serial verb construction.

4.2 'Adjectives'

Strictly speaking, there is no class of words in Chinese that we can call 'adjective'. That is, while there are certainly words which denote qualities or properties of entities, from a grammatical point of view it is difficult to distinguish 'adjectives' from 'verbs'. There are at least three ways in which 'adjectives' can be seen to behave like verbs.

First, in Chinese, words denoting qualities and properties do not occur with a copula as they do in Indo-European languages. For example, the English and Běijīng Mandarin versions of a sentence such as *Molly is very intelligent* differ with respect to the presence or absence of the copular verb.

> mǎlì　　hěn　　cōngming
> Molly　very　intelligent
> 'Molly is very intelligent.'

Thus, in English, adjectives have the distinguishing characteristic of occurring with a copula when they are used predicatively. In Chinese, on the other hand, such words appear without any copula, just as verbs do.

Secondly, quality and property words in Chinese are negated by the same particle *bù* as are verbs:

tā   bù   kāixīn
s/he not   happy
'S/he is not happy.'

tā   bù   chī   ròu
s/he not   eat   meat
'S/he does not eat meat.'

Thirdly, when an 'adjective' modifies a noun, it occurs with the same nominalising particle *de* as verb phrases do:

kāixīn   -de   rén
happy   noms.   person
'people who are happy'

chī   ròu   de   rén
eat   meat noms.   person
'people who eat meat'

For these reasons, it is sensible to consider quality and property words in Chinese simply as a subclass of verbs, one which we might call 'adjectival verbs'.

4.3 Questions

4.3.1 Question-word Questions
Question-word questions are formed in Chinese by the use of question words whose position is the same as non-question words having the same function. For example, consider the positions of *shéi?* 'who?' and *shénme?* 'what?' in the following examples:

tā   zhǎo   *shéi?*
s/he look-for   who
'Who is s/he looking for?'

shéi zhǎo   tā?
who   look-for s/he
'Who is looking for him/her?'

nǐ   shuō   *shénme?*
you   say   what
'What are you saying?'

shénme   guì?
what   expensive
'What is expensive?'

Similarly, *nǎlǐ?* 'where?' can occur wherever a locative noun phrase can occur:

tā   zài   *nǎlǐ*   yóuyǒng?
s/he at   where   swim
'Where does s/he swim?'

As would be expected, question words which modify nouns occur before the noun, the position in which ordinary noun modifiers are found. The following sentence illustrates the prenominal position of *duōshǎo?* 'how many?':

nǐ   mǎi-le   *duōshǎo*   rìlì?
you   buy-perf.   how many   calendar
'How many calendars did you buy?'

4.3.2 Yes-no Questions
Chinese has several processes for forming 'yes-no' questions. First, such a question can be signalled by intonation: a rising intonation with a declarative clause has an interrogative force, as in most languages.

Another way to signal yes-no questions is to use a question particle at the end of the sentence. In Běijīng Mandarin the particles *ma* and *ne* are used for this purpose, as in:

nǐ   xǐhuan   Xīān *ma*?
you   like   Xīān Q
'Do you like Xīān?'

nǐ   jiějie   shì   gōngchéngshī, nǐ   mèimei   *ne*?
you   elder-sister   be   engineer   you   younger-sister   Q
'Your elder sister is an engineer — what about your younger sister?'

Chinese also has another way of forming yes-no questions: an affirmative and a negative version of the same proposition can be combined to make what is known as an 'A-not-A' question. Here are some examples from Běijīng Mandarin:

nǐ   *xǐhuan-bu -xǐhuan*   tā?
you   like -not-like   s/he
'Do you like him/her?'

tā   *chī-bu -chī*   píngguǒ?
s/he   eat-not-eat   apple
'Does s/he eat apples?'

5 The Writing System

The Chinese writing system is called a logographic or character system, because each symbol is a character/logograph. There are five processes by which the characters are created. We will briefly discuss those five processes in the following:

5.1 Pictographs

Writing in China began over 4,000 years ago with drawings of natural objects. The pictures were gradually simplified and formalised, giving rise to pictorial characters, called pictographs. For example:

Table 5.6: Pictographs in Chinese Writing

Old form	Modern form	Meaning
林	林 /lín/	'forest'
巛	川 /chuān/	'river'
☉	日 /rì/	'sun'

5.2 Ideographs

Ideographs are characters derived from diagrams symbolising ideas or abstract notions. For example, the diagrams ˙— and ⁻˙ were created to symbolise the notions 'above' and 'below'. Today the characters denoting 'above' and 'below' have become 上 /shàng/ and 下 /xià/ respectively.

5.3 Compound Ideographs

A compound ideograph is a character whose meaning is in some way represented by the combination of the meanings of its parts. For example, the character 譶 /tà/, meaning 'loquacious', is formed by combining the character 言 /yán/ 'speak' three times; and the character 明 /míng/ 'bright' is a compound of the character 日 /rì/ 'sun' and the character 月 /yuè/ 'moon', because the sun and the moon are the natural sources of light.

5.4 Loan Characters

Loan characters result from borrowing a character for a word whose pronunciation is the same as that of another word represented by that character. For example, in an earlier stage of the Chinese language, the character 易 /yì/ denoting 'scorpion' was borrowed to stand for the word meaning 'easy' because 'easy' and 'scorpion' had the same pronunciation. In modern Chinese, a new character has been created for the word 'scorpion' and the character, 易 /yì/, denotes 'easy'.

5.5 Phonetic Compounds

A phonetic compound is the combination of two characters, one representing a semantic feature of the word, the other representing the phonetic, i.e. the pronunciation of the word. Consider the character, 鈾 /yóu/ 'uranium', for example. The character is composed of the two characters, 金 /jīn/ and 由 /yóu/. The first, 金 /jīn/, has the meaning 'metal', signifying the metallic nature of uranium. The second character, 由 /yóu/, has a pronunciation which approximates the first syllable of the English word *uranium*, because when the new chemical element, uranium, was discovered, it was decided that the Chinese character should approximate the sound of the first syllable of the English word, *uranium*. Over 90 per cent of all modern Chinese characters are phonetic compounds and the process of forming phonetic compounds remains the standard method for creating new characters.

5.6 Simplification of the Writing System

The movement to simplify the Chinese writing system originated in the 1890s. However, it did not crystallise into an official policy enforced by the government throughout the country until the 1950s. The strategy of simplification involves a reduction in the number of strokes of commonly used characters. This reduction is achieved by eliminating parts of a

Appendix I

The Pīnyīn symbols and their corresponding IPA values

A. Consonants

Pīnyīn symbol	IPA
b	p
p	p^h
m	m
f	f
d	t
t	t^h
n	n
l	l
z	ts
c	ts^h
zh	tṣ
ch	$tṣ^h$
sh	ṣ
r	r
j	tɕ
q	$tɕ^h$
x	ɕ
g	k
k	k^h
h	x
ng	ŋ
w	w
y	j

character, condensing several strokes into one and replacing a complex character or parts of a complex character with a simpler one. Some examples are provided in table 5.7:

Table 5.7: Simplified Characters

Meaning	Original Version	Simplified version	Pronunciation (Pīnyīn)
'to bid farewell'	辭	辞	cí
'to cross'	過	过	guò
'should'	應	应	yīng
'solid'	實	实	shí
'door'	門	门	mén
'strong'	鞏	巩	gǒng

B. Vowels

Pīnyīn symbol	IPA	Context
a	$\begin{cases} [\varepsilon] \\ [a] \end{cases}$	/i___n
o	$\begin{cases} [o] \\ [u] \end{cases}$	$/ \begin{Bmatrix} u\_\_ \\ C\_\# \end{Bmatrix}$ $/ \begin{Bmatrix} a\_\_ \\ \_\_ng \end{Bmatrix}$
e	$\begin{cases} [\partial] \\ [\varepsilon] \\ [i] \\ [\gamma] \end{cases}$	/___N $/ \begin{Bmatrix} i \\ \ddot{u} \end{Bmatrix}$ — /___i
i	$\begin{cases} [\iota] \\ [\imath] \\ [ɿ] \end{cases}$	$/ \begin{Bmatrix} zh \\ ch \\ sh \\ r \end{Bmatrix}$ — $/ \begin{Bmatrix} z \\ c \\ s \end{Bmatrix}$ —
u	$\begin{cases} [y] \\ [u] \end{cases}$	/y___
ü	[y]	
er	[ɚ]	

Bibliography

Newnham (1971) is a popular introduction to the Chinese language. Alleton (1973) is an introductory sketch of Chinese grammar. More thorough reference grammars are Chao (1968), a rich source of insightful observations and data, and Li and Thompson (1981), a major description of the syntactic and morphological structures of Chinese from the viewpoint of the communicative function of language. Rygaloff (1973) contains some interesting descriptive observations on Chinese grammar, while Henne et al. (1977) is pedagogical.

For sociolinguistics, Dil (1976) is a collection of articles on Chinese dialects, the Chinese writing system and issues on language and society by Y.-R. Chao; all are informative and comprehensible. DeFrancis (1967) is an informative article describing in detail the history of and governmental policies concerning the Chinese writing system. For Chinese dialects, Egerod (1967) is an important and valuable survey of the dialects themselves as well as of research into them. Hashimoto (1973) is a modern description of the Hakka dialect with a strong tilt towards historical phonology. Li (1983) offers a glimpse of the complex language-contact situation in western China.

Karlgren (1923) is an introduction to Chinese from the viewpoint of historical phonology. Yang (1974) is a useful source book for research, especially in the area of historical phonology.

Acknowledgement

During the preparation of this chapter, Charles N. Li was partially supported by National Science Foundation Grant #BNS 83 08220.

References

Alleton, V. 1973. *Grammaire du chinois* (Presses Universitaires de France, Paris)
Chao, Y.-R. 1968. *A Grammar of Spoken Chinese* (University of California Press, Berkeley and Los Angeles)
DeFrancis, J. 1967. 'Language and Script Reform', in T. Sebeok (ed.), *Current Trends in Linguistics*, vol. 2, *Linguistics in East Asia and South East Asia* (Mouton, The Hague)
Dil, A.S. (ed.) 1976. *Aspects of Chinese Sociolinguistics: Essays by Yuen Ren Chao* (Stanford University Press, Stanford)
Egerod, S. 1967. 'Dialectology', in T. Sebeok (ed.), *Current Trends in Linguistics*, vol. 2, *Linguistics in East Asia and South East Asia* (Mouton, The Hague)
Forrest, R.A.D. 1965. *The Chinese Language* (Faber and Faber, London)
Hashimoto, M.J. 1973. *The Hakka Dialect: A Linguistic Study of its Phonology, Syntax and Lexicon* (Cambridge University Press, Cambridge)
Henne, H., O.B. Rongen and L.J. Hansen. 1977. *A Handbook on Chinese Language Structure* (Universitetsforlaget, Oslo)
Karlgren, B. 1923. *Sound and Symbol in Chinese* (Oxford University Press, London)
Li, C.N. 1983. 'Language in Contact in Western China', *Journal of East Asian Languages*, vol. 1, pp. 31–54
—— and S. Thompson. 1981. *Mandarin Chinese: A Functional Reference Grammar* (University of California Press, Berkeley and Los Angeles)
Newnham, R. 1971. *About Chinese* (Penguin Books, Harmondsworth and Baltimore)

Rygaloff, A. 1973. *Grammaire élémentaire du chinois* (Presses Universitaires de France, Paris)
Yang, P.F.-M. 1974. *Chinese Linguistics: A Selected and Classified Bibliography* (The Chinese University, Hong Kong)

6 Burmese

Julian K. Wheatley

1 Historical Background

Burmese is the official language of the Socialist Republic of the Union of Burma, a nation situated between the Tibetan plateau and the Malay peninsula and sharing borders with Bangladesh and India to the north-west, with China to the north-east and with Thailand to the south-east. Burmese belongs to the Burmish sub-branch of the Lolo-Burmese (or Burmese-Yi) branch of the Tibeto-Burman family and is one of the two languages in that family with an extensive written history (the other being Tibetan).

Standard Burmese has evolved from a 'central' dialect spoken by the Burman population of the lower valleys of the Irrawaddy and Chindwin rivers. Although it is now spoken over a large part of the country, regional variation remains relatively minor; apart from a few localisms, the speech of Mandalay in Upper Burma, for example, is indistinguishable from that of Rangoon, 400 miles to the south. A number of non-standard dialects, showing profound differences in pronunciation and vocabulary, are found in peripheral regions. The best known of these are Arakanese in the south-west, Tavoyan in the south-east and Intha in the east. Despite being heavily influenced in formal registers by the national language, the dialects preserve many features attested in the modern orthography but lost in standard speech.

Burma is a multi-national state. About two thirds of its population are Burmans. The other third is made up of a variety of ethnic groups, including other Tibeto-Burman-speaking peoples such as the Chin, Naga and Karen, Mon-Khmer peoples such as the Mon and Padaung, the Shan, whose language is closely related to Thai, and Chinese and Indians, who live mostly in the towns. The minority languages are partially differentiated from the national language by function, speakers tending to utilise the former in the family and in daily transactions and the latter in school, in dealing with authority and in cross-cultural communication. Most of the population of the country, provisionally put at about 37 million, speaks Burmese as either a first or second language.

The linguistic, as well as the historical evidence, shows that the ancestor of the Burmese language spread westwards from a centre in southwestern China, where its next of kin, the Yi (or Loloish) languages remain to this day. In doing so, it passed from the margins of the Tai and Chinese cultural sphere to a region profoundly influenced by Indian tradition. By the time the Burmese emerge on the historical scene, they have already begun to take on the religious and political features of the Indianised states that flourished in what is now the heart of Burma and from the first inscriptions their language shows the admixture of specialised Indic lexical stock and original Tibeto-Burman roots and grammatical structure that is so salient a feature of the Burmese language today.

It is difficult to be sure of the early history of the Burmese people. They seem to have appeared in central Burma near modern Mandalay in the ninth century AD, possibly in conjunction with raids by Nan Chao, a kingdom that flourished in southwestern China at that time. At any rate, by the tenth century they had established a state with a capital at Pagan and from the beginning of the eleventh to near the end of the thirteenth century, when Pagan was sacked by the Mongols, they were the dominant political power in much of what is now modern Burma. In the course of this rise to power, they apparently absorbed the remnants of the Pyu state. (The Pyu language, thought to have been Tibeto-Burman, is known only through inscriptions.) But their expansion was mainly at the expense of the Indianised Mon state that controlled much of Lower Burma and large parts of (modern) Thailand at that time. The Mon state, whose ruling class spoke the Mon-Khmer language of the same name, was to survive until the middle of the eighteenth century, its political fortunes tending to fluctuate inversely with those of the Burmese. Though the direction of cultural influence was ultimately reversed, the Mons were initially the donors. They were, for example, the source of the Theravada variety of Buddhism that is now dominant in Burma; according to tradition, the Burmese first acquired the Theravada scriptures, written in the old Indian canonical language of Pali, after defeating the Mons in AD 1057, and it is likely that Mon monks, brought to Pagan after that campaign, assisted in adapting their Indic script to the writing of Burmese. The earliest specimens of Burmese writing appear early in the next century. The best known of these is the Rajakumar (or Myazedi) inscription from central Burma, dated AD 1113, which records the offering of a gold Buddha image in four languages, Pali, Mon, Pyu and Burmese. By the end of the twelfth century, Burmese had become the main language of the inscriptions.

As the major substrate language in Lower Burma, Mon is the source of a number of words having to do with the natural and man-made environment; in addition, many Indic loanwords show the effects of transmission by way of Mon. Later we will see that it has also left its mark on the Burmese phonological system.

After the Mongol conquest of Pagan, Burmese rule in the south disintegrated, while political power in Upper Burma passed to a series of Shan rulers. The Shan probably arrived in Burma not long after the Burmans, part of the migration of Tai peoples that peaked in the early thirteenth century. But Shan rule in Upper Burma was nominal; inscriptions continued to be written in Burmese and in fact non-inscriptional literature, mainly poetry, made its appearance during this period. Later the Burmese came into contact with the Thais to the east, close kin of the Shan. Twice they conquered the Thai capital of Ayutthaya and Burmese secular drama owes its beginnings to Thai influence following the last of these invasions. But Shan and Thai influence on the Burmese language — though still inadequately researched — seems to be limited to loanwords for cultural items.

The first notable European presence in Burma was that of the Portuguese in the sixteenth century, followed in the next by small numbers of British, Dutch and French. The nineteenth century brought Burma into conflict with the British in India, who eventually annexed the country in three stages between 1826 and 1886; from 1886 until 1937, it was administered as a province of British India. Independence was restored in 1948.

British rule introduced a large number of words of English origin into Burmese. Many of these were later replaced by Burmese or Indic forms, but large numbers remain and new ones continue to appear, particularly in the fields of science, technology, business and politics. Loanwords tend to be fully adapted to Burmese segmental phonology (though the assignment of tones in the process is unpredictable), but in many cases they remain identifiable by their polysyllabic morphemes and their resistance to internal sandhi processes.

Rather than adapting English or other foreign phonetic material, the Burmese often form neologisms from their own lexical stock or from the highly esteemed classical languages of India, which are to Burmese (and many South-East Asian languages) what Latin and Greek are to European languages. Thus the word for 'spaceship', $ʔa+ka+θáyin$ (plusses represent phonological boundaries: see page 113) is composed of $ʔa+ka+θá$, a learned term meaning 'space, expanse', originally from Pali ĀKĀSA (transliterations are capitalised) and yin, spelled YAN, derived from Pali YĀNA 'vehicle'. Yin also appears with $yəhaʔ$ 'a reel', originally from Hindi, in the word for 'helicopter', $yəhaʔyin$, a compound coexisting with the English loan, $hɛli+kɔ́+pəta$. Similar competition between a native formation and a loanword is seen in the two words for 'television', the transparent $yoʔmyin+θancà$, 'image-see sound-hear', and the opaque $tɛlibìhyìn$.

Pali has been one of the main sources of new lexical material throughout the attested history of Burmese, with the result that the Burmese lexicon has come to have a two-tiered structure not unlike that of English, with its learned Romance and classical elements side by side with older and more colloquial Germanic forms. In Burmese the most common locutions, including grammatical words and formatives, nouns referring to basic cultural material and almost all verbs, tend to be composed of monosyllabic morphemes of Tibeto-Burman stock. Learned or specialised words (many of which must have entered the spoken language by way of the 'literary' language) often contain Pali material, frequently compounded with native stock. Pali is phonotactically quite compatible with Burmese, having no initial clusters and few stem-final consonants. Its morphemes are generally not monosyllabic, however. Disyllabic Pali words ending in a short A are usually rendered as a single syllable in Burmese, e.g.: *kan*, spelled KAM, 'fortune; deeds', from Pali KAMMA; *yo?*, spelled RUP, 'image', from Pali RŪPA. But otherwise, Pali loans (like those of English) are set off by the length of their morphemes: cf. *taya* 'constellation (of stars)', from Pali TĀRĀ, versus *cɛ* 'star', a Tibeto-Burman root; *htaná*, spelled ṬHĀNA 'place; department (in a university etc.)', from Pali ṬHĀNA, versus *neya* 'place', a compound of the native morphemes *ne* 'to live; be at' and *(ʔə)ya* 'place; thing'.

It is not uncommon to find two versions of a Pali word in Burmese, one closer to the Pali prototype than the other, e.g.: *man* and *maná*, both 'pride, arrogance' and both from Pali MĀNA, which occur together in the pleonastic expression *man maná hyí-* 'to be haughty, arrogant'.

Often a Pali prototype will be represented in a number of South-East Asian languages, providing a pan-South-East Asian technical lexicon comparable to the 'international' scientific vocabulary based on Latin and Greek: cf. Burmese *se?*, Mon *cɒt*, Khmer *cɤt*, Thai *cìt*, all from Pali CITTA 'mind'.

Despite inconsistent spelling and a restricted subject matter, the early inscriptional records probably render the spoken language of the time — Old Burmese — fairly directly. The inscriptional orthography, which can be interpreted in terms of Mon and, ultimately, Indic sound values, reveals a language phonetically very different from the modern spoken standard. It also shows major differences in lexical content, particularly among grammatical words and suffixes. But the grammatical categories and the order of words have remained relatively stable over the intervening 900 years.

The orthography underwent a number of changes after the inscriptional period, apparently reflecting a redistribution of certain vowels and a reduction in the number of medial consonants (see pages 844–5). By the end of the sixteenth century the orthography had assumed more or less its modern form, though there have been modifications in the spelling of individual words since. Pronunciation continued to change though, so there is now a wide gap between the spoken and literal values of the script, e.g.: *cɛ?* 'chicken' is spelled KRAK; *-θɛ*, an agentive suffix, is spelled -SAÑ.

The modern orthography (sometimes called 'Written Burmese') is often taken as the reflection of an intermediate stage in the history of the language, i.e. Middle Burmese. The construct is a useful one, though the precise nature of the relationship still needs to be worked out.

Along with the orthography, some grammatical and lexical forms from earlier stages of Burmese live on in the language used for literature and most written communication, literary Burmese. Particularly in this century, differences between literary and spoken styles have tended to diminish, so that nowadays, although other 'classical' elements may still appear in literary Burmese, the only feature consistently distinguishing the two is the choice of the textually frequent post-nominal and post-verbal particles and other grammatical words. Literary Burmese retains a set of archaic grammatical morphemes, some reflecting earlier versions of their spoken equivalents, others reflecting forms that have been replaced in the spoken language. For example, instead of the locative postposition -*hma* 'in, at', literary Burmese uses -NHUIK (read -*hnai?*) or -TWAṄ (read -*twin*); instead of the interrogative particles -*là* and -*lè*, it has -LO (read -*lɔ́*) and -NAÑ: (read -*nì*), respectively; instead of the possessive marker -*yé* (-RAI?), it has -?E̩? (read -*ʔí*).

Not all the literary particles are functionally homologous with spoken forms. Whereas the spoken language makes use of a single postposition, -*ko* (-KUI), to mark both objects and goals of motion, the literary language makes use of three: -KUI 'object', -?Ā: (read -*ʔà*) '(usually) second or indirect object', and -SUI? (read -*θó*) 'goal of motion'.

It is possible to write Burmese as it is spoken, i.e. using the standard orthography with the syntax and lexicon of the spoken language. Indeed, in the 1960s an association of writers based in Mandalay advocated the development of such a 'colloquially based' literary style. Despite the appearance of a number of works in the new style, it was not generally adopted. This was partly because it lacked official sanction, but also because no style evolved which could convey the seriousness of purpose connoted by formal literary Burmese.

Particularly in the older and more classical styles of literary Burmese, the influence of Pali grammatical structures can also be seen; for until the nineteenth century, prose writing was mostly translations, adaptations and studies of Pali texts. The extreme case is that of the 'nissaya' texts, which have a history dating from the inscriptional period to the present day (cf. Okell 1965). In these, Burmese forms are inserted after each word or phrase of a Pali text; in many cases the Pali is omitted, resulting in a Burmese 'calque' on the original — Burmese words with Pali grammar. The interesting point is that in addition to mirroring Pali syntax, the nissaya authors developed conventions for representing Pali inflectional categories in Burmese, an uninflected language. For example, the Pali past participle, a category quite alien to Burmese, was sometimes represented periphrastically by placing the 'auxiliary' ?AP 'be right, proper' after the verb: KHYAK

ʔAP SO CHWAM: 'the food that [should be] cooked, the cooked food'. In the spoken Burmese equivalent no auxiliary is required.

Not surprisingly, given the exalted position of Pali studies in Burmese culture, nissaya forms spread to other kinds of prose, so that Pali can be considered a significant substratum in many and perhaps all styles of literary Burmese.

2 Phonology

In presenting the inventory of phonological oppositions in Burmese, it is necessary to distinguish between full, or 'major' syllables, and reduced, or 'minor' ones. In reduced syllables the functional load is borne by the initial; no medial or final consonants are possible, and there are no tonal contrasts; the vowel is mid central and lax. Minor syllables occur singly or, occasionally, in pairs, always bound to a following major syllable. They can often be related to full syllables, if not synchronically, then historically: the first syllable of *səpwè* 'table' is shown from the spelling to derive from *sà* 'to eat': the word arose as a compound of 'eat' + 'feast'.

The iambic pattern of major preceded by minor syllable is more typical of Mon-Khmer languages than Tibeto-Burman. In fact, in Burmese, where closely bound *major* syllables are involved, it is the first that tends to be more prominent. Burmese probably absorbed the iambic pattern from Mon.

In major syllables, phonological oppositions are concentrated at two points, the initial and the vowel. There are two possible medial consonants, only one final consonant and four tonal contrasts, one of which is partially realised as final consonantism. The inventory of phonological oppositions can be discussed in terms of five syntagmatic positions: initial (C_i), medial (C_m), vowel (V), final (C_f) and tone (T). Of these, C_i, V and T are always present (though the glottal initial is represented by 'zero' in some transcriptions).

There are 34 possible C_i. Three of these are marginal: *r* may be found in learned loanwords; *hw* and *ð* are very rare. In table 6.1, C_i are arranged in three series, labelled 'aspirate', 'plain' and 'voiced'. The aspirates consist of aspirated stops and fricatives and voiceless nasals and resonants; the plain, of voiceless unaspirated stops and fricatives and voiced nasals and resonants; the voiced of voiced stops and fricatives only. The basis of this classification is morphological. First of all, while the plain and aspirate series may appear in absolute initial position (i.e. after pause) in both major word classes, the voiced series is restricted in that position mainly to nouns. The fact that such nouns can often be matched to verbs with plain or aspirate initials (e.g. *bì* 'a comb', *hpì* 'to comb') suggests that deverbative prefixes or other syllables are responsible for the voiced initials; assimilatory processes such as voicing

Table 6.1: Burmese Phonological Oppositions

		Stops and affricates	Fricatives	Nasals	Resonants
C_i	Aspirate	hp ht hc hk	hs	hm hn hɲ hŋ	hl hy (hw) h
	Plain	p t c k	s θ	m n ɲ ŋ	l y w(r) ʔ
	Voiced	b d j g	z(ð)		

V Syllable type

Open   (-∅) i   e   ɛ   a   ɔ   o u

Closed (-n) ɪ   eɪ   a   aɪ aʊ oʊ ʊ

       (-ʔ) ɪ   eɪ ɛ a   aɪ aʊ oʊ ʊ

Transcribed as:

                  i   e   ɛ   a   ɔ   ai au o u

C_m -y-, -w- C_f -n, (-ʔ)

T ´(creaky), ∅ (low), ` (high), -ʔ (checked)

are characteristic of word-internal positions in Burmese (see page 113). The incidence of nouns with C_i in the voiced series has been enlarged by loanwords, but the functional yield of the voiced series remains relatively low.

The aspirate series of C_i is not restricted to a particular class of words like the voiced, but it is associated with one member of derivationally related pairs of verbs such as the following: *pyɛʔ* 'be ruined', *hpyɛʔ* 'destroy'; *myín* 'be high', *hmyín* 'raise, make higher'. In these, the stative or intransitive member has a plain C_i, the causative or transitive, an aspirate. The alternation is represented by over 100 pairs of verbs, but it is not productive. The aspirates in these verbs record the effects of a sibilant causativising prefix, reconstructed at the Proto-Tibeto-Burman level as **s-* (see page 81). The original value of this prefix is reflected in 'irregular' pairs such as *ʔeʔ* 'sleep', *θeʔ* 'put to sleep' (the latter spelled SIP). The process has contributed to the incidence of the typologically rare voiceless nasals (*hm-, hn-, hɲ-, hŋ-*). As in many of the modern transcriptions of Burmese, the members of the aspirate series are consistently transcribed with a prescript 'h'; *hl-* and *hw-*, the latter found only in onomatopoeic words, are voiceless; *hy-* is actually a sibilant, [ʃ] or [ç], linked with *y-* in pairs such as *yɔ́* 'be reduced; be slack', *hyɔ́* [ʃɔ́] 'reduce; slacken'.

The medials are *-y-* and *-w-*. The second co-occurs with most C_i, but the first is only found with labials and occasionally with laterals.

In terms of our transcription there are two C_fs, *-n* and *-ʔ*, but in phonological terms -ʔ can be regarded as a fourth tone; it precludes the possibility of any of the other tones and, though it almost always has some segmental realisation, it is also associated with a very short, high and even pitch contour. The reasons for transcribing it as though it were a C_f are partly historical: -ʔ derives from an earlier set of final oral stops and is symbolised in the writing system as such.

To discuss the realisation of -n and -ʔ, it is necessary to begin with the topic of sandhi. The shape of a syllable in Burmese varies according to the degree of syllable juncture. At least two degrees of juncture need to be recognised: open, representing minimal assimilation between syllables, and close, representing maximal. The distinction is realised mainly in terms of the duration, tonal contour and C_f-articulation of the first syllable and the manner of the C_i of the second. Phonetic values vary with tempo but can be generalised as follows: successive major syllables linked in *open* juncture preserve citation values of all variables; for the C_fs -n and -ʔ, these are nasalisation of the preceding vowel (θòn, [θoũ]) and (along with pitch and other features) final glottal stop (hyiʔ, [çıʔ]), respectively. In successive major syllables in *close* juncture, the first is shortened and has a truncated pitch contour, while the C_f of the first and the C_i of the second undergo varying degrees of mutual assimilation, the final tending to adopt the *position* of articulation of the following initial, the initial tending to adopt the *manner* of articulation of the preceding final, e.g.: *lè-hkàn* 'four rooms' is realised [lègà], with perseverative voicing on the internal velar stop; *θòn-hkàn* 'three rooms' is realised [θoũŋgà] with the same voicing but, additionally, anticipation of the velar stop by the nasal final; while *hyiʔ-hkàn* 'eight rooms' is realised [ʃıkkʰà], the aspirate remaining after the checked final, the final taking on the position of the following stop. In this last case, the phonetic final segment associated with -ʔ may disappear, leaving only pitch, duration and, in some cases, allophonic vowel quality, to signal the checked tone ([ʃıkʰà]). In the first two cases — those involving smooth (-Ø, -n) syllables — these phonological processes result in the neutralisation of manner distinctions for some C_i in favour of the voiced, e.g.: *hk-, k-,* and *g-* are all realised [g-].

Sandhi affects combinations of minor and major syllables slightly differently, with interesting results. When the first syllable of two is a minor one, the voicing process does not extend to the aspirates: in *səpwè* 'table', internal *-p-* is voiced, but in *təkhàn* 'one room', the internal *-kh-* remains aspirated. In addition, the initial of a minor syllable often harmonises with the voicing of the following consonant: *səpwè* is most often pronounced [zəbwè], with voicing throughout; but *təkhàn* is realised [təkʰà] with both stops voiceless. This sporadic process of consonant harmony reduces even further the number of initial oppositions available for minor syllables.

Close juncture is characteristic of certain grammatical environments, e.g.: noun + classifier, illustrated above, and noun + adjectival verb: (ʔen –

θiʔ 'new house', is pronounced [ʔẽɪndɪʔ]). Most particles are also attached to preceding syllables in close juncture: θwà - hpó 'in order to go', is pronounced [θwàbó]. But within compounds the degree of juncture between syllables is unpredictable; the constituents of disyllabic compound nouns (other than recent loanwords) tend to be closely linked, but compound verbs vary, some with open, some with close juncture.

In our transcription, syllabic boundaries are shown as follows: open juncture is represented by a space between syllables and open juncture within a compound by a plus (hkwè+hkwa 'to separate; leave' is pronounced [kʰwèkʰwa]). Close juncture within a compound is indicated by lack of a space between the syllables (hkúhkan 'to resist' is pronounced [kʰúgã]), while close juncture between phrasal constituents is marked with a hyphen (as in the examples of the previous paragraph).

Moving on to the vowels, we find that the number of vocalic contrasts varies according to the type of syllable (see table 6.1): in smooth syllables (-∅, -n), there are seven contrasts, in checked (-ʔ), eight. In phonetic terms, however, the line of cleavage is not between smooth and checked but between open and closed: vowels in closed syllables (-n, -ʔ) tend to be noticeably centralised or diphthongised compared to those in open syllables. For purposes of transcription it is of course possible to identify certain elements of the different systems, as in the chart. And it would be possible to reduce the number of symbols even further by identifying the ɔ of open syllables with either the ai or au of closed. Historically (and in the writing system) ɔ is connected with au (and o with ai). Such an analysis is not motivated synchronically, nor does it have much practical value, so, like most of the transcriptions in use, we indicate nine vowels (plus the ə of reduced syllables).

Four tonal distinctions can be recognised, the 'creaky', the 'low' (or 'level'), the 'high' (or 'heavy') and the 'checked', the last symbolised by -ʔ. Tone in Burmese has a complex realisation of which pitch is only one feature. In the case of the checked tone, segmental features of vowel quality and final consonantism as well as suprasegmental features of pitch and duration are involved. The relative presence of these features varies with context. It has been observed, for example, that in disyllabic words such as zaʔpwè '(a) play', the pitch of the checked tone (high, in citation) may range from high to low. The same kind of variation is characteristic of creaky tone as well.

In citation form, the three tones that appear in smooth syllables have the following features: the 'creaky', (transcribed ́): tense or creaky phonation (sometimes with final lax glottal stop), medium duration, high intensity and high, often slightly falling pitch; the 'low' (unmarked): normal phonation, medium duration, low intensity and low, often slightly rising pitch; the 'high' (transcribed ̀): sometimes slightly breathy, relatively long, high intensity and high pitch, often with a fall before a pause.

In citation form, the creaky tone is much less common than the others, a fact accounted for by its relatively late development from affixal elements. The balance is partially restored, however, by the incidence of morphologically conditioned creaky tone (see pages 120–1).

3 The Writing System

The Burmese script is an adaptation of the Mon, which in turn, is derived through uncertain intermediaries from the Brāhmī script, the antecedent of all Indian scripts now in use. Like the Mon, it preserves the main features of its Indian prototype, including signs that originally represented non-Burmese sounds, such as the Indic retroflex and voiced aspirated series. These usually appear only in the spelling of Indic loanwords.

The script is alphabetic in principle, with 'letters' representing phonemes, though the sound values of many of these letters have changed considerably since it was first introduced, as we showed earlier. A few very common literary Burmese grammatical morphemes are represented by logograms — word signs — but these originated as abbreviations of phonographic combinations. Like all Indic scripts, the Burmese differs from European alphabetic scripts in two important respects. First, neither the sequence in

Table 6.2: The Burmese Writing System: Consonants

		i	ii	iii	iv	v	*Transliteration* i	ii	iii	iv	v	*Transcription* i	ii	iii	iv	v
C₁	I	က	ခ	ဂ	ဃ	င	K	KH	G	GH	Ṅ	k	hk	g	g	ŋ
	II	စ	ဆ	ဇ	ဈ	ည/ဉ	C	CH	J	JH	Ñ	s	hs	z	z	ɲ
	III	ဋ	ဌ	ဍ	ဎ	ဏ	Ṭ	ṬH	Ḍ	ḌH	Ṇ	t	ht	d	d	n
	IV	တ	ထ	ဒ	ဓ	န	T	TH	D	DH	N	t	ht	d	d	n
	V	ပ	ဖ	ဗ	ဘ	မ	P	PH	B	BH	M	p	hp	b	b	m
	VI	ယ	ရ	လ	ဝ	သ	Y	R	L	W	S	y	y	l	w	θ
	VII	ဟ	ဠ	အ			H	Ḷ	ʔ			h	l	ʔ		

C_M   ◌ျ ◌ြ ◌ွ ◌ှ
       -Y- -R- -W- -H-
       -y- -y- -w- h -

which the letters appear, nor the order in which they are written, reflects the temporal order of phonemes. Vowel signs appear before, after, above or below C_I signs. (Abbreviations with capitalised subscripts refer to positions in the written syllable.) Secondly, a consonant sign without any vowel sign implies the vowel *a*. It is this use of 'zero' that sometimes leads to Indic writing systems being incorrectly labelled 'syllabic'.

Table 6.2 shows the consonant signs together with a Romanised transliteration based on original Indic values and a transcription of their regular modern pronunciation. The transliteration is a capitalised and otherwise slightly modified version of the widely used Duroiselle system (see Okell 1971). Many of the differences between the transliteration and the transcription reflect changes in the spoken language since the writing system was introduced. Some of these are discussed below.

The 33 consonant signs are given in the traditional Burmese (and Indian) order, which is also the basis of ordering entries in dictionaries. Almost all the consonant signs can appear initially, but only the plain series (K, C, T, P), their nasal counterparts (Ṅ, Ñ, N, M), and Y occur finally in native words. The boxed row (III) representing the Indian retroflex series, is pronounced like the dental series. The boxed columns (iii, iv), representing the Indian voiced and voiced aspirated series, are usually pronounced alike. The *spoken* voiced series, discussed earlier, is often written with the plain or aspirate voiceless consonant signs.

There are four medial consonant signs: Y, R, W, H. The last is subscribed to nasal and resonant C_Is to indicate the aspirates of those series, e.g.: LHA, *hlá* 'beautiful'. In Old Burmese writing, a medial -L- was also found (see below).

The writing system reflects a number of consonantal changes. The development of C_fs will be discussed separately below. As initials, some consonants have undergone phonetic changes, but distinctions have generally been preserved. Row II in table 6.2 shows a shift from palatal affricate to dental sibilant. From the representation of Burmese words in certain Portuguese and English records of the eighteenth and nineteenth centuries, the Burmese scholar, Pe Maung Tin ('Phonetics in a Passport', *Journal of the Burma Research Society*, 1922, vol. 12, pp. 129–31) concluded that this change and the shift from $s > \theta$ (VI,v) began in the late eighteenth century and were followed by the palatalisation of velar stops before medial -y- (written -Y- and -R-). The three shifts form a 'drag chain', the first clearing the way for the second, the second for the third ($s>\theta, c>s, ky>c$, etc.). Two typologically rare consonants arose as a result of these developments: θ, pronounced [t^θ], and *hs*-, an aspirated sibilant ($< c^h$). The functional yield of the latter is very low.

Contrasts among medial consonants have been reduced from four in Old Burmese to three in Middle Burmese (reflected in the standard orthography), to two in the modern spoken language. The medial -*l*-

attested by the inscriptions merged with either -*y*- or -*r*-, according to whether the initial consonant was velar or labial, respectively, i.e.: OBs. *kl-* > MBs. *ky-*, OBs. *pl-* > MBs. *pr-*. MBs. *r* then merged with *y* in all positions, initial as well as medial (so that 'Rangoon' is now transcribed as *Yankon*). Some of the dialects attest to the earlier stages. In Tavoyan, the medial -*l*- of Old Burmese usually survives as such, while earlier -*r*- and -*y*- merge as -*y*-: cf. standard *cá* 'to fall', spelled KYA in the orthography and KLA in the inscriptions, pronounced *klá* in Tavoyan. In Arakanese, on the other hand, earlier -*l*- is distributed between -*r*- and -*y*- with the latter two remaining distinct, e.g. standard *cɛʔ* 'chicken', spelled KRAK, is *kraʔ* in Arakanese, the -*r*- realised as a retroflex continuant.

Whether we are dealing with the script or the spoken language, vowel, final consonant and tone are conveniently treated as a unit, the 'rhyme'. Table 6.3 shows the main (or 'regular') rhymes of Burmese, arranged according to written vowels. (To save space, tonal markings are only indicated where they are incorporated in a vowel sign.) Comparing the transliteration with the transcription reveals both a large reduction in the number of C_fs and a major restructuring of the vowel system.

Consonant signs are marked as final by the superscript hook, or 'killer' stroke. The orthography shows four positions of final oral and nasal stops, and -Y, which — in native words — represents only the rhyme -*ɛ*. ('Little Ñ', the second of the two signs for Ñ, is a modern variant of the first, used to signal the pronunciation -*in* over the otherwise unpredictable alternatives, -*i, e* and *ɛ*.) From the table, it can be seen that many combinations of written final and vowel do not occur. Finals -C and -Ñ, for instance, occur only with the 'intrinsic' vowel A. Comparative evidence shows that the 'extra' A-rhymes derive from earlier *-*ik* and *-*iŋ*, respectively, the 'missing' velar rhymes of the high front series (row II). Palatal finals are rare in Tibeto-Burman languages, but common in Mon-Khmer; it is likely that the appearance of these finals in Burmese is another result of Mon influence.

Neither the distributional evidence nor the comparative evidence is clear enough to explain the other gaps in the system of orthographic rhymes.

All positions of final stops have been reduced to just one in the modern language, represented by -*ʔ* for oral stops, -*n* for nasal. The association of high pitch with the former can probably be attributed to the well documented pitch-raising effects of final tense glottal stop. This glottal stop is quite different from the lax glottal stop that sometimes appears in creaky-toned syllables. The latter would be expected to depress pitch.

From table 6.3, vowels can be seen to have split according to the type of syllable they were in, open or closed; thus written I is read *i* or *e*, written U, *u* or *o*, written UI, *o* or *ai*, written O, *ɔ* or *au*, with the first, higher vowel quality found in reflexes of open syllables. (Written UI and O are both digraphs in the script, but only the first is transliterated according to its parts, U + I; the symbol was a Mon invention for representing a mid front rounded

Table 6.3: The Burmese Writing System: Regular Rhymes

	Open		Closed									
I	◌ိ / I / i		X	ိ◌် / IN / en	ိ◌ံ / IM / en	X	ိ◌် / IT / e?	ိ◌ပ် / IP / e?	◌င် / WAṄ / (win)	◌ွန် / WAN / un	◌ွမ် / WAM / un	◌ွက် / WAK / (we?)	◌ွတ် / WAT / u?	◌ွပ် / WAP / u?
II	◌ူ / Ū / ū	◌ု / U / u							X	◌ွန် / UN / on	◌ွမ် / UM / on	X	◌ွတ် / UT / o?	◌ွပ် / UP / o?
III	ေ◌ / E / e								◌ိုင် / UIṄ / ain	X	X	◌ိုက် / UIK / ai?	X	X
IV	ဲ◌ / AI / ε	ေ◌း / AY / ε							ေ◌ာင် / OṄ / aun	◌ / O / ɔ	◌ / OW / ɔ	ေ◌ာက် / OK / au?	X	X
V	◌ / - / à	◌ါ / ◌ာ / A / a					◌ / AṄ / in		◌ / AC / i?	◌ / AT / a?	◌ / AP / a?		

Note: Tones not contained in a vowel sign are written as follows: ◌ (originally -ဆ) for *creaky*; ◌း ('visarga') for *high*; unmarked for *low*.

vowel and it probably had the same value in Old Burmese.) Written A attests to a three-way split of *a* into *a*, *i* and *ε*, conditioned by the final. To an extent, these developments, coupled with the reduction in the number of final consonants, filled the gaps in the pattern of (written) rhymes, so that the only asymmetries in the modern system are the missing nasal rhyme, *-εn*, and the uncertain relationship between open *ɔ* and closed *ai* and *au*, discussed above (see table 6.1).

Table 6.3 also shows the relationship between V- and C_f-signs and the representation of tones in Burmese. Much of the complicated system for indicating tone derives from Mon orthographic conventions. Neither Mon nor the Indic languages were tonal. But Old Mon did have short syllables ending in a glottal stop, which must have sounded very similar to the short, creaky-toned syllables of Burmese. In Mon, final *-ʔ* was generally written with the same sign as glottal onset, the 'vowel support'; but with the three vowels I, U and A — the 'short' vowels of the Indian prototype — the symbol for *-ʔ* could be omitted. Both practices were taken over and eventually systematised in the Burmese writing system. From table 42.3, we see that the three 'corner' vowels (II, V) have two written forms; in Indian terms — also the basis of our transliteration — the first is short, the second (with the additional stroke) long ($\bar{V}$). The first indicates a creaky-toned syllable, the second, a low-toned syllable. With all other finals, creaky tone was indicated by the sign for glottal onset, reduced to just a dot in the modern orthography (but, for clarity, still transcribed as ʔ herein: UIʔ = *ó*).

There was, apparently, no clear analogue in Mon to the opposition between high and low tones and for some six centuries the two were not consistently distinguished in the orthography. In the modern script, the lower-mid vowel signs (IV) are intrinsically high-toned, with additional strokes ('killed-Y' in one case, the killer alone — originally a superscript killed-W — in the other) changing them to low. Elsewhere, high tone is indicated by two post-scriptal dots ('visarga'): UI: = *ò*. The modern use of visarga (which represents final *-h* in Old Mon) to signal the high tone was occasionally anticipated in the earliest inscriptions, which suggests that breathiness has long been a feature of that tone.

Except in those cases in which the vowel sign is intrinsically creaky or high, the low tone is unmarked: UI = *o*. The checked tone is symbolised by the presence of a final oral stop.

One of the characteristics of Indic alphabets is that vowels are written with special signs when they are in syllable-initial position. Such 'initial-vowel symbols', based on Mon forms, exist for all but three of the Burmese vowels (table 6.4). Nowadays, they are found only in a small number of words — most of them, loanwords. In the modern orthography, 'initial' vowels — actually vowels with glottal onset — are generally written with a combination of the vowel support sign (which represents ʔ-) and ordinary vowel signs.

A few other signs also appear in the script; for these and other irregularities, the reader is referred to Roop (1972).

Table 6.4: The Burmese Writing System: Miscellaneous Symbols

Initial vowel signs:

အ	ဤ			ʔi	ʔí	
ဉ	ဥ	ဦ		ʔú	ʔu	ʔù
	ဧ	(ဧ)			ʔe	ʔè
ဩ	ဪ				ʔɔ	ʔɔ̀

Numerals:

၁	၂	၃	၄	၅	၆	၇	၈	၉	၀
1	2	3	4	5	6	7	8	9	0

4 Morphology

Morphology in Burmese is primarily derivational morphology and compounding; there is little to discuss under the heading of 'inflection'. Grammatical functions that might be realised as inflections in other languages are mostly carried out by word order or by grammatical particles. There is, however, one phenomenon that can be considered inflectional, and that is the 'induced creaky tone' (Okell's term). Under certain conditions, words with otherwise low tones and sometimes those with high shift to the creaky tone. This shift has a number of apparently disparate functions (cf. Allott 1967). Some of them seem to exploit the sound symbolism of the features of creaky phonation and high intensity: with sentence-final 'appellatives' (kin terms, titles etc. that pick out the audience and convey information about social distance) the induced creaky tone suggests abruptness and urgency. It also appears with the first occurrence of certain repeated words, e.g. ʔinmətan 'very', but ʔinmətán ʔinmətan 'very, very'.

At other times, the induced creaky tone has a specific grammatical function. Usually only with pronouns and nouns of personal reference, it may signal 'possession' or 'attribution': θu 'he; she', θú ʔəmyò+θəmì 'his wife'. In such cases, the creaky tone looks like an allomorph of the creaky-toned possessive particle, -yé (-ké after checked syllables); but although the two often alternate, they may also cooccur, so their relationship is now only historical.

The induced creaky tone also tends to appear — again, mainly with personal referents — before the locative postposition, -hma 'in, at', and the 'accusative' postposition, -ko 'object, goal, extent'. With objects in particular, -ko is often omitted, leaving the creaky tone to mark the grammatical role: θú(-ko) mè-lai?-pa 'ask him!'. The origin of the creaky tone in these contexts is uncertain.

Apart from the regular but non-productive patterns involving aspiration and voicing illustrated earlier, almost all derivational morphology in Burmese involves prefixation of a minor syllable, partial or complete reduplication or combinations of the two. Derivational processes generally act on verbs, turning them into nouns or noun-like expressions that can often function as either nominals or adverbials. Verbs themselves are very rarely derived (just as they are very rarely borrowed). The verbal inventory is expanded through compounding or through the lexicalisation of verb + complement constructions, e.g. ʔəyè cì- 'affair-be big = be important'; the latter retain most of the syntactic properties of phrases. In contrast to verbs, adverbials are almost always derived.

The general function of the productive derivational processes in Burmese is to subordinate verbs. Complete reduplication of stative verbs (with close juncture distinguishing them from iterative repetition) forms manner adverbials: ca 'be long (time)', caca 'for (some) time'; θehca 'be sure, exact', θeθe+hcahca 'exactly, definitely'. Prefixation of action verbs by the nominalising prefix ʔə- creates action nominals: kai? 'to bite', but ʔəkai? hkan-yá- 'biting-suffer-get = get bitten' (a 'passive of adversity', see page 125); hcɛ? 'to cook', but ʔəhcɛ? θin- 'cooking-learn = learn to cook'. The same process forms adverbials: myan 'be fast', but ʔəmyan θwà- 'go in haste, go quickly'; or, with a different prefix, ʔəyè+təcì 'urgently', from the syntactic compound meaning 'be important', mentioned at the end of the last paragraph. Whether reduplicated or prefixed, the verbs may retain nominal complements: təlá caca nei- 'one-month-long-stay = to stay for a month'; hcin (ʔə)kai? hkan-yá- 'get bitten by a mosquito'. In the latter type, the prefix is often deleted and the verbal noun appears in close juncture with the preceding complement as a kind of nonce compound.

Prefixation, but not complete reduplication, is also attested in lexicalised form, e.g. ʔəhkwá 'fork (of a tree)', from the verb hkwá 'to fork in two'. In cases involving a prefixed verb and a complement, the lexicalised version becomes a syntactic compound, e.g. htəmìnhcɛ? 'a cook', derived from the deverbal ʔəhcɛ? with the generic object, htəmìn 'rice; food'. In principle, derived forms such as these can be interpreted literally or idiomatically; htəmìnhcɛ? is also an action nominal with the meaning of 'cooking'.

Other kinds of compounding are well utilised in Burmese as a means of deriving nouns and verbs. Nominal patterns are more varied and several are recursive; compound verbs are usually composed of pairs of verbs. Compounding is a favourite way of coining new technical vocabulary, e.g. kon+tin+kon+hcá+maùn, lit. 'an arm (that) loads (and) unloads goods', i.e. 'a crane'; mainhnòn+pyá+dainkwɛ? 'a dial (that) shows mile-rate', i.e.

'a speedometer'. *Mainhnòn* and *dainhkwɛʔ* are themselves compounds that combine loanwords from English (*main* from 'mile', *dain* from 'dial') with words from Burmese, a practice that is quite common.

Burmese vocabulary also attests to a variety of processes that straddle the line between derivation and compounding. They apparently satisfy an urge, most noticeable in formal and literary styles, to add weight and colour to the monosyllabic root. Nouns and verbs often have pleonastic versions formed by the addition of a near synonym: *yè* and *yè+θà*, both 'write', the latter containing the verb *θà* 'inscribe'; *cí* and *cí+hyú* both 'look at', with *hyú*, a less common verb than *cí*, meaning 'to behold'. The enlarged version may be phonologically as well as semantically matched: *po* and *pomo*, both meaning 'more', the latter with the rhyming and nearly synonymous *mo*. Or it may be phonologically matched but semantically empty: *hkɔ* and *hkɔwɔ* 'call', the latter containing the otherwise meaningless rhyming syllable *-wɔ*; *ɲi* and *ɲiɲa* 'be even', with the meaningless 'chiming' syllable *-ɲa*. In the 'elaborate' adverbial *wòdò+wàdà* 'blurred, unclear', rhyme and chime are intermeshed.

The pattern of four rhythmically or euphonically balanced syllables is prolific. Elaborate nouns are frequently formed by the addition of *ʔə-* to both parts of a compound verb: *hnáun+hyɛʔ* 'annoy', *ʔəhnáun+ʔəhyɛʔ* 'annoyance'. Elaborate adverbs may contain any of a variety of minor syllables: *bəyòn+bəyìn* 'tumultuously'; *kəbyàun+kəbyan* 'in an illogical, backwards way'; *təsì+təlòn* 'in unity'. As these examples show, the language has vast resources for expressing fine nuances through the adverbial position. Many adverbials are onomatopoeic or ideophonic, e.g. the pattern *tə-* plus reduplication, as in *təzizi* 'buzzing with noise'; or the pattern of an imitative syllable plus the suffix *-hkənè*, the latter associated with sudden movement: *hyuʔhkənè* 'whoosh'; *htwihkənè* 'ptui' (spitting sound, expressing disgust).

5 Syntax

In Burmese the verb and its modifiers occupy the final position in the clause, with nominals and other complements 'freely' ordered before it. There is neither agreement between constituents nor concord within them. The grammatical apparatus consists mainly of postpositional particles — many of them deriving from nouns or verbs — whose relative ordering, though often fixed, tends to accord with their semantic scope: *yu-la-se-hcin-tɛ* 'carry-come-cause-want-realis = (he) wanted to make (him) bring (it)'; *cènaun hsəya-ká-lè-hpὲ* (*cènaun tì-tɛ*) 'gong-master-contrastive subject-additive-restrictive = and the gong-master, for his part, just (plays the gong)'. The only obligatory grammatical categories involve the verb; with some exceptions, final verb phrases are followed by one of a small set of functionally disparate particles that signal, simultaneously, features of polarity and mood, or polarity, mood and aspect. Thus, *-tɛ*, *-mɛ* and *-pi* carry, in addition to the meanings 'positive' and 'non-imperative', the aspectual distinctions of realis, irrealis, and punctative, respectively. The punctative expresses the realisation of a state (*to-pi* '(that)'s enough') or the initiation of an action (*sà-pi* '(I)'m eating (now)'), different manifestations of the notion 'change of state'. Grammatical categories of voice, tense and definiteness are not found at all; number is an optional category, expressed by a suffix.

The verbal phrase itself, as we saw in the earlier example, often consists of a string of verbs, verb-like morphemes and particles. These exhibit a variety of syntactic and semantic properties. In the phrase *hté θwà* 'put in-go = to take (it) in (it)', two verbs combine in open juncture and retain their lexical meanings; in *hté pè*, 'put (something) in for (someone)', open juncture is still usual, but the second morpheme, *pè*, has its benefactive meaning of 'for the sake of' rather than its literal meaning of 'give'; in *hté-laiʔ* 'just put (it) in', *hté* is followed in close juncture by a morpheme whose lexical meaning is 'to follow' but which, as a verbal modifier, signals an 'increase in transitivity', and is often translated as 'effective or abrupt action'. The functions of the verbal modifiers are surprisingly diverse: *-hya*, the 'commiserating' particle (with no verbal prototype) conveys 'pity or compassion, usually towards a third person': *la-yá-pyan-hya-tɛ* 'come-had to-again-pity-realis = [she] had to come back, unfortunately'. The directional particle, *-hké* (again, with no obvious lexical prototype), signifies 'displacement in space or time', as in *Pəgan myó-ká wɛ-hké-tɛ* 'Pagan-town-from-buy-there-realis = (we) bought (it) back in Pagan'.

Within the noun phrase, the order of constituents is primarily modifier before modified, with the main exception being stative verb modifiers which follow their head nouns either in close juncture or with the nominalising prefix *ʔə-*. Demonstratives precede their head: *di mìpon* 'this/these lantern(s)'. So do genitive phrases and other nominal modifiers: *ʔəpyó ʔen* 'the young woman's house' (with induced creaky tone on *ʔəpyo* marking possession). So, too, do most relative clauses: *baθa+səkà léla-té lu-te* 'language-study-realis (with induced creaky tone showing subordination)-person-plural = people that study language'. Unlike English, the original semantic role of the relativised noun is not indicated: *θu gàun səpwè-né taiʔ-mí-tɛ* 'he-head-table-with-hit-inadvertently-realis = he hit (his) head on the table', but *θu gàun taiʔ-mí-té səpwè* 'the table that he hit (his) head (on)'.

Burmese, like many of the languages spoken on the mainland of South-East Asia, requires classifiers (or 'measures') for the quantification of what in English would be called count nouns. Numeral and classifier follow the quantified noun in an appositional relationship: *θwà lè-hcàun* 'tooth-four-peg = four teeth'; *θəhcìn lè-poʔ* 'song-four-stanza = four songs'. Some nouns can be self-classifying: *ʔen lè-ʔen* 'four houses'. Classifiers often reflect the shape or some other salient feature of a nominal referent. In many cases, nouns may be classified in several ways, according to the particular aspect of an object the speaker chooses to emphasise; in the case of animate nouns the choice usually reflects status: *lu təyauʔ* 'one (ordinary) person', *lu təʔù* 'one (esteemed) person'. But probably as a result of material and cultural change, the semantic or conceptual basis of classification in Burmese is now often obscure, so possible classifiers must be listed with nouns in the dictionary as lexical facts.

Although certain orders of clause elements are much more common than others — agent–beneficiary–patient, for example — order of elements before the verb is, in principle, free. As a result, a sentence such as *Maun Hlá Maun Ŋɛ yaiʔ-tɛ* is ambiguous, each nominal capable of being interpreted as agent or patient: 'Maung Hla struck Maung Nge' or 'Maung Hla was struck by Maung Nge'. Where context is insufficient to ensure the intended interpretation, semantic relations can be marked by postpositional particles. In this case, the agent can be signalled by *-ká*, the patient by *-ko*: *Maun Hlá-ko Maun Ŋɛ-ká yaiʔ-tɛ* 'Maung Hla was struck by Maung Nge'. These, like many of the other postpositional particles, have several different senses. With locations they mark 'source' and 'goal', respectively: *Yankon-ká Mandəlè-ko θwà-tɛ* '(he) went from Rangoon to Mandalay'. Other functions of *-ko*, such as the marking of beneficiary and extent or degree can be subsumed under the notion of 'goal'. But *-ká* has one other very common function that is not obviously related to the notion of source: where *-ká* does not serve a disambiguating function — in intransitive clauses, for example — it signals 'contrastive topic'; *di-ká təcaʔ, ho-ká caʔ-hkwè* 'this-*ká* (costs) one kyat, that-*ká*, one and a half'. *-ká* in this sense may appear with nominals already marked for semantic roles: *ʔəhtè-htè-hma-ká* 'inside-in-at-*ká*', as in '**inside** it's crowded but outside it's not'.

The last example illustrates the origin of the many of the more specific relational markers. *ʔəhtè* is a noun meaning 'the inside', which can function as head to a genitive phrase with the meaning 'the inside of': *yehkwɛʔ ʔəhtè* 'the inside of the cup'. Without its prefix, and closely bound to the preceding syllable, the morpheme occurs in locative phrases that may be explicitly marked as such by the particle *-hma: yehkwɛʔ-htè-hma* 'in the cup'.

Although word order is 'free' in the sense that it does not indicate the grammatical or semantic roles of constituents, it is not without significance. It is conditioned by the pragmatic notions of topic, which establishes a point of departure from previous discourse or from context, and 'comment', which contains the communicative focus of the utterance. It is this pragmatic organisation that leads us to translate the sentence *Maun Hlá-ko Maun Ŋɛ-ká yaiʔ-tɛ* with the English passive, i.e. 'Maung Hla was struck by Maung Nge', rather than the active 'Maung Nge struck Maung Hla'. For, by mentioning Maung Hla first, we take the patient's point of view, just as we do when using the passive in English. But unlike the English, topicalising the patient changes neither the grammatical relations of the nominals (the agent is not demoted) nor the valence of the verb (which keeps the same form), so the term 'passive' does not apply. The closest Burmese gets to a passive construction is a 'passive of adversity', which, as the name suggests, is associated primarily with events that affect a person (or patient) unpleasantly. Thus the unlikely perspective of the sentence, *kà θú-ko tai?-tɛ* 'car-he-obj.-hit-realis = the car hit him', can be reversed by making *tai?* a nominal complement of a verb phrase containing the verbs *hkan* 'suffer; endure', and *yá* 'get; manage to': *θu kàtai? hkan-yá-tɛ* 'he-car hitting-suffer-get-realis = he got hit by a car'. But even this construction is not nearly as frequent as the passive is in English.

A topic, once established, may remain activated over several sentences. Its pragmatic role, in other words, may be 'given'. English typically leaves a pronominal trace in such cases; Burmese generally does not. Nominals, topical or otherwise, whose reference can be recovered from previous discourse or context can be omitted, a process sometimes known as 'zero-pronominalisation'; *pyin pè-mɛ* 'fix-(give)-irrealis = (I)'ll fix (it) for (you)'. Such sentences are grammatically complete like their English counterparts. Pronouns, which almost always have human referents in Burmese, are used either as a hedge against misinterpretation or as a means of making the relative status of the participants explicit.

The primacy of the topic-comment organisation of the sentence in Burmese is also illustrated by sentences of the following type: *di hkəlè θwà cò-θwà-tɛ* 'this-child-teeth-break (intransitive)-(go)-realis = this child has broken (his) teeth'. The verb is intransitive (its corresponding transitive is aspirated) and the two noun phrases are not in a possessive relationship but are clausal constituents; a more literal translation would read 'the child, teeth have been broken'. In such cases, the first topic, *hkəlè*, is a locus for the second topic, *θwà*, and only the second is matched to the selectional requirements of the verb.

Bibliography

Okell (1969) is the most thorough and useful grammatical description of Burmese; part 1 is a structural analysis, part 2 a conspectus of grammatical morphemes. Judson (1888) is still the best English description of formal literary Burmese. For phonology, Bernot (1963) is a functional analysis of standard Burmese phonology, while Allott (1967) deals with grammatical tone. Bernot (1980) is a detailed study of the form and function of the elements of the verb phrase, including data on cooccurrence restrictions.

For the writing system, reference may be made to Roop (1972), a programmed course, and for Romanisation to Okell (1971). Allott (1985) is an important sociolinguistic study. Nissaya Burmese is discussed by Okell (1965).

Acknowledgements

I would like to express my gratitude to the following people: to Anna Allott and John Okell, who, over a number of years, have shared their own materials with me and guided me in my study of Burmese; to them, to Jim Matisoff and to Graham Thurgood, for providing extremely helpful comments on an earlier draft of this paper; to the Social Science Research Council, who supported my research on Burmese in London and Burma from 1978–9; and to the many Burmese people who have looked after me and assisted me in my endeavours to learn their language.

References

Allott, A. 1967. 'Grammatical Tone in Modern Spoken Burmese', *Wissenschaftliche Zeitschrift der Karl-Marx Universität Leipzig, Gesellschafts- und Sprachwissenschaftliche Reihe*, vol. 16, pp. 157–62.
—— 1985. 'Language Policy and Language Planning in Burma', in D. Bradley (ed.) *Papers in South-East Asian Linguistics*, No. 9, *Language Planning and Sociolinguistics in South-East Asia*, pp.131–54. Pacific Linguistics A-67, 1985.
Bernot, D. 1963. 'Esquisse d'une description phonologique du birman', *Bulletin de la Société Linguistique de Paris*, vol. 58, pp. 164–224.
—— 1980. *Le Prédicat en birman parlé* (Centre Nationale de la Recherche Scientifique, Paris)
Judson, Rev. A. 1888. *A Grammar of the Burmese Language* (Baptist Board of Publications, Rangoon)
Okell, J. 1965. 'Nissaya Burmese: A Case of Systematic Adaptation to a Foreign Grammar and Syntax', *Lingua*, vol. 15, pp. 186–227.
—— 1969. *A Reference Grammar of Colloquial Burmese*, 2 vols. (Oxford University Press, London)
—— 1971. *A Guide to the Romanization of Burmese* (Luzac and Co., London)
Roop, D.H. 1972. *An Introduction to the Burmese Writing System* (Yale University Press, New Haven)

7 JAPANESE

Masayoshi Shibatani

1 Introduction

Japanese is spoken by virtually the entire population of Japan — some 115 million people as of 1 March 1980. In terms of the number of native speakers, it is thus comparable to German and ranks sixth among the languages of the world. Yet, despite its status as a world's major language and its long literary history, Japanese is surrounded by numerous myths, some of which are perpetuated by Japanese and non-Japanese alike. There are a number of factors which contribute to these myths, e.g. the uncertainty of the genetic relationship of Japanese to other languages, its complex writing system and the relatively small number of non-Japanese (especially Westerners) who speak it.

One of the persistent myths held by the Japanese concerning their language is that it is somehow unique. This myth derives mainly from the superficial comparison between Japanese and closely related Indo-European languages such as English, German and French and the obvious disparities which such work reveals. Another persistent myth is that Japanese, compared to Western languages, notably French, is illogical and/or vague. This belief, remarkable as it may be, is most conspicuously professed by certain Japanese intellectuals well versed in European languages and philosophy. Their conviction is undoubtedly a reflection of the inferiority complex on the part of Japanese intellectuals toward Western civilisation. After all, Japan's modernisation effort started only after the Meiji Restoration (1867). Prior to this, Japan had maintained a feudalistic society and a closed-door policy to the rest of the world for nearly 250 years.

However understandable the historical or cultural causes may be, widespread characterisation of Japanese as a unique and illogical language grossly misrepresents the true nature of the language. In fact, in terms of grammatical structure, Japanese is a rather 'ordinary' human language. Its basic word order — subject–object–verb — is widespread among the world's languages. Also other characteristics associated with an SOV language are consistently exhibited in Japanese (see section 5). In the realm of phonology too, it is a commonplace language, with five hardly exotic vowels, a rather simple set of consonants and the basic CV syllable structure (see section 4).

As for the claim that Japanese is illogical or vague, one can argue that Japanese is in fact structurally superior to Western languages in the domain of discourse organisation. As we shall see in section 6, Japanese enables the speaker to distinguish clearly between the simple description of an event and a judgement about someone or something.

While the notion of uniqueness as applied to the entire domain of a given language is dubious, especially in the case of Japanese as pointed out above, each language does possess certain features that are unique or salient in comparison to other languages. For Japanese, these include honorifics, certain grammatical particles, some of which are distinct for male and female speakers, and the writing system. In this chapter, I shall attempt to include in the discussion those aspects of Japanese that constitute a notable feature of this language which I believe is not shared by many other languages and which makes learning Japanese difficult for many foreigners.

2 Historical Setting

Like Korean, its geographical neighbour, Japanese has long been the target of attempts to establish a genetic relationship between it and other languages and language families. Hypotheses have been presented assigning Japanese to virtually all major language families: Altaic, Austronesian, Sino-Tibetan, Indo-European, and Dravidian. The most persuasive is the Altaic theory, but even here evidence is hardly as firm as that which relates the languages of the Indo-European family, as can be seen in ongoing speculations among both scholars and linguistic amateurs.

With regard to individual languages, Ryūkyūan, Ainu and Korean have been the strongest candidates proposed as possible sister languages. Among these, the Japanese-Ryūkyūan connection has been firmly established. Ryūkyūan, spoken in Okinawa, is, in fact, now considered to be a dialect of Japanese. A Japanese-Ainu relationship has been hypothesised, but evidence is scanty. On the other hand, the Japanese-Korean hypothesis stands on firmer ground and perhaps it is safe to assume that they are related, though remotely.

The earliest written records of the Japanese language date back to the eighth century. The oldest among them, the *Kojiki* ('Record of Ancient Matters') (AD 712) is written in Chinese characters. The preface to this work is written in Chinese syntax as well. What was done is that the characters whose meanings were equivalent to Japanese expressions were arranged according to Chinese syntax. Thus, the document is not readily intelligible to those who do not know how the Chinese ordering of elements corresponds to the Japanese ordering, since Chinese word order is similar to English, e.g. *Mary likes fish*, as opposed to the Japanese order of *Mary fish likes*. Furthermore, it is not clear how such characters were read; they may have been read purely in the Chinese style in imitation of the Chinese pronunciation of the characters used or they may have been read in a Japanese way, i.e. by uttering those Japanese words corresponding in meaning to the written Chinese characters and inverting the order of elements so as to follow the Japanese syntax. Perhaps both methods were used. This means that a character such as 山 'mountain' was read both as *san*, the Chinese reading, and as *yama*, the semantically equivalent Japanese word for the character. This practice of reading Chinese characters both in the Chinese way and in terms of the semantically equivalent Japanese words persists even today.

By the time the *Manyōshū* ('Collection of a Myriad Leaves'), an anthology of Japanese verse, was completed (AD 759), the Japanese had learned to use Chinese characters as phonetic symbols. Thus, the Japanese word *yama* 'mountain' could be written phonetically by using a character with the sound *ya* (e.g. 夜 'evening') and another with the sound *ma* (e.g. 麻 'hemp'), as 夜麻. In other words, what stands for 'mountain' could be written in two ways. One used the Chinese word 山, as discussed above. The other way was to choose Chinese characters read as *ya* and *ma*. It is this latter phonetic way of writing which gave rise to the two uniquely Japanese syllabary writings known as *kana*.

Since things Chinese were regarded as culturally superior to their native equivalents, the Chinese manner was a formal way of writing. The phonetic representation of Japanese was considered only 'temporary' or mnemonic in nature. Thus, the phonetic writing was called *karina* 'temporary letters' while the Chinese way of writing was called *mana* 'true letters'.

Present-day *karina* (now pronounced as *kana*) have developed as simplified Chinese characters used phonetically. There are two kinds of *kana*. The original *kana* were used as mnemonic symbols in reading characters and were written alongside them; hence they are called *kata-kana* 'side *kana*'. *Hira-gana* 'plain *kana*' have developed by simplifying the grass style (i.e. cursive) writing of characters. These two *kana* syllabaries are set out in table 7.1.

Table 7.1: Japanese *Kana* Syllabaries

Hiragana

A	KA	SA	TA	NA	HA	MA	YA	RA	WA	
あ	か	さ	た	な	は	ま	や	ら	わ	
I	KI	SI	TI	NI	HI	MI		RI		
い	き	し	ち	に	ひ	み		り		
U	KU	SU	TU	NU	HU	MU	YU	RU		
う	く	す	つ	ぬ	ふ	む	ゆ	る		
E	KE	SE	TE	NE	HE	ME		RE		
え	け	せ	て	ね	へ	め		れ		
O	KO	SO	TO	NO	HO	MO	YO	RO	WO	N
お	こ	そ	と	の	ほ	も	よ	ろ	を	ん

Katakana

A	KA	SA	TA	NA	HA	MA	YA	RA	WA	
ア	カ	サ	タ	ナ	ハ	マ	ヤ	ラ	ワ	
I	KI	SI	TI	NI	HI	MI		RI		
イ	キ	シ	チ	ニ	ヒ	ミ		リ		
U	KU	SU	TU	NU	HU	MU	YU	RU		
ウ	ク	ス	ツ	ヌ	フ	ム	ユ	ル		
E	KE	SE	TE	NE	HE	ME		RE		
エ	ケ	セ	テ	ネ	ヘ	メ		レ		
O	KO	SO	TO	NO	HO	MO	YO	RO	WO	N
オ	コ	ソ	ト	ノ	ホ	モ	ヨ	ロ	ヲ	ン

Note: Voicing oppositions, where applicable, are indicated by the diacritical dots on the upper right hand corner of each *kana*; e.g. *gi* ギ as opposed to *ki* キ.

Katakana were originally used in combination with Chinese characters. *Hiragana*, on the other hand, were mainly used by women and were not mixed with characters. The contemporary practice is to use Chinese characters, called *kanji*, for content words, and *hiragana* for grammatical function words such as particles and inflectional endings. *Katakana* is used to write foreign loanwords, telegrams and in certain onomatopoeic expressions.

In addition, there is *rōmaji*, which is another phonetic writing system using the Roman alphabet. *Rōmaji* is mainly employed in writing station names as an aid for foreigners, in signing documents written in Western languages and in writing foreign acronyms (e.g. *ILO*, *IMF*). It is also used in advertising. Thus the word for 'mountain' can be written as 山 in *kanji*, as ヤマ in *katakana*, as やま in *hiragana* and as *yama* in *rōmaji*. Sometimes all these four ways of writing can be found in one sentence; e.g. the sentence *Hanako is an OL* (< *office lady* i.e. 'office girl') *working in that building* can be written as below:

```
      花子 は あのビル    で  働いている    OL  です。
      Hanako wa ano biru  de  hataraite-iru  ooeru desu.
             top. that building at  work-ing      OL   cop.
```

The traditional way of writing is to write vertically, lines progressing from right to left. Today both vertical writing and horizontal writing, as illustrated above, are practised.

As may be surmised from the above discussion, learning how to write Japanese involves considerable effort. Japanese children must master all four ways of writing by the time they complete nine years of Japan's compulsory education. Of these, the most difficult is the Chinese system. For each *kanji*, at least two ways of reading must be learned: one the *on-yomi*, the Sino-Japanese reading, and the other the *kun-yomi*, the Japanese reading. For the character 山 'mountain', *san* is the Sino-Japanese reading and *yama* the Japanese. Normally, the Sino-Japanese reading is employed in compounds consisting of two or more Chinese characters, while in isolation the Japanese reading is adopted.

An additional complication is the multiplicity of Sino-Japanese readings. This is due to the fact that Chinese characters, or rather their pronunciations, were borrowed from different parts of China as well as at different times. Thus, dialectal differences in pronunciation also had to be learned by the Japanese. One of the two major sources of borrowing was the Wu area of China during the Six Dynasties period. The reading reflecting this dialect is called *go'on*. The other reading called *kan'on* reflects a newer dialect of *Chang-an*, which is believed to be the standard language of the Tang period. The character 米 for 'rice' is pronounced *mai* in *go'on*, *bei* in *kan'on* and *kome* and *yone* in the Japanese reading. Unlike the *on-yomi* versus *kun-yomi*, there is no systematic rule for determining whether a given character is to be read in *kan'on* or in *go'on*; each expression must be learned as to which way it is read. The character 米 for 'rice', for example, will be read in *go'on* in a form like 外米 *gai mai* 'imported rice', but in *kan'on* in a form like 米国 *bei koku* 'America'. That is, the *go'on/kan'on* distinction is purely historical and speakers of Japanese must simply live with the fact that in addition to the Japanese way of reading, most *kanji* have two or more Chinese ways of reading them and that the same *kanji* is likely to be pronounced differently depending on which expression it is used in.

Because of this kind of complexity caused by retaining all these writing methods, there have been movements for abolishing Chinese characters in favour of *kana* writing and even movements for completely Romanising the Japanese language. All these, however, have so far failed and it is safe to say that Chinese characters are here to stay. What has been done instead of abolishing Chinese characters altogether is to limit the number of commonly used characters. In 1946, the Japanese government issued a list of 1,850 characters for this purpose. The list was revised in 1981, and the new list, called *Jōyō Kanji Hyō* ('List of Characters for Daily Use'), contains 1,945 characters recommended for daily use. This is now regarded as the basic list of Chinese characters to be learned during elementary and intermediate education. Also, most newspapers try to limit the use of characters to these

1,945 characters; when those outside the list are used, the reading in *hiragana* accompanies them.

Japan, a mountainous country with many islands, has a setting ideal for fostering language diversification; and, indeed, Japanese is rich in dialectal variation. Many dialects are mutually unintelligible. For example, speakers of the Kagoshima dialect of the southern island of Kyūshū would not be understood by the majority of the speakers on the main island of Honshū. Likewise, northern dialect speakers of Aomori and Akita would not be understood by the people of metropolitan Tōkyō or by anyone from western Japan. Communication among people of different dialects has been made possible through the spread of the so-called *kyootuu-go* 'common language', which consists essentially of versions of local dialects modified according to the 'ideal' form called *hyoozyun-go* 'standard language', which in turn is based on the dialect of the capital Tōkyō.

Hyoozyun-go is used in broadcasting and it is this form of Japanese which elementary education aims at in teaching children. The following description is based on this dialect, sometimes referred to as the standard dialect.

3 Lexicon

The fact that Japan has never been invaded by a foreign force or colonised by a foreign interest causes surprise when one examines the Japanese lexicon, for it shows a characteristic of those languages whose lands have been under foreign control at one time or another. Namely, Japanese vocabulary abounds in foreign words. In this regard, Japanese is similar to Turkish, which has borrowed a large number of Arabic and Persian words without ever being ruled by Arabs or Persians, and contrasts with English and others that have incorporated a large quantity of words from invaders' languages.

In addition to the abundance of foreign words, the Japanese lexicon is characterised by the presence of a large number of onomatopoeic words. This section, still in the spirit of presenting an overall picture of Japanese, surveys these two characteristic aspects of the Japanese lexicon.

Japanese has borrowed words from neighbouring languages such as Ainu and Korean, but by far the most numerous are Chinese loanwords. Traditionally, the Japanese lexicon is characterised in terms of three strata. The terms *wago* 'Japanese words' or *Yamato-kotoba* 'Yamato (Japanese) words' refer to the stratum of the native vocabulary and *kango* 'Chinese words' refers to loanwords of Chinese origin (hereafter called Sino-Japanese words). All other loanwords from European languages are designated by the term *gairaigo* 'foreign words' (lit. 'foreign coming words'). The relative proportions of these loanwords in the *Genkai* dictionary (1859) were: Sino-Japanese words — 60 per cent, foreign words — 1.4 per cent, the rest being native words. Although the proportion of foreign words has been steadily increasing (see below), that of the Sino-Japanese words remains fairly constant.

The effect of loanwords on the Japanese language is not insignificant. In particular, the effects of Sino-Japanese borrowing have been felt in all aspects of the Japanese language, including syntax. Restricting our discussion to the domain of the lexicon, however, Sino-Japanese and foreign loanwords have resulted in a large number of synonymous expressions. This demonstrates that Japanese has borrowed even those words whose equivalents already existed in the language. This may appear at first to be unmotivated and uneconomical. However, synonymous words are often associated with different shades of meaning and stylistic values, thereby enriching the Japanese vocabulary and allowing for a greater range of expression. For example, some interesting observations can be made with regard to the following sets of synonymous triplets:

Gloss	'inn'	'idea'	'acrobat'	'detour'	'cancellation'
Native	yadoya	omoituki	karuwaza	mawarimiti	torikesi
S-J	ryokan	tyakusoo	kyokugei	ukairo	kaiyaku
Foreign	hoteru	aidea	akurobatto	baipasu	kyanseru

In general, the native words have broader meanings than their loan counterparts. For example, *torikesi* can be applied to various kinds of cancellation-type acts, even in taking back one's words. The Sino-Japanese word *kaiyaku* is normally used with reference to the cancellation of contracts and other formal transactions. The foreign word *kyanseru*, on the other hand, is used for the cancellation of appointments or ticket reservations etc. The Sino-Japanese words, which generally convey a more formal impression, tend to be used with reference to higher-quality objects than do the native equivalents. On the other hand, the foreign words have a modern and stylish flavour.

Though various factors can be pointed out to account for the ready acceptance of loanwords in Japanese, the main linguistic reasons have to do with the lack of nominal inflections and the presence of a syllabic writing system. Since Japanese does not mark gender, person or number in nouns and since cases are indicated by separate particles, a loanword can simply be inserted into any position where a native nominal might appear with no morphological readjustment. For the borrowing of verbal expressions, Japanese utilises the verb *suru*, which has the very general meaning 'do'. This useful verb can attach to the nominal forms of loanwords to create verbal expressions; e.g. the Sino-Japanese word *hukusya* 'copy' yields *hukusya-suru* 'to copy' and the English loan *kopii* 'copy' yields *kopii-suru* 'to copy'.

The proportion and the status of the Sino-Japanese words in Japanese are strikingly similar to those of the Latinate words in English. The proportion of Latinate words in English vocabulary is estimated to be around 55 per cent, while that of Germanic (Anglo-Saxon) words and of other foreign loans are 35 per cent and 10 per cent, respectively. Furthermore, the status of the Sino-Japanese words in Japanese is quite similar to that of Latinate words in English. As they tend to express abstract concepts, Sino-Japanese words make up the great majority of learned vocabulary items.

Loanwords other than those belonging to the stratum of Sino-Japanese words are called *gairaigo*. The first Japanese contacts with the western world came about in the middle of the sixteenth century, when a drifting Portuguese merchant ship reached the island of Tanegashima off Kyūshū. The Portuguese were followed by the Spaniards and Dutch. Thus, most of the earliest foreign words were from Portuguese, Spanish and especially Dutch. Toward the latter part of the nineteenth century, English replaced Dutch as the language of foreign studies; and presently, roughly 80 per cent of the foreign vocabulary of Japanese are words of English origin.

English terms were first translated into Japanese semantically using Chinese characters, which resulted in a large number of *kango* 'Chinese words' coined in Japan. This was in keeping with the traditional practice of assigning semantically appropriate Chinese characters to foreign loanwords. In order to represent the original sounds, a *katakana* rendering of the original pronunciation accompanied the translated word. Thus, in the initial phase of loan translation, there were, for each word, both character and *katakana* representations; the former representing the meaning and the latter the sound. These foreign words then had two paths open to them; some retained the character rendering and began to be pronounced according to the readings of the characters, while others preserved the *katakana* rendering. A good number of words took both paths, resulting in the formation of many doublets — the *kango* version and the foreign (phonetic) version; e.g. *kentiku:birudingu* 'building', *sikihu:siitu* 'sheet', *tetyoo:nooto* 'notebook', and more recently *densikeisanki:konpyuutaa* 'computer'.

Contemporary practice now is to borrow by directly representing just the sounds using *katakana*. But when foreign loanwords are rendered in *katakana*, the original pronunciation is most often grossly altered. Since all the *katakana* except ン end in a vowel, consonant clusters and a final consonant of a loanword are altered into sequences consisting of a consonant and a vowel. Thus, a one-syllable word like *strike* becomes the five-mora word *sutoraiku* (see section 4). As a consequence, many Japanese words of English origin are totally incomprehensible to the ears of the native English speaker, much to the chagrin of the Japanese. Japanese-born American historian and former ambassador to Japan, E.O. Reischauer, comments, 'It is pathetic to see the frustration of Japanese in finding that English speakers cannot recognise, much less understand, many of the English words they use.'

In addition to the phonological process, there are three other factors which annoy non-Japanese when encountering Japanised borrowings from their native tongues. They are: (1) change in semantics, e.g. *sutoobu* (< *stove*) exclusively designates a room heater; (2) Japanese coinages, e.g. *bakku miraa* (< *back* + *mirror*) for the rear-view mirror of an automobile; and (3) change in form due to simplification, *pan-suto* (< *panty stockings*) 'panty hose, tights'.

Foreign words are conspicuous not only in number (they abound in commercial messages and inundate Japanese daily life), but also in form, as they are written in *katakana*. The ubiquity and conspicuousness of foreign words in contemporary Japan as well as the fact that they are often used without precise understanding of their original meanings alarm language purists. Occasional public outcries are heard and opinions for curbing the use of foreign words are voiced. However, such purists are fighting a losing battle and, to their dismay, foreign words are gaining a firm footing in the Japanese language.

Foreign loanwords, like slang expressions, are quickly adopted and then abandoned. Only those that are firmly entrenched in the language can be found in dictionaries. The proportion of foreign loanwords in dictionaries is, however, steadily increasing. The ratio of the foreign words in the *Genkai*, published in 1859, was only 1.4 per cent. The rate increased to 3.5 per cent in the *Reikai Kokugojiten* published in 1956. The 1972 version of *Shin Meikai Kokugojiten* has *gairaigo* comprising 7.8 per cent of its entries. It is predicted that foreign words would claim at least a 10 per cent share of the entries in a dictionary compiled today.

Onomatopoeic and other sound symbolic words form another conspicuous group of words in the Japanese lexicon. In a narrow sense, onomatopoeia refers to those conventionalised mimetic expressions of natural sounds. These words are called *giongo* 'phonomimes' in Japanese; e.g. *wan-wan* 'bow-wow', *gata-gata* '(clattering noise)'. In addition to phonomimes, the Japanese lexicon has two other classes of sound symbolic or synaesthetic expressions. They are *gitaigo* 'phenomimes' and *gisyoogo* 'psychomimes'. Phenomimes 'depict' states, conditions or manners of the external world (e.g. *yoboyobo* 'wobbly', *kossori* 'stealthily'), while psychomimes symbolise mental conditions or states (e.g. *ziin* 'poignantly', *tikutiku* 'stingingly'). In the following discussion, all these classes of sound symbolic words will be collectively referred to as onomatopoeic words.

In comparison to English, many Japanese verbs have very general meanings. *Naku*, for example, covers all manners of crying that are expressed in specific English verbs such as *weep* and *sob*. Similarly, *warau* is a general term for laughing. This lack of specificness of the verb meaning is compensated by the presence of onomatopoeic words. Indeed, one may argue that the differences between *weep* and *sob* and between *chuckle* and *smile* etc. are more expressive in Japanese. Some examples follow: 'cry' *waa-waa naku*, 'weep' *meso-meso naku*, 'sob' *kusun-kusun naku*, 'blubber' *oi-oi naku*, 'whimper' *siku-siku naku*, 'howl' *wan-wan naku*, 'pule' *hii-hii naku*, 'mewl' *een-een to naku*; 'laugh' *ha-ha-ha to warau*, 'smile' *niko-niko to warau*, 'chuckle' *kutu-kutu to warau*, 'haw-haw' *wa-ha-ha to warau*, 'giggle' *gera-gera to warau*, 'snigger' *nita-nita warau*, 'simper' *ohoho to warau*, 'grin' *nikori to warau*, 'titter' *kusu-kusu warau*.

Sound qualities and synaesthetic effects are correlated to a certain extent, especially with regard to the voicing opposition and differences in vowel quality. In reference to the voicing opposition, the voiced versions relate to heavier or louder sounds or stronger, bigger, rougher actions or states and the voiceless versions to lighter or softer sounds or crisper or more delicate actions or states.

Differences in vowel quality also correlate with differences in the texture of observed phenomena. High or closed vowels are associated with higher or softer sounds or activities involving smaller objects, with low vowels correlating with the opposite phenomena. The front-back opposition is similarly correlated with loudness and size, as is the high-low opposition. Thus, *kiin* is a shrill metallic sound, while *kaan* is the sound of a fairly large bell and *goon* the sound of a heavy bell of a Buddhist temple. *Boro-boro* symbolises the vertical dropping of relatively small objects such as tear drops, as opposed to *bara-bara*, which depicts the dropping of objects by scattering them. A small whistle sounds *pippii* and a steam whistle goes *poppoo*. A goat bleats *mee*, and a cow lows *moo*. *Gero-gero* is the way a frog croaks, but *goro-goro* is the rumbling of thunder.

Onomatopoeic expressions permeate Japanese life. They occur in animated speech and abound in literary works to the chagrin of the translators of Japanese literature. In baby-talk, many animals are referred to by the words that mimic their cries; *buu-buu* 'pig', *wan-wan* 'dog', *nyan-nyan* 'cat', *moo-moo* 'cow'. Indeed, names of many noise-making insects and certain objects are derived by a similar process; *kakkoo* 'cuckoo', *kirigirisu* '(a type of grass-hopper)', *gatya-gatya* '(a noise-making cricket)'. There are said to be more than thirty kinds of cicadas in Japan and many of them are named after the noises they make: *tuku-tuku-boosi*, *kana-kana*, *min-min-zemi*, *tii-tii-zemi* etc. A hammer is sometimes called *tonkati* and a favourite pastime of the Japanese is *patinko* 'pinball game', which is sometimes referred to by the more expressive form *tinzyara*, mimicking the noise of the *patinko* parlour.

4 Phonology

Although different phonemic interpretations are possible, perhaps the most orthodox inventories of Japanese segmental phonemes are those set out in table 7.2.

The basic vowel phonemes of the standard dialect are rather straightforward. However, a great deal of dialectal variation in the vocalic

Table 7.2: Segmental Phonemes of Japanese

Vowels					
	i		u		
	e		o		
		a			
Consonants					
	p	t	k		
	b	d	g		
		s		h	
		z			
		r			
	m	n			
	w	j			
			N	Q	

system is observed. Dialectal systems range from a three-vowel system (/i/, /u/, /a/) in the Yonaguni dialect of Okinawa to an eight-vowel system in the Nagoya dialect, which, in addition to the five vowels of the standard dialect, possesses the central vowels /ü/ and /ö/, as well as the low front vowel /æ/. Despite these variations, it is generally believed that the basic vowels of the Japanese language are those five vowels set out in table 7.2, which are observed in the major dialects of Tōkyō, Kyōto, Ōsaka etc., and that the other dialectal systems have evolved from the five-vowel system.

In the standard dialect, there are two characteristics concerning vowels. One is the articulation of /u/; it is unrounded [ɯ]. The other is the devoicing of high vowels /u/ and /i/ in a voiceless environment; [kɯtsɯ] 'shoe', [haʃi] 'chopstick', [sɯsɯki] 'eulalia'. Specifying the notion of voiceless environment precisely is not easy, but the following factors have been identified so far: (1) /i/ and /u/ will only devoice if not contiguous to a voiced sound; (2) the high vowels do not devoice when they are initial even followed by a voiceless sound; and (3) accented high vowels do not devoice even if flanked by voiceless consonants. The phenomenon also depends on speech tempo; in slow, deliberate speech, devoicing is less frequent.

Among the consonants, notable phenomena are two pervasive allophonic rules: the palatalisation and affrication of dental consonants. The former involves /s/, /z/, /t/ and /d/ and the latter /t/, /d/ and /z/.

In the non-Sino-Japanese vocabulary of the Japanese lexicon (cf. section 3), the dental consonants and their palatalised or affricated versions are in complementary distribution:

/s/: [ʃ]   before *i*
      [s]   elsewhere
/z/: [dʒ]   before *i*
      [dz]   before *u*
      [z]   elsewhere

/t/:   [tʃ]   before *i*
       [ts]   before *u*
       [t]   elsewhere
/d/:   [dʒ]   before *i*
       [dz]   before *u*
       [d]   elsewhere

In the Sino-Japanese vocabulary, there is a contrast between the dentals and their palatalised versions; e.g. [sa] 'difference': [ʃa] 'diagonal', but these are generally analysed as /sa/ and /sya/, the latter of which undergoes the palatalisation process just like the /si/ sequence seen above. (Except for proper nouns, which are transliterated in *rōmaji*, the Japanese expressions in this text are transliterated according to the phonemic representation; thus what is transliterated as *si*, *ti*, *tu* etc. should be read with appropriate palatalisation and affrication as [ʃi], [tʃi], [tsɯ] etc. according to the above distributional pattern.)

The palatalisation and the affrication described here are very pervasive and cause morphophonemic alternations. Thus, when verb stems that end in a dental consonant are affixed with suffixes beginning in a high vowel, palatalisation or affrication occurs. Observe the alternations: [kas-ɯ] 'lend-pres.': [kas-anai] 'lend-neg.': [kas-e] 'lend-imper.': [kaʃ-imas-ɯ] 'lend-polite-pres.', [kats-ɯ] 'win-pres.': [kat-anai] 'win-neg.': [kat-e] 'win-imper.': [katʃ-imas-ɯ] 'win-polite-pres.'.

The same rules apply to loanwords; e.g. [ʃiidzün] *season*, [tʃiimɯ] *team*, [tsɯaa] *tour*. Many younger speakers have begun to pronounce forms such as *party* and other recent loans with [t]. On the other hand, the pronunciation of [s] before [i] appears to be more difficult, so that words such as *seat* and *system* are almost invariably pronounced with [ʃi].

Other pervasive phonological rules are seen in verb inflection, which involves affixation of various suffixes. The most important consideration here is the distinction between verb stems ending in a consonant (C-stems) and those ending in a vowel (V-stems), for this distinction largely determines the shape of the suffixes. The clearest such case is the choice of an imperative suffix: C-stems take *-e* and V-stems *-ro*; *kak-e* 'write-imper.', *mi-ro* 'look-imper.'.

In other situations, phonological rules intervene to resolve consonant clusters and vowel clusters resulting from the joining of C-stems and consonant-initial suffixes (C-suffixes) and of V-stems and vowel-initial suffixes (V-suffixes). In the former case, the suffix-initial consonants are elided and in the latter, the suffix-initial vowels are elided. For example, the initial consonant of the present tense suffix /-ru/ is elided after a C-stem verb like /kak-/ 'to write', while it is retained after a V-stem verb like /mi-/ 'to see', as seen in the contrast, *kak-u*:*mi-ru*. As an example of a suffix with an initial vowel, take the negative /-anai/. With /kak-/, it retains the initial vowel, while it is lost after /mi-/: *kak-anai:mi-nai*. The other inflectional categories are exemplified in the chart of verb inflection.

Japanese Verb Inflection

	C-stem 'to cut'	*V-stem* 'to wear (clothes)'	
Imperative	kir-e	ki-ro	⎫
Present	kir-u	ki-ru	
Past	kit-ta	ki-ta	
Participial	kit-te	ki-te	⎬ C-suffixes
Provisional	kir-eba	ki-reba	
Tentative	kir-oo	ki-yoo	
Passive	kir-are-ru	ki-rare-ru*	
Causative	kir-ase-ru	ki-sase-ru	⎭
Negative	kir-ana-i	ki-na-i**	⎫
Polite	kir-imas-u	ki-mas-u	⎬ V-suffixes
Desiderative	kir-ita-i	ki-ta-i	
Infinitive	kir-i	ki	⎭

Note:* /-ru/ here and in the causative and /-u/ in the polite form are the present tense suffix. ** /-i/ is the present tense suffix for adjectives.

The basic syllable structure of Japanese is CV and this canonical pattern is also imposed on loanwords. A consonant cluster and a syllable-final consonant will be made into a CV sequence by inserting [ɯ] (or [o] after a dental stop; remember that [tɯ] or [dɯ] do not occur phonetically in Japanese). Thus, a word like *strike* will be turned into [sɯtoraikɯ]. As this word indicates, a vowel by itself forms a syllable — or more precisely a mora (see page 140) — and sequences of vowels occur. This is one deviation from the basic CV pattern. The other deviation has to do with two types of consonants that may close a syllable. They are non-nasal consonants followed by homorganic consonants of the following syllable and a nasal that closes a syllable; e.g. [jappari] 'as expected', [jatto] 'finally', [jɯkkɯri] 'slowly', [hontoo] 'truly', [hampa] 'haphazard', [koŋgari] 'crisply', [hoN] 'book'.

Since the phonetic values of all these syllable-final consonants, except the word-final nasal in [hoN] and other such words, are entirely predictable from the nature of the following consonants, they are assigned to two archiphonemes: /Q/ for the non-nasal consonants and /N/ for the nasal consonants. When /N/ occurs word-finally it assumes the value of the uvular nasal [N] or simply nasalisation of the vowel identical to the preceding vowel. Thus, /hoN/ 'book' will be [hoN] or [hoõ]. (Words such as *pen* and *spoon*, which end in [n], are borrowed with the [N] replacing the final nasal, as [peN] and [sɯpɯɯN], respectively.)

The syllable-final consonants constitute one rhythmic unit, much like the syllabic [ṇ] and [ḷ] in English. This leads us to a discussion of an important phonological unit of Japanese, namely the *mora*. In Japanese phonology, a distinction needs to be made between the suprasegmental units syllable and mora. A form such as *sinbun* 'newspaper' consists of two syllables *sin* and *bun*, but a Japanese speaker further subdivides the form into four units *si*, *n*, *bu* and *n*, which correspond to the four letters of *kana* in writing the word. A mora in Japanese is a unit which can be represented by one letter of *kana* and which functions as a rhythmic unit in the composition of Japanese *waka* and *haiku*, the Japanese traditional poems. Thus, in poetic compositions, *sinbun* is counted as having four, rather than two, rhythmic units, and would be equivalent in length to *hatimaki* 'headband'.

While ordinary syllables include a vowel, morae need not. In addition to the moraic nasal seen in *sinbun* above, there are consonantal morae. These occur as the first element in geminate consonants discussed above, e.g. *hakkiri* 'clearly', *yappari* 'as expected', *tatta* 'stood up'. Although these geminate consonants have different phonetic values, the first segments, which constitute morae, are written in *hiragana* with a small っ ([tsu]). *Hakkiri* is written with four letters and counted as having four morae — *ha-k-ki-ri*. If a native speaker is asked to pronounce this word slowly marking off each mora unit, he would pronounce it according to the way it is written in *hiragana*, namely as, *ha-tu-ki-ri*.

Long vowels, written with two of the same *kana* or with one *kana* followed by a bar indicating length, also count as two morae; e.g. *ookii* 'big' is a two-syllable (*oo-kii*), four-mora (*o-o-ki-i*) word.

Both morae and syllables play an important role in the Japanese accentual system. For one thing, pitch change occurs at the mora level. The one-syllable word *kan* 'completion', for example, has a pitch drop after the first mora as ka̅n. This contrasts with another *kan* 'sense', which has the pitch configuration ka̱n̄. Moreover, in the standard dialect the initial low pitch can be only one mora in length. Thus, if the first syllable contains two morae, as in *ooi* 'many' or *hantai* 'opposite', only the first mora will have the low pitch: o̱o̅i̅, ha̱nta̅i̅. If the initial syllable has just one mora, it of course will have the low pitch (unless it is accented); ha̱tu̅me̅i̅ 'invention'. (Forms beginning with high pitch can also have high pitch but only for one mora, the second mora and the rest being low pitched.)

The concept of syllable also plays a role in Japanese accentuation. In the standard dialect, it is the syllabic unit which carries accent or the mark of pitch fall. This is seen from the fact that two-mora syllables always have the accent on the first mora. That is, while there are forms like *ko'orogi* 'cricket', which is realised as ko̅o̅rogi, there is no form like *koo'rogi*, with an accent on the second mora of the first syllable, which would be pronounced as ko̱o̅rogi. This does not mean that there is no form with a high-pitched second mora. Such forms occur in two situations. One case occurs when the word contains no accent, e.g. _koōru_ 'to freeze'. The other case is when the second mora is an independent syllable and carries the accent as in _koga'isya_ (_kogāisya_) 'subsidiary company'. The same applies with other types of mora. There are forms like _ga'nko_ 'stubborn', but none like _gan'ko_, with an accent on the second mora of the first syllable. If a mora were an accentual unit, there should be no reason for such a restriction. Thus, Japanese accentuation rules must refer to both moraic and syllabic units.

Incidentally, not all Japanese dialects have both syllabic and moraic units. Certain dialects in the northern Tohoku region and the southern Kyūshū region do not count forms like _matti_ 'match' and _honya_ 'book-store' as having three rhythmic units. Rather they are separated into only two units, _mat-ti_ and _hon-ya_. A syllable with a long vowel is also counted as one unit in these dialects. Furthermore, in these dialects the syllable is also the unit of pitch assignment.

Since these dialects which recognise only syllabic units occur in the peripheral areas of northern and southern Japan, the Japanese dialectologist Takesi Sibata hypothesises that Japanese was once a syllable language from which the more contemporary mora dialects have developed.

As the preceding discussion indicates, Japanese accentuation involves pitch differences. If a textbook definition were to be applied to Japanese, most Japanese dialects would be called tone languages. In the Kyōto dialect, for example, the segmental form _hasi_ has three pitch patterns each associated with a distinct meaning: _hasi_ with H(igh) H(igh) is 'edge', _hasi_ with L(ow) H is 'chopsticks', and _hasi_ with HL is 'bridge'. In certain dialects not only the level tones H and L, but also a contour tone H-L is observed. Again, in Kyōto, _saru_ 'monkey' is L H-L; that is, the second mora _ru_ begins high and falls to low.

However, the Japanese accentual system is characteristically distinct from the archetypal tone languages of the Chinese type. In this type of language, it is necessary to specify the tone for each syllable. If a word or phrase has two or more syllables, each syllable needs to have a tone specified for it; there is no way of predicting the tone of each syllable of a word or phrase from something else. This is not the case for Japanese. In the majority of Japanese dialects, given diacritic accent markers and a set of rules, the pitch of each syllable of a phrase can be predicted, thereby making the specification of the pitch for each individual syllable unnecessary. In other words, the phonemic nature of the Japanese accentuation is reducible to the abstract accent marker that indicates the location of pitch fall.

Rules that predict actual pitch shapes differ slightly from one dialect to another, but in the standard dialect, the following three ordered rules assign correct pitches (indicated in parentheses) to phonemic representations of such words as /sakura/ (LHH) 'cherry', /za'kuro/ (HLL) 'pomegranate', /koko'ro/ (LHL) 'heart', as well as to those of phrases like /sakura ga/ (LHH H) 'cherry nom.', /miyako' ga/ (LHH L) 'capital nom.' etc.:

(a) Assign high pitch to all morae.
(b) Assign low pitch to all morae following the accent.
(c) Assign low pitch to the first mora if the second is high pitched.

In the standard dialect, one only needs to know the location of pitch fall in predicting the phonetic pitch shape. However, in other dialects additional information may be called for. In some dialects (e.g. Kyōto, Ōsaka) more than the location of pitch change needs be specified in order to assign the pitch contour to a word; specifically, whether a word begins with high pitch or with low pitch must be indicated. The standard dialect has predominant high pitch, as can be noticed from the first of the rules given above, but some dialects (e.g. Kagoshima) have a system with predominant low pitch, in which pitch changes all entail the raising of pitch. Finally, some dialects (e.g. Miyakonojō) have just one accentual pattern, which perforce makes the system non-phonemic.

5 Syntax

The basic word order in Japanese is subject, (indirect object) direct object, verb; e.g.

(a) Taroo ga   Hanako ni   sono hon   o   yatta.
     nom.   dat.   that book   acc. gave
     'Taro gave that book to Hanako.'

However, emphatic fronting may move a non-subject element to sentence-initial position and therefore variously reordered sentences are possible — an important consideration being that the verb always remains in final position. But there seems to be a restriction: when more than one element is fronted, the resulting sentences are not so well formed as the ones that involve the movement of one element. Thus, the above sentence has the following well formed and less well formed variations:

(b) Hanako ni Taroo ga sono hon o yatta (fronting of the indirect object).
(c) Sono hon o Taroo ga Hanako ni yatta (fronting of the direct object).
(d) ?Hanako ni sono hon o Taroo ga yatta (fronting of both indirect and direct object).
(e) ?Sono hon o Hanako ni Taroo ga yatta (fronting of both indirect and direct object).
(f) Taroo ga sono hon o Hanako ni yatta (reversing the order of indirect and direct object).

Related to the basic SOV word order are the following characteristics that are shared by a large number of other SOV languages:

(a) Nominal relations are expressed by postpositional (as opposed to prepositional) particles. (See the above examples.)

(b) The demonstrative, numeral (plus classifier) and descriptive adjective precede the noun in that order; e.g. *sono san-nin no ookii kodomo* (that three person of big child) 'those three big children'. (In this kind of combination, the numeral and adjective expressions may be in reverse order.)

(c) The genitive noun precedes the possessed noun; e.g. *Taroo no hon* (Taro of book) 'Taro's book'.

(d) The relative clause precedes the noun modified; e.g. [*Taroo ga katta*] *hon* ([Taroo nom. bought] book) 'the book which Taro bought'.

(e) The proper noun precedes the common noun; e.g. *Taroo ozisan* (Taro uncle) 'Uncle Taro'.

(f) The adverb precedes the verb; e.g. *hayaku hasiru* (quickly run) 'run quickly'.

(g) Auxiliaries follow the main verb; e.g. *ik-itai* (go-want) 'want to go', *ik-eru* (go can) 'can go'.

(h) The comparative expression takes the order standard–marker of comparison–adjective; e.g. *Taroo yori kasikoi* (Taroo-than-smart) 'smarter than Taro'.

(i) Questions are formed by the addition of the sentence-final particle *ka*; e.g. *Taroo ga kita* 'Taro came' → *Taroo ga kita ka* 'did Taro come?'. Also, unlike English, there is no movement of a *wh*-element in a *wh*-question. Thus, the question word *nani* 'what' remains in object position in the question: *Taroo wa nani o katta ka* (Taroo top. what acc. bought Q) 'What did Taro buy?'

The basic Japanese sentence type exhibits the nominative-accusative case marking pattern, whereby the subjects of both transitive and intransitive sentences are marked by the particle *ga* and the object of a transitive sentence with a distinct particle, *o*. There are, however, three noteworthy deviations from this basic pattern. They are illustrated below along with the basic pattern.

(a) Taroo ga kita.
    nom. came
'Taro came.'

(b) Taroo ga hebi o korosita.
    nom. snake acc. killed
'Taro killed the snake.'

(c) Taroo ga Hanako ni atta.
    nom. dat. met
'Taro met Hanako.'

(d) Taroo ni eigo ga wakaru.
    dat. English nom. understand
'Taro understands English.'

(e) Taroo ga Hanako ga suki da.
    nom. nom. like copula
'Taro likes Hanako.'

While English consistently exhibits the basic transitive sentence pattern for all these expressions, it is rather exceptional in this regard. Many other languages belonging to different language families show similar deviations along the lines of Japanese. The nominative-dative pattern of (c) is seen in German with verbs like *helfen* 'help' and *danken* 'thank'. The dative-nominative pattern seen in (d) is also very frequently seen in Indo-European languages as well; e.g. Spanish *me gusta la cerveza* 'I like beer', Russian *mne nravitsja kniga* 'I like a book'. In Japanese, predicates like *aru* 'have', *dekiru* 'can do' and *hituyoo da* 'necessary' govern the dative-nominative pattern.

Less frequently seen is the nominative-nominative pattern in (e). As the above examples from Spanish and Russian indicate, the predicate 'like' is normally subsumed under the dative-nominative pattern in those languages that exhibit this pattern. Japanese has a distinct nominative-nominative pattern for predicates such as *suki da* 'like', *zyoozu da* 'good at', *hosii* 'want' etc. Another language that has this pattern regularly with predicates similar to those given here is Korean.

Just as in many other languages, many important syntactic phenomena centre around the subject noun phrase. We will discuss some of them, but since they can be best treated in comparison to the topic noun phrase, we shall now turn to discourse-related phenomena.

6 Discourse Phenomena

One of the most important aspects of Japanese grammar has to do with the construction involving the particle *wa*. This particle, generally regarded as a topic marker, attaches to various nominals and adverbials, as seen below, and those constructions with a *wa*-marked constituent are called the topic construction.

(a) Taroo ga   Hanako ni   sono hon o   nitiyoobi ni watasita.
    nom.   dat.   that book acc. Sunday on   gave
    'Taro gave that book to Hanako on Sunday.'
(b) Taroo wa Hanako ni sono hon o nitiyoobi ni watasita.
    (Topicalisation of the subject)
(c) Hanako ni wa Taroo ga sono hon o nitiyoobi ni watasita.
    (Topicalisation of the indirect object)
(d) Sono hon wa Taroo ga Hanako ni nitiyoobi ni watasita.
    (Topicalisation of the direct object)
(e) Nitiyoobi ni wa Taroo ga sono hon o Hanako ni watasita.
    (Topicalisation of the adverbial)

As seen above, the nominative particle *ga* as well as the accusative *o* drop when *wa* is attached, while other particles tend to be retained (see the dative *ni* in (c), for example).

It is also possible to have two or more *wa*-attached constituents, as in the following example:

(f) Taroo wa nitiyoobi ni wa Hanako ni sono hon o watasita.
     (Topicalisation of the subject and the adverbial)

In the above examples, the topic has been 'extracted' from clause-internal position. While these are typical topic constructions, there are others whose topics cannot be related to a non-topic structure, i.e. the comment is itself a complete clause structure. For example:

(a) Sakana wa   tai   ga   ii.
     fish   top. red snapper   nom.   good
     'As for fish, red snappers are good.'
(b) Huro   wa   kimoti   ga   ii.
     bath   top.   feeling   nom.   good
     'As for the bath, it feels good.'

Recent discussion in the literature of Japanese grammar published in English has concentrated mainly on identifying those factors which determine the attachment of *wa*. What has been explicated are those factors which pertain to the nature of 'topic' or 'theme', namely, that the entity must be old information or given.

What has been lacking in the discussion of *wa* in these treatments is the notion of sentence type, which figures importantly in the tradition of Japanese grammar. The relevant distinction here is the difference between a sentence of description and that of judgement. When one describes an event or a state, no topic construction is used, while when one is to make a certain judgement about an entity, then that entity would be marked by *wa* and the topic construction results. Thus, if someone were just describing the sky, he would say: *sora ga aoi* (sky nom. blue) 'the sky is blue', but if someone were to make a judgement about the sky (in this case that the sky is blue), he would use the topic construction and say: *sora wa aoi*, which would have to be also translated as 'the sky is blue' in English.

In fact, one has a certain degree of freedom as to the use and non-use of the topic construction depending on whether the narration involves making judgement or not. For example, in the following narrative, there is no topic construction involved:

(a) Hitori no   kodomo ga   aruite   kita.
     one   of   child nom.   walking   came
     'A child came walking.'
(b) Soko   e   inu   ga   hasitte   kita.
     there   at   dog   nom.   running   came
     'There came a dog running.'
(c) Sosite   sono   inu   ga   kodomo ni   kamituita.
     and then   that   dog   nom.   child to   bit
     'And then, the dog bit the child.'

In the conventional account, *wa* is attached to an entity referring to old information. *Inu* 'dog' in sentence (c) is expected to be marked *wa*, for it has been previously introduced into the discourse and is hence old information. But the sentences (a)–(c) constitute a perfectly well formed chunk of a narrative. Of course, the *inu* in question can be topicalised, as below, but then there is a slight difference between the two versions of the narrative.

(c′) Sosite   sono inu wa   kodomo ni   kamituita.
      and then   that dog top. child   to   bit
      'And then, the dog, it bit the child.'

The difference is this: in the (a)–(c) version, each event is described as if witnessed afresh. To seek analogy in cinema, the (a)–(c) version involves three scenes in succession. In the (a)–(c′) version, on the other hand, the first two sentences describe two successive events, presented as two discrete scenes, but the (c′) sentence does not constitute a different scene; it rather dwells on the scene introduced by the (b) sentence by detailing on the dog introduced there. In uttering (c′), the speaker is not simply saying what has happened next; rather he is making a 'judgement' regarding the dog, i.e. what can be said about the dog that came running.

The discussion of the topic construction along these lines accounts naturally for a number of facts. The restriction that only what is identifiable (i.e. old information or given) can be topicalised follows naturally from the notion of making a judgement; one would not make a judgement about something which is not part of the hearer's presumed knowledge. Also, the fact that subordinate clauses do not admit the topic construction is understandable in view of the fact that subordinate clauses normally describe background events and, as seen above, descriptions of events are done in non-topic sentences.

In the tradition of Japanese grammar, the notions of topic and subject are often confused, for, as seen above, they are not clearly separated in languages like English. However, the topic has a status distinct from that of the grammatical subject. That is, the Japanese topic does not participate in any syntactic processes that the subject does. The only exception is the topic that is 'converted' from the subject such as the *sono inu wa* (that dog top.) in (c′) above. We will show this in terms of two grammatical phenomena in which the subject figures importantly, namely reflexivisation and subject honorification.

In Japanese, there is a general constraint that the antecedent of the reflexive form *zibun* 'self' must be the subject at some stage of derivation. Thus, in the following sentence, the reflexive form is coreferential only with the subject Taro.

(a) Taroo ga   Hanako ni   zibun   no   hon   o   watasita.
     nom.   dat.   self   of   book   acc.   handed
     'Taro handed his own book to Hanako.'

Taroo in (a) functions like a subject even if it is topicalised, but that the subject function is not the property of the topic is seen from the fact that when non-subjects are topicalised, they exhibit no subject properties. In other words, the topicalisation of the indirect object *Hanako* of (a) confers no subject properties on it, as the following sentence cannot be understood to mean that Hanako and *zibun* are coreferential.

(b) Hanako ni wa Taroo ga zibun no hon o watasita.
'As for Hanako, Taro handed his own book.'

Just as the term 'subject honorification' indicates, there is an honorific phenomenon that is 'triggered' when the subject refers to someone worthy of the speaker's respect. The process essentially involves attaching the prefix *o* to the infinitive form of the verb and then extending the sentence with the verbal form *naru* 'become'. This converts a plain sentence like (a) below into an honorific form as in (b).

(a) Sensei ga waratta.
teacher nom. laughed
'The teacher laughed.'
(b) Sensei ga o-warai-ni natta.
lit. 'The teacher became to be laughing.'

Again, the subject-based topic can trigger subject honorification and the conversion of the *sensei ga* in (b) above into *sensei wa* results in a good sentence. But, the topic 'deriving' from non-subjects cannot trigger this process and (b) below is inappropriate; it expresses deference toward the speaker himself.

(a) Boku ga sensei o tasuketa.
I   nom. teacher acc. helped
'I helped the teacher.'
(b) #Sensei wa boku ga o-tasuke-ni natta.
teacher top. I   nom. helped (honorific)
'As for the teacher, I helped him.'

What is called for in a situation like (a)–(b) above is the other honorification process, called 'object honorification', which expresses the speaker's deference toward the referent of a non-subject nominal.

(c) Boku ga sensei o o-tasuke sita.
I   nom. teacher acc. helping did
lit. 'I did the helping of the teacher.'
(d) Sensei wa boku ga o-tasuke sita.
lit. 'As for the teacher, I did helping of him.'

The topic and the subject also show an important difference with respect to the scope of discourse domain. Although both subject and topic can function as a reference for a gapped element, the topic has a far larger scope in this function. In an English coordinate expression such as the following, the gap, indicated by Ø, in the second clause is understood to be identical with the subject of the first clause.

(a) John came and Ø took off his coat.

When the first clause is a subordinate clause, gapping of the subject of the main clause is not permitted; thus the following are not well formed.

(b) *When John came, Ø took off his coat.
(c) *As soon as John came, Ø took off his coat.

In Japanese, all of the above sentences are grammatical, for it allows elliptical expressions for a situation where English typically has pronominal expressions. However, note that the coordinate and subordinate clauses are in this respect grammatically distinct. In the case of coordination, as exemplified in (a) below, the gapped subject of the second clause must be interpreted as identical with the subject of the first clause. But in the case of subordination, as exemplified in (b)–(c) below, the gapped subjects of the main clause must be interpreted as different from the subject of the subordinate clause.

(a) Taroo ga   ki-te,   suguni   Ø   uwagi o   nuida.
         nom.   came   immediately   coat   acc. took off
     'Taro$_i$ came, and immediately Ø$_i$ took off the coat.'
(b) Taroo ga   kuru-to,   suguni Ø uwagi o nuida.
                  come-when
     'When Taro$_i$ came, immediately Ø$_j$ took off the coat.'
(c) Taroo ga   kuru-ya   inaya,   suguni Ø uwagi o nuida.
                  come-as   soon as
     'As soon as Taro$_i$ came, immediately Ø$_j$ took off the coat.'

In the above examples, the subject of the first coordinate clause and the subject of the subordinate clauses are retained. The same situation obtains even in the reverse expressions, where the subject of the second coordinate clause and that of the main clause are retained.

(a) Ø kite, suguni Taroo ga uwagi o nuida.
     'Ø$_i$ came, and immediately Taro$_i$ took off the coat.'
(b) Ø kuruto, suguni Taroo ga uwagi o nuida.
     'When Ø$_i$ came, immediately Taro$_j$ took off the coat.'
(c) Ø kuru-ya ina ya, suguni Taroo ga uwagi o nuida.
     'As soon as Ø$_i$ came, immediately Taro$_j$ took off the coat.'

However, when the topic form is used, the restriction on (b)–(c) does not obtain and the topic can function in reference to both the subject of the subordinate clause and that of the main clause.

(b') Taroo wa, kuru-to, suguni uwagi o nuida.
     top. come-when immediately coat acc. took off
    'As for Taro$_i$, Ø$_i$ immediately took off the coat when Ø$_i$ came.'
(c') Taroo wa, kuru-ya inaya, suguni uwagi o nuida.
    'As for Taro$_i$, Ø$_i$ took off the coat as soon as Ø$_i$ came.'

As the comma after the topic in (b')–(c') above indicates, the structure of these differs from that underlying the non-topic sentences (b)–(c). That is, while the non-topic subordinate structure is like (a) below, the topic version is like (b):

(a) [Taroo ga kuru]-to suguni Ø uwagi o nuida
(b) Taroo wa [Ø kuru]-to suguni Ø uwagi o nuida

While the (b) structure above is the normal pattern, the topic can be retained in the subject position of the main clause, but still the topic functions as a reference for the gapped subject of the subordinate clause; e.g.

(c) [Ø kuru]-to suguni Taroo wa uwagi o nuida

In other words, the topic has the scope over the entire sentence with the role of a reference for the gapped subject of both the subordinate and the main clause. The subject of the subordinate clause or of the main clause, on the other hand, has no such wide scope of reference.

7 Contextual Dependency

Compared to English, Japanese utterances are more context-dependent. This can be seen in assessing the appropriateness of the following two 'equivalent' expressions.

(a) I'd see him.
(b) Atasi kare ni au wa.
    I he dat. meet

Aside from semantic and discourse factors that preclude the possibility of (a), it is rather difficult to find a context in which the English sentence (a) is inappropriate. However, this is not the case for (b); there are a number of contextual factors that must be satisfied in order for the sentence to be an appropriate utterance. First, the sex of the speaker must be considered. Only a female speaker can utter this sentence. The first person pronoun *atasi* is a form exclusively used by a female speaker. And the sentence-final particle *wa*, which has the effect of softening the assertion, is also from the repertory of the particles for female speakers. If a comparable expression were to be uttered by a male speaker, it would be something like the following, where the pronoun for a male *boku* and a sex-neutral particle, *yo*, are used:

(c)　　Boku kare ni au yo.

Secondly, the (b) sentence is only appropriate when uttered in a very informal setting. The sentence-final particle like *wa* would not be used in a formal setting and the first person pronoun *atasi* is a rather vulgar or coquettish form. Related to this is the status of the addressee. If the addressee is someone superior to the speaker, the addressee honorific ending *-imasu* needs to be employed. Thus, a more appropriate form for a little more formal setting would require the dropping of the sentence-final particle *wa*, the replacement of the pronoun *atasi* by the more formal form *watakusi* and the adjustment of the verbal ending. In other words, (b) would be replaced by the following expression on a little more formal occasion.

(b')　　Watakusi kare ni a-imasu.

The sentence (b') can still be inappropriate depending on the person being referred to by the third person pronoun *kare* 'he'. If the person referred to is someone to whom the speaker is obliged to be deferential, then it is not quite appropriate to refer to him as *kare*; such a person is better referred to by *sono kata* 'that person' (lit. 'that direction'). Referring to the person by *sono kata* requires the use of the object honorific form of the verb, *o-ai suru* (see section 5). Should one want to make the utterance even politer, the suppletive form of 'to see/meet' *o-me ni kakaru* would be used. These modifications yield the following forms:

(b")　　Watakusi sono kata ni o-ai s-imasu.
(b''')　　Watakusi sono kata ni o-me ni kakar-imasu.

One can still go on elaborating the sentence, but the point should be clear. Japanese has different sets of personal pronouns for male and female speakers and for appropriate levels of politeness. Some of the sentence-final particles, which are used in moderating or strengthening the assertion one way or another, also differ for men and women. Thus, an adequate command of Japanese means both grammatical and sociolinguistic knowledge of the appropriate forms of subject or object honorific address. (Notice that at the elevated level of speech, speech style distinctions according to sex tend to be neutralised; thus, a form such as (b''') above can be used by both male and female speakers.)

All these considerations mean that there are many synonyms that are differently used in reference to the speaker's sex, the addressee, as well as the referents of the nominals within a sentence. Addressee honorification and subject and object honorification are in general regular, but there are sufficient suppletive forms that are used regularly and so need to be learned separately. Thus, while speech levels are observed in other languages including English, Japanese has a highly grammaticalised system, which entails many synonymous expressions which must be used appropriately according to the context.

We have seen that numerous synonyms have also been created due to borrowing from Chinese and other foreign languages. In addition, one must contend with four kinds of writing systems. It is this multiplicity of coding possibilities which constitutes one unique aspect of Japanese and it is the multitude of synonymous expressions and the complexity of the contextual factors determining the appropriate choice that make the learning of Japanese very difficult for non-Japanese.

Bibliography

Miller (1967) is a comprehensible general account of Japanese with emphasis on the historical development; Miller (1971) presents documentation of the hypothesis relating Japanese to the Altaic family. Sansom (1928) is an excellent account of the grammar of Old Japanese, with a detailed discussion of the development of the writing system.

Martin (1975) is the most comprehensible account of the grammar of modern Japanese written in English, with numerous examples taken from actual published materials. Alfonso (1966) is a useful introduction to the structure of Japanese, while Kuno (1973) is particularly useful on particles and the topic construction. Hinds (1986) is written in a format convenient for looking up specific constructions and phenomena for contrastive and comparative studies. It is also unique among the available reference works for its inclusion of a large amount of actual conversational data. For phonology, McCawley (1968) is a generative treatment, including a useful survey of the accentual systems of Japanese dialects. Shibatani (1976) is a collection of papers dealing with selected topics in Japanese syntax within the framework of generative grammar. Shibatani (1982), another collection of papers, includes papers dealing with Japanese dialectology and sociolinguistics.

Acknowledgement

I am grateful to Charles M. De Wolf of Chiba University for discussing with me a number of topics covered here, as well as providing me with useful suggestions for the improvement of the present essay.

References

Alfonso, A. 1966. *Japanese Language Patterns*, 2 vols. (Sophia University Press, Tokyo)

Hinds, J. 1986. *Japanese* (Croom Helm Descriptive Grammars; Croom Helm, London)
Kuno, S. 1973. *The Structure of the Japanese Language* (MIT Press, Cambridge, Mass.)
McCawley, J.D. 1968. *The Phonological Component of the Grammar of Japanese* (Mouton, The Hague)
Martin, S.E. 1975. *A Reference Grammar of Japanese* (Yale University Press, New Haven)
Miller, R.A. 1967. *The Japanese Language* (University of Chicago Press, Chicago)
—— 1971. *Japanese and the Other Altaic Languages* (University of Chicago Press, Chicago)
Sansom, G. 1928. *An Historical Grammar of Japanese* (Oxford University Press, Oxford)
Shibatani, M. (ed.) 1976. *Japanese Generative Grammar* (Academic Press, New York)
—— (ed.) 1982. *Studies in Japanese Linguistics* (= *Lingua*, vol. 57, nos. 2–4) (North-Holland, Amsterdam)

8 KOREAN

Nam-Kil Kim

1 Historical Background

For a long time scholars have tried to associate the Korean language to one of the major language families but have not been successful in this venture. There have been many theories proposed on the origin of Korean. Based on the views as to where the Korean language first originated, two prominent views, which are called the Southern theory and the Northern theory, have been advocated by some scholars. According to the Southern theory, the Korean people and language originated in the south, namely the South Pacific region. There are two versions of this theory. One is that the Korean language is related to the Dravidian languages of India. This view is not taken seriously by contemporary linguists, but it was strongly advocated by the British scholar Homer B. Hulbert at the end of nineteenth century. Hulbert's argument was based on the syntactic similarities of Korean and the Dravidian languages. For instance, both languages have the same syntactic characteristics: the word order subject–object–verb, postpositions instead of prepositions, no relative pronouns, modifiers in front of the head noun, copula and existential as two distinct grammatical parts of speech etc.

The other version of the Southern theory is the view that Korean may be related to the Austronesian languages. There are some linguistic as well as anthropological and archeological findings which may support this view. The linguistic features of Korean which are shared by some Polynesian languages include the phonological structure of open syllables, the honorific system, numerals and the names of various body parts. The anthropological and archeological elements shared by Koreans and the people in other regions of the South Pacific are rice cultivation, tattooing, a matrilineal family system, the myth of an egg as the birth place of royalty and other recent discoveries in paleolithic or preceramic cultures. Although this Southern theory has been brought to the attention of many linguists, it is not accepted as convincing by linguists.

The Northern theory is the view that Korean is related to the Altaic family. Although this view is not wholly accepted by the linguistic community, the majority of Korean linguists and some western scholars seem inclined towards believing this view. The major language branches which belong to the Altaic family are Turkic, Mongolian and Tungusic. The area in which the Altaic languages are spoken runs from the Balkans to the Kamchatka Peninsula in the North Pacific. The Northern theory stipulates that the Tungusic branch of Altaic tribesmen migrated towards the south and reached the Korean peninsula. The Tungusic languages would include two major languages: Korean and Manchu. The view that Korean is a branch of the Altaic family is supported by anthro-archeological evidence such as comb ceramics (pottery with comb-surface design), bronze-ware, dolmens, menhirs and shamanism. All these findings are similar to those found in Central Asia, Siberia and northern Manchuria. Korean is similar to the Altaic languages with respect to the absence of grammatical elements such as number, genders, articles, fusional morphology, voice, relative pronouns and conjunctions. Vowel harmony and agglutination are also found in Korean as well as in the Altaic languages. Comparing the two theories, it is apparent that the Northern influence in the Korean language is more dominant than the Southern.

It has been discovered in recent archeological excavations that the early race called Paleosiberians lived in the Korean peninsula and Manchuria before the Altaic race migrated to these areas. The Paleosiberians, who include the Chukchi, Koryaks, Kamchadals, Ainu, Eskimos etc., were either driven away to the farther north by the newly arrived race or assimilated by the conquerors when they came to the Korean peninsula. It is believed that the migration of the new race towards the Korean peninsula took place around 4000 BC. Nothing is known about the languages of the earliest settlers. After migration, some ancient Koreans settled down in the regions of Manchuria and northern Korea while others moved farther to the south. Many small tribal states were established in the general region of Manchuria and the Korean peninsula from the first century BC to the first century AD. The ancient Korean language is divided into two dialects: the Puyŏ language and the Han language. The Puyŏ language was spoken by the people of tribal states such as Puyŏ, Kokuryŏ, Okchŏ and Yemaek in

Manchuria and northern Korea. The Han language was spoken by the people of the three Han tribal states of Mahan, Chinhan and Byŏnhan which were created in southern Korea.

Around the fourth century AD the small tribal states were vanquished and three kingdoms with strong central governments appeared in Manchuria and the Korean peninsula. Of these three kingdoms, the biggest kingdom, Kokuryŏ, occupied the territory of Manchuria and the northern portion of the Korean peninsula. The other two kingdoms, Paekche and Silla, established states in the southwestern and the southeastern regions of the Korean peninsula respectively. It is believed that the Kokuryŏ people spoke the Puyŏ language and the Silla people spoke the Han language; however, it is not certain what language the Paekche people spoke because the ruling class of the Paekche kingdom consisted of Puyŏ tribesmen who spoke the Puyŏ language. When the Korea peninsula was unified by Silla in the seventh century, the Han language became the dominant dialect paving the way for the emergence of a homogeneous language. The Han language finally became the sole Korean language through the two succeeding dynasties of Koryŏ (936–1392) and Chosŏn (1392–1910).

Since Silla's unification of the Korean peninsula in the seventh century, it appears that the language spoken in the capital has been the standard dialect. Thus, the Silla capital, Kyŏngju, dialect was the standard dialect during the unified Silla period from the seventh century to the tenth century. When Silla was succeeded by Koryŏ in the tenth century, the capital was moved from Kyŏngju, which was located in the southeastern region of the Korean peninsula, to Kaegyŏng in the central region of Korea and subsequently the dialect spoken in this new capital became the standard language in Koryŏ from the tenth century to the end of the fourteenth century. When the Yi (or Chosŏn) Dynasty succeeded Koryŏ at the end of the fourteenth century, the capital was established at Seoul, the present capital of South Korea, and the language spoken in this area became the standard dialect and has continued as a standard dialect to the present time. Thus, it is obvious that the formation of the standard dialect has been dominated by political decisions. We can find this even in the twentieth century. There are officially two standard dialects existing in Korea; one is the Seoul dialect in South Korea and the other the P^{h}yŏng'yang dialect in North Korea. Each government has established prescriptive criteria for its own standard dialect and made separate policies on language.

Though the dialect distinction of one region from the other is not drastic owing to the relatively small size of the Korean peninsula, each region has its own characteristic dialects. For instance, in the Hamgyŏng dialect of northern Korea the final p. of verb bases ending in p is pronounced as [b] before suffixed morphemes starting in a vowel, while in the standard Seoul dialect this final p is pronounced as [w] before a vowel; tǝp- 'hot' is pronounced [tǝbǝ] in the Hamgyŏng dialect but [tǝwǝ] in the standard dialect. As another example, in the standard dialect palatalisation is normal but in the P^{h}yŏng'yang dialect palatalisation does not take place: *kat^{h}i* 'together' is pronounced as [kac^{h}i] in the standard dialect but as [kat^{h}i] in the P^{h}yŏng'yang dialect. Historically, both Hamgyŏng and P^{h}yŏng'yang dialects reflect archaic forms. That is, in the nineteenth-century Yi Dynasty language the words *təp-* and *kat^{h}i* were pronounced as they are pronounced in the Hamyŏng and P^{h}yŏng'yang dialects; and the pronunciation of these words in the standard dialect reflects this historical change.

The Korean language spoken before the fifteenth century is not well known because there are not many records or documents revealing how the language was used before the fifteenth century. It was in the fifteenth century that the alphabetic script (Han'gŭl) for writing Korean was invented by King Sejong. Before the Korean script was invented, only Chinese characters were used for the purpose of writing. But Chinese characters could not depict the living language spoken by Korean people, since Chinese characters were meaning-based and the grammar of classical Chinese did not have any connection with Korean grammar. Even after the Korean script was invented, Chinese characters were continuously used as the main means of writing until the twentieth century. In traditional Korean society, the learning and study of Chinese characters and classical Chinese were entirely monopolised by a small class of elite aristocrats. For average commoners, the time-consuming learning of Chinese characters was not only a luxury but also useless, because they were busy making a living and knowledge of Chinese characters did not help in improving their lives.

The use of Chinese characters imported a massive quantity of loanwords into the Korean lexicon. More than half of Korean words are Chinese-originated loanwords. Although Chinese loanwords and Korean-originated words have always coexisted, the Chinese loanwords came to dominate the original Korean words and subsequently many native Korean words completely vanished from use. A movement by people who wanted to restore native culture at the end of the nineteenth century tried to stimulate mass interest in the study of the Korean language. When the government proclaimed that the official governmental documents would be written both in Korean script and Chinese characters, the first newspapers and magazines were published in Korean script and the use of the Korean alphabet expanded. In the early twentieth century, more systematic studies on the Korean language were started and a few scholars published Korean grammar books. However, the active study of Korean grammar was discontinued owing to the Japanese colonial policy suppressing the study of Korean.

The study of the Korean language resumed after the end of World War II, but Korea was divided into two countries by the Big Powers. The language policies proposed and implemented by the two governments in the South and the North were different from each other. While both the Korean alphabet and Chinese characters were used in the South, only the Korean alphabet was used in the North. In the North the policy on the use of Chinese characters has been firm; that is, no instruction in Chinese characters has been given to students and Chinese characters are not used in newspapers, magazines or books. This policy has never been changed in the North. Contrary to this, in the South the policy on the instruction of Chinese characters has been inconsistent; whenever a new regime has come to power, both proponents and opponents of the use of Chinese characters have tried to persuade the government to adopt their views. Though the instruction of Chinese characters was abolished a couple of times by the government in the past, this abolition never lasted more than a few years. At the present time in the South, the government has adopted a policy which forces students in secondary schools to learn 1,800 basic Chinese characters.

The South and the North also have different policies on the so-called 'purification' of Korean. The purification of Korean means the sole use of native Korean words in everyday life by discontinuing the use of foreign-originated words. The main targets of this campaign are Sino-Korean words. In the North, the government has been actively involved in this campaign, mobilising newspapers and magazines to spread the newly translated or discovered pure Korean words to a wide audience of readers. In the South, some interested scholars and language study organisations have tried to advocate the purification of Korean through the media and academic journals, but the government has never officially participated in this kind of movement. It will be interesting to see what course each of the two governments will take in future with respect to language policy.

2 Phonology

The sound system of Korean consists of 21 consonants and ten vowels. The vowels can be classified by the three positions formed by the vocal organs. The first is the height of the tongue, the second is the front or the back of the tongue and the third is the shape of the lips. The vowel systems of Korean can be represented as in table 8.1.

Table 8.1: Korean Vowels

| | *Front* | | *Back* | |
	Unrounded	Rounded	Unrounded	Rounded
High	i	ü	ŭ	u
Mid	e	ö	ə	o
Low	æ		a	

The vowels /ü/ and /ö/ have free variants [wi] and [we] respectively; thus, /kü/ 'ear' is pronounced either [kü] or [kwi] and /kömul/ 'strange creature' is pronounced either [kömul] or [kwemul]. The vowel ŭ is always pronounced [u] after labial sounds; sŭlpʰŭta is pronounced as [sŭlpʰuda] and kamŭm 'draught' is pronounced as [kamum].

Korean has a large number of morphophonemic alternations. As major examples of Korean morphophonemic processes involving vowels, we can name the following kinds: vowel harmony, glide formation, vowel contraction and vowel deletion. When non-finite endings starting with ə are attached to verbal bases, the initial ə of the ending is changed to a after a and o as in nok-əsə 'melting' → [nokasə], and mac-əsə 'be hit' → [macasə]; elsewhere ə is not changed as in mək-əsə 'eat' → [məkəsə], kipʰəsə 'deep' → [kipʰəsə], kæ-əsə 'clear' → [kæəsə] and so on.

The vowels o, i and a undergo vowel contraction with the vowel i when the vowels in verbal bases and other morphemes such as the causative and passive are combined with each other. Korean has the following kinds of vowel contraction; o+i → ö: po-i-ta 'be seen' → [pöta]; ə+i → e: sə-iu-ta 'raise' → [seuta]; a+i → æ: ca-iu-ta 'make sleep' → [cæuta]; u+i → ü: pak'u-i-ta 'be changed' → [pak'üta].

The front vowel i and the back vowels u and o of verbal bases undergo glide formation when they are immediately connected to ə or a of suffixes such as -ə and -əsə; i becomes y and u and o become w: ki-əsə 'crawl' → [kyəsə], tu-əsə 'leave' → [twəsə] and po-asə → [pwasə]. As examples of vowel deletion, Korean has two kinds: ŭ-deletion and ə-deletion. When verbal bases ending in the vowel ŭ are attached to an ending starting with the vowel ə, the vowel ŭ is deleted: s'ŭ-ə 'write' → [s'ə] and k'ŭ-əsə 'extinguish' → [k'əsə].

Finally, ə-deletion occurs when endings starting with the vowel ə are combined with verbal bases ending with the vowels e, æ, ə and a; thus we have the following examples: se-əs'ta 'counted' → [ses'ta], kæ-əsə 'clear' → [kæsə], sə-ə 'stand' → [sə] and ka-əto 'even if he goes' → [kato]. Interestingly, the vowels which force ə-deletion are those vowels which do not undergo either glide formation or ŭ-deletion, i.e. i, u and o undergo glide formation; ü and ö have free variant forms [wi] and [we] respectively as in tü-əs'-ta 'jumped' → [twiəs'ta] and k'ö-əs'ta 'lure' → [kweəs'ta]; ŭ is deleted before ə. From the above discussion of glide formation and vowel deletion, we can see that all the vowels in the Korean vowel system participate in phonological processes without exception when verbal bases are combined with suffixes starting in ə.

Of the 21 consonants, there are 9 stops, 3 affricates, 3 fricatives, 3 nasals, 1 liquid and 2 semi-vowels. The Korean consonants can be illustrated as in table 8.2.

Let us now briefly describe the sound of Korean obstruents (stops, affricates and fricatives). The Korean laxed obstruents are weaker than English voiceless obstruents with respect to the degree of voicelessness. This seems to be due to the fact that Korean obstruents have two other stronger

Table 8.2: Korean Consonants

	Manner	Point	Labial	Dental	Palatal	Velar	Glottal
Stops	voiceless	laxed aspirated tensed	p p^h p'	t t^h t'		k k^h k'	
Affricates	voiceless	laxed aspirated tensed			c c^h c'		
Fricatives	voiceless	laxed tensed		s s'			h
Nasals	voiced		m	n		ŋ	
Liquid	voiced			l			
Semi-vowels			w	y			

voiceless consonants, the tensed and the aspirated. The laxed obstruents are produced without voice and without aspiration and glottal tension. However, the laxed stops and affricates /p,t,k,c/ are pronounced as the voiced obstruents [b,d,g,j] when they occur between two voiced sounds. Even if some voiceless obstruents have voiced allophones, Korean speakers are not aware of this change. For instance, the word /aka/ 'baby' is pronounced [aga] because /k/ occurs between two vowels, which are voiced sounds.

The Korean aspirated obstruents are produced with stronger aspiration than English aspirated sounds. The Korean tensed obstruents are one of the most peculiar sounds among Korean consonants. The tensed obstruents are produced with glottal tension, but these sounds are not glottal sounds or ejectives. For instance, the Korean /t'/ is phonetically similar to the sound [t'] in English which is pronounced after [s] in the word *stop* [stap]; however, the Korean tensed obstruent must be pronounced with more glottal tension.

Liquids and semi-vowels need some explanation. The Korean liquid /l/ has two variants; one is the lateral [l] and the other the flap [r]. The liquid /l/ is pronounced as the lateral [l] in word-final position and in front of another consonant, and as the flap [r] in word-initial position and between two vowels. The Korean semi-vowels, /w/ and /y/, occur only as on-glides, never as off-glides.

In the above, the general qualities of Korean consonants were briefly described. Let us now discuss some of the phonological processes affecting Korean consonants. In pronunciation, consonants are always unreleased in word-final position and before another obstruent. Because of this, consonants belonging to a given phonetic group are pronounced identically in word-final position and before other obstruents. For instance, the labial stops /p/, /p^h/ and /p'/ are all neutralised into /p/ in word-final position; in the same manner, the velar stops /k/, /k^h/ and /k'/ are neutralised to /k/. The largest group of consonants comprises the dental and palatal obstruents, which are pronounced /t/: /t/, /tʰ/, /t'/, /c/, /cʰ/, /c'/, /s/ and /s'/. When examining consonant clusters, it is found that only single consonants occur in both initial and final position of words. Consonant clusters occur only in medial position in words and only clusters of two consonants are permitted to occur there. Some words have final two-consonant clusters in their base forms, but only one consonant is pronounced and the other consonant is deleted; for instance, the word /talk/ 'chicken' has the *lk* cluster in its base, but it is pronounced [tak], losing *l* when it is pronounced alone. However, the cluster *lk* occurs in intervocalic positions: /talk/ + /i/ → [talki]. When the final cluster occurs before a consonant, again one consonant must be deleted as in word-final position to obey the two consonant constraint; e.g. /talk/ 'chicken' + /tali/ 'leg' [taktali] 'chicken leg'.

One of the most interesting characteristics of Korean phonology is its rich consonant assimilation. Korean consonant assimilation comprises nasalisation, labialisation, dentalisation, velarisation, palatalisation and liquid assimilation. Of these, nasalisation is the most productive; for instance, the stops *k*, *t* and *p* (including the neutralised stops) become *ŋ*, *n* and *m* respectively before nasals: /kukmul/ 'soup' → [kuŋmul], /patnŭnta/ 'receive' → [pannŭnda], and /capnŭnta/ 'catch' → [camnŭnda]. As another example of nasalisation, the liquid *l* becomes *n* after the nasals *m* and *ŋ* and the stops *k*, *t*, *p*: e.g. /kamlo/ 'sweet' → [kamno], /pækli/ 'one hundred *li*' → [pækni], /matlyaŋpan/ 'first son' → [matnyaŋpan] and /aplyək/ 'press' → [apnyək]. Interestingly, in the last three examples, the stop sounds which caused *l* to nasalise assimilate to the following new nasals and become nasals themselves: [pækni] → [pæŋni], [matnyaŋban] → [mannyaŋban] and [apnyək] → [amnyək]; thus these three examples undergo two nasalisation processes.

The consonant *h* behaves interestingly in medial positions; when *h* occurs in intervocalic position, it is deleted: /cohŭn/ 'good' → [coŭn]; and when *h* occurs before laxed stops and affricates, metathesis takes place as in the following example: /hayah-ta/ 'white' → [hayatha] → [hayatʰa]. As another example of consonant deletion, we can name *l*-deletion: when the consonant *l* occurs in the initial position, it is deleted: /lyaŋpan/ 'aristocrat' → [yaŋban]. However, *l*-deletion in the initial position is not absolute, because *l* is changed to *n* in the same position depending on the following vowels, as in /lokuk/ 'Russia' → [noguk]. Thus, the right way of explaining the *l* phenomena would be to say that the consonant *l* does not occur in initial position.

Thus far, we have seen the Korean phonemic system and some of its phonological processes. In the remaining portion of this section, the Korean writing system will be briefly presented.

As can be seen from table 8.3, the Korean alphabet, which is called *Han'gŭl*, consists of 40 letters: 10 pure vowels, 11 compound vowels, 14 basic consonants and 5 double consonants. The Korean writing system is

Table 8.3: Korean Alphabet

Letter	Transcription	Letter	Transcription
Pure vowels:			
ㅣ	/i/	ㅡ	/ŭ/
ㅔ	/e/	ㅓ	/ə/
ㅐ	/æ/	ㅏ	/a/
ㅟ	/ü/	ㅜ	/u/
ㅚ	/ö/	ㅗ	/o/
Compound vowels:			
ㅑ	/ya/	ㅘ	/wa/
ㅒ	/yæ/	ㅙ	/wæ/
ㅕ	/yə/	ㅝ	/wə/
ㅖ	/ye/	ㅞ	/we/
ㅛ	/yo/	ㅢ	/ŭi/
ㅠ	/yu/		
Consonants:			
ㄱ	/k/	ㅇ	/ŋ/
ㄴ	/n/	ㅈ	/c/
ㄷ	/t/	ㅊ	/cʰ/
ㄹ	/l/	ㅋ	/kʰ/
ㅁ	/m/	ㅌ	/tʰ/
ㅂ	/p/	ㅍ	/pʰ/
ㅅ	/s/	ㅎ	/h/
Double consonants:			
ㄲ	/k'/	ㅆ	/s'/
ㄸ	/t'/	ㅉ	/c'/
ㅃ	/p'/		

based on the 'one letter per phoneme' principle. However, comparing the number of phonemes with the number of letters, it is found that the writing system has nine more letters. This is because the diphthongs are also represented by their own letters. Thus, the semi-vowels *y* and *w* do not have their own independent letters. They are always represented together with other vowels occurring with them. For instance, the letter ㅑ is a combination of *y* and *a*, and the letter ㅘ is a combination of *w* and *a*.

As a general rule, in writing, Korean letters are formed with strokes from top to bottom and from left to right. The letters forming a syllable have a sequence of CV(C)(C) and they are arranged as a rebus: e.g. *ka* 'go' → 가; *kak* 'each' → 각; *talk* 'chicken' → 닭. One interesting thing about the Korean writing system is that a vowel cannot be written alone; for instance, *a* cannot be written as ㅏ and *i* cannot be written as ㅣ. In the Korean writing system, the absence of a consonant is represented by a Ø consonant, which is shown by the symbol ㅇ and written to the left of the vowel. Thus, *a* is written as 아 and *i* is written as 이. For instance, a word *ai* 'child' which consists of the two vowels, *a* and *i*, is written as 아이.

3 Morphology

Korean words can be divided into two classes: inflected and uninflected. The uninflected words are nouns, particles, adverbs and interjections. Inflected words are classed as action verbs, descriptive verbs, copula and existential. The distinction between action and descriptive verbs can be shown by the way in which paradigmatic forms such as propositive and processive are combined with verbal forms. For instance, a descriptive verb lacks propositive and processive forms. Thus, whereas the action verb plus the propositive *ca* or the processive *nŭn* is grammatical, the combinations of descriptive verbs with the same endings are not: *mək-ca* 'let's eat' and *mək-nŭn-ta* 'is eating' but **alŭmtap-ca* 'let's be beautiful' and **alŭmtap-nŭn-ta* 'is being beautiful'. While the copula behaves like a descriptive verb, the existential behaves like an action verb with respect to conjugation; thus, **i-ca* 'let's be' and **i-n-ta* 'is being' are ungrammatical but *is'-ca* 'let's stay' and *is'-nŭn-ta* 'is staying' are grammatical.

As predictable from the above discussion, each inflected form consists of a base plus an ending. Bases and endings can be classed into groups according to the ways in which alternant shapes of bases are combined with endings. There are two kinds of ending: one-shape endings such as *-ko*, *-ta*, *-ci* and *-kes'* and two-shape endings such as *-sŭpnita/-ŭpnita*, *-ŭna/-na* and *-ŭn/-n*. Two-shape endings are phonologically conditioned alternants; thus, for instance, the formal form *-sŭpnita* occurs only with base forms ending in a consonant, but the alternant form of the formal form *-pnita* occurs only with base forms ending in a vowel. Based on these classes of endings, verb bases can be divided into two groups: consonant bases (i.e. bases ending in a consonant) and vowel bases (i.e. bases ending in a vowel). There are, however, some classes of bases whose final sounds are changed when attached to endings. Thus, in addition to regular bases which do not alter when combined with the ending, there are about five classes of consonant bases which alter with the ending: bases ending in *t*, bases ending in *w*, bases ending in *h*, bases ending in sonorants and *s*-dropping bases. Vowel bases have three classes in addition to the regular vowel bases: *l*-extending vowel bases, *l*-doubling bases and *l*-inserting vowel bases.

In order to see how the base form is changed when it is attached to the endings, the partial conjugation of regular and irregular bases ending in *t* is illustrated:

	Irregular	*Regular*
Base	/mut-/ 'ask'	/tat-/ 'close'
Gerund	[muk-ko]	[tak-ko]
Suspective	[muc-ci]	[tac-ci]
Formal Statement	[mus-sŭmnita]	[tas-sŭmnita]
Infinitive	[mul-ə]	[tat-ə]
Adversative	[mul-ŭna]	[tat-ŭna]

When comparing the two base forms, *mut* 'ask' and *tat* 'close', ending in *t*, it is found that both forms undergo morphophonemic changes when combined with endings starting with a consonant. These morphophonemic changes are phonologically conditioned; *t* is changed to *k* before *k*; *t* is changed to *s* before *s* and so on. However, *t* is changed to *l* before vowels only in the base *mut*, but not in the base *tat*.

Below, the partial conjugation of an *l*-inserting vowel base is illustrated together with the conjugation of an ordinary vowel base.

	Irregular	*Regular*
Base	/pʰulŭ-/ 'be blue'	/t'alŭ-/ 'obey'
Gerund	[pʰulŭ-ko]	[t'alŭ-ko]
Suspective	[pʰulŭ-ci]	[t'alŭ-ci]
Formal Statement	[pʰulŭ-mnita]	[t'alŭ-mnita]
Infinitive	[pʰulŭl-ə]	[t'al-ə]
Adversative	[pʰulŭl-ŭna]	[t'al-ŭna]

In regular vowel bases such as *t'alŭ-*, the final vowel is deleted when attached to the endings starting with a vowel, as shown in the conjugation of the infinitive and the adversative. However, in the case of irregular vowel bases such as *pʰulŭ-*, *l* is inserted before the same endings.

The number of endings which can be attached to the base is said to be over 400. In finite verb forms, there are seven sequence positions where different endings can occur: honorific, tense, aspect, modal, formal, aspect and mood. The honorific marker *si* (or *ŭsi*) is attached to the base to show the speaker's intention or behaviour honouring the social status of the subject of the sentence. Tense has marked and unmarked forms; the marked form is past and the unmarked form present. The past marker *əs'/s'* has the meaning of a definite, completed action or state.

Aspect occurs in two different positions because there are two different aspects: experiential-contrastive and retrospective, which are mutually exclusive, i.e. if one occurs, then the other cannot. The experiential-contrastive *əs'/s'*, which has the same form as the past tense marker and only occurs after the past tense, has been called 'the double past'. The two sentences, *John i hakkyo e ka-s'-ta* and *John i hakkyo e ka-s'-əs'-ta*, are usually translated in the same way as 'John went to school'. However, this does not mean that they have the same meaning. To translate them more precisely, the first sentence merely indicates the fact that the subject has gone to school and is there now. But the second sentence has the meaning that the subject has had the experience of being in school or that he had been in school before but has come back to the place where he is now. Thus, the two sentences have quite different meanings. Only the second sentence has an aspectual meaning of experiential-contrastive.

The retrospective *tə* indicates that the speaker recollects what he observed in the past and reports it in the present situation. The sentence *John i cip e ka-tə la* has roughly the meaning 'I observed that John was going home and now I report to you what I observed'.

The modal *kes'* has the meaning indicating the speaker's volition or supposition and is used both for a definite future and a probable present or past. When the modal *kes'* is attached to a verb whose subject is first person, the sentence only has the volitional meaning and is used only with reference to the future: *næ ka næil ka-kes'-ta* 'I will go tomorrow' but **næ ka næil ka-s'-kes-ta*. When the modal *kes'* occurs in a sentence whose subject is second or third person, the sentence has only the suppositional meaning and is used for both a definite future and a probable present or past: *Mary ka næil ka-kes'-ta* 'I suppose that Mary will go tomorrow' and *Mary ka əce ka-s'-kes'-ta* 'I suppose that Mary left yesterday'.

The formal form *sŭpni/pni* is used for the speaker to express politeness or respect to the hearer: *onŭl təp-sŭpni-ta* 'it is hot today' and *onŭl təp-ta* 'it is hot today'. The only difference between the two sentences is the presence or absence of the polite form *sŭpni* in the verbal form. The first sentence could be used for addressing those whose social status is superior to the speaker's but the second sentence would be used for addressing one who is inferior or equal to the speaker in social status (here, social status includes social position, age, sex, job etc.).

Among a large number of mood morphemes, the most typical moods are declarative, interrogative, imperative and propositive. In Korean, sentence types such as declarative, interrogative, imperative and propositive sentences are identified by the mood morphemes: *ta, k'a, la* and *ca*. These mood morphemes occur in the final position of finite verbal forms, e.g. declarative: *ka-pni-ta* 'he is going'; interrogative: *ka-pni-k'a?* 'is he going?'; imperative: *ka-la* 'go'; propositive: *ka-ca* 'let's go'.

Passive and causative verbal forms can be derived by adding suffixes to bases. There are a number of passive and causative suffixes such as *i, hi* and *li* which have common shapes. Generally, causative suffixes can be divided into three groups according to the vowel in the suffix: *i*-theme causatives, *u*-theme causatives and *æ*-theme causatives. Passive suffixes can be grouped with the *i*-theme causative because their theme vowel is only *i*. Because both causative and passive suffixes have identical shapes, homonymous causative and passive verbal forms are frequently produced from the same base: *k'ak'-i* 'cause to cut' and *k'ak'-i* 'be cut' from the base *k'ak'* 'cut'; *anc-hi* 'seat' and *anc-hi* 'be seated' from *anc* 'sit'. Besides the causative morphemes *-i-*

and -hi-, there are -ki-, uk^hi-, $-ik^h$-, -li-, -liu- and -iu- morphemes in i-theme causatives.

In addition to lexical causatives and passives which are derived from the combination of verb bases with the causative or passive suffixes, Korean has periphrastic causatives and passives. The periphrastic causative is formed by the combination of verb base with the adverbial ending -ke followed by the verb ha 'do', e.g. ip-ke-ha-n-ta 'make (someone) put on'. Some verbs take both lexical and periphrastic causatives, but some other verbs take only periphrastic causatives. Comparing the two types of causative, periphrastic causatives are more productive than lexical causatives in Korean.

In Korean, passives are not so commonly used as in some other languages, such as English or Japanese. There are many transitive verbs which do not undergo passivisation; for instance, the verb cu 'give' does not undergo either lexical or periphrastic passivisation. Thus, the number of transitive verbs which undergo passive formation with the passive suffix is limited to a certain group of verbs. There are two kinds of verbs which undergo periphrastic passivisation: one is a group of verbs which take an inchoative verb ci and the other a group of verbs which take an inchoative verb tö in their passive formation. The passive of the first group is formed by adding the infinitive ending ə to the base followed by the inchoative verb ci: pusu-ə ci-ta 'be broken'. All the transitive verbs which take the inchoative verb tö in passive formation are derived from Chinese-originated loan verbs plus the verbaliser ha. In the passive formation of these verbs, the verbaliser ha is changed to the inchoative verb tö; thus, the passive of sæŋkakha-ta 'think' is sæŋkaktö-ta 'be thought'.

Finally, there are a great number of nouns which are derived from verbs by adding the nominalising morphemes to verbal bases. There are three nominalisers ki, ŭm/m and i which can be added to the base. As examples of derived nouns, we have the following: ki-derived nouns: talliki 'running', næki 'bet', $c^h aki$ 'kicking' and poki 'example'; ŭm/m-derived nouns: əlŭm 'ice', cam 'sleep', k'um 'dream' and $c^h um$ 'dance'; i-derived nouns: kəli 'hanger', noli 'game', kili 'length' and nəlpi 'width'. Though there is no general rule deciding which nominaliser is attached to which base, more nouns are derived from verbal bases by adding the nominalisers ŭm/m and i than the nominaliser ki.

4 Syntax

In this brief sketch of Korean syntax, the discussion will concentrate on representative examples which make Korean different from many Indo-European languages, especially English. One of the most frequently cited features of Korean syntax is the word order. Korean is a SOV language, meaning that the basic word order of transitive sentences is subject–object–verb. Korean has a relatively free word order compared to

English; here, the phrase 'relatively free' means that Korean is not a completely free word order language. The Korean language obeys a strict grammatical constraint requiring that the sentence end with a verb. As long as the sentence obeys this constraint, a permutation of the major constituents in a sentence is permissible; thus, the sentence *John i Mary eke c^hæk ŭl cu-əs'-ta* 'John gave a book to Mary' can also be said in the following ways: *John i c^hæk ŭl Mary eke cu-əs'-ta*; *Mary eke John i c^hæk ŭl cu-əs'-ta*; *c^hæk ŭl John i Mary eke cu-əs'-ta*; *c^hæk ŭl Mary eke John i cu-əs'-ta*. However, the following sentences are ungrammatical: **John i Mary eke cu-əs'-ta c^hæk ŭl*; **John i cu-əs'-ta c^hæk ŭl Mary eke*. The ungrammaticality of the last two sentences is due to the violation of the verb-final constraint.

In the above examples of Korean sentences, the grammatical elements *i*, *eke* and *ŭl* are postpositional particles corresponding to the cases nominative, dative and accusative. There are other kinds of postpositional particles such as *e* 'to/at', *esə* 'at/in', *to* 'also', *nŭn* 'topic', *put^hə* 'from' and *k'aci* 'to/till'. All these particles must occur after nouns, but some of them can occur after other particles; *ice put^hə to ha-l-su is'-ta* 'we can do it from now, too'; *uli tosəkwan e nŭn c^hæk i manh-ta* 'in our library, there are many books'.

Comparing the Korean example with its English translation, it is found that *c^hæk* 'book' in Korean does not have any number marker, singular or plural, whereas *books* in the English translation has a plural marker *s*. This does not mean that Korean does not have a plural marker. In Korean, the plural marker attachment is not so obligatory as in English. Especially in cases where quantifiers or numerals appear in sentences as in the above example, the plural marker is usually not attached to the noun. Another characteristic of number in Korean is that the plural marker can be attached to adverbs, e.g. *p'alli-tŭl il ŭl ha-n-ta* 'they do work fast'. In the example, the plural marker *tŭl* is attached to the adverb *p'alli* 'fast'. Usually, in this kind of sentence, the subject is deleted, but it is understood that the subject of the sentence is plural instead of singular owing to the presence of the plural marker on the adverb.

When nouns occur with numerals, classifiers are attached to numerals almost obligatorily. Korean has a rich system of classifiers. Each classifier is related to a class of nouns. In other words, a certain classifier occurs only with a certain class of nouns, e.g. *c^hæk han-kwən* 'one volume of a book'; *mækcu tu-pyəŋ* 'two bottles of beer'; *namu han-kŭlu* 'one tree'; *coŋi han-caŋ* 'one piece of paper'. Another interesting thing with respect to numerals is that there is an alternative word order. Thus, the sequence of numeral + classifier, which occurs after nouns in the above examples, can also occur before nouns. When this floating takes place, the genitive particle *ŭi* is inserted between numeral + classifier and the noun: *han-kwən ŭi c^hæk* 'one volume of a book'; *tu-pyəŋ ŭi mækcu* 'two bottles of beer'; *han-kŭlu ŭi namu* 'one tree'; *han-caŋ ŭi coŋi* 'one piece of paper'.

As may have been noticed in some of the examples, deletion of subjects is allowable as long as subjects are recoverable from linguistic or non-linguistic context. Deletion of the first person and second person in Korean is especially free, as in *c^{h}æk ul sa tŭli-kes'-ŭpni-ta* 'I will buy you a book'; *ənce t'əna-seyo?* 'when do you leave?' In the first sentence, the first person subject is deleted and in the second, the second person subject is deleted because these subjects are recoverable in a discourse context. Although deletion of the third person subject is not so common as deletion of first and second person subjects, it is also possible: *Mary ka cip e kass-ŭlt'æ* Ø up^{h}yənpætalpu lŭl manna-s'-ta* 'when Mary went home, she met the mailman'. The zero indicates the position where the third person subject is deleted. In the last example, we discover another difference between Korean and English. In the English translation of the last Korean example, the noun *mailman* is preceded by the definite article *the*. This same noun could be preceded by the indefinite article *a*. This means that English has distinct definite and indefinite articles. But Korean does not have articles indicating definiteness or indefiniteness. Although definiteness is indicated by demonstratives in some cases, the distinction between definite and indefinite, in general, is not made in Korean.

Modifiers such as demonstratives, genitives, adjectives and relative clauses precede head nouns in Korean, e.g. *i c^{h}æk ŭn cæmiis'ta* 'this book is interesting'; **John** *ŭi apəci nŭn ŭisa-ta* 'John's father is a doctor'; **yep'ŭn** *k'oc^{h}i is'-ta* 'there is a pretty flower'; **hakkyo e ka-ko is'-nŭn** *haksæŋ ŭn na ŭi c^{h}inku-ta* 'the student who is going to school is my friend'. All constituents in bold print are located to the left of the head noun. These modifying constituents make Korean a left-branching language. The notion of left-branching becomes clear in the following sentence containing three relative clauses [[[[*næ ka a-nŭn*] *haksæŋ i tani-nŭn*] *hakkyo ka is'-nŭn*] *tosi nŭn k^{h}ŭ-ta*] '[the city [where the school is [where my friend goes [who I know is big]]]]'. One of the characteristics of the relative clause in Korean is that it lacks relative pronouns. Demonstratives can also be classified as one class of modifiers. Korean demonstratives have two distinct characteristics which differ from English demonstratives. First, Korean demonstratives cannot occur independently, i.e. they must occur with nouns. The second difference is that Korean demonstratives have a triple system, unlike that of English. In addition to the demonstratives 'this' and 'that', Korean has a demonstrative which has the meaning 'that over there': *i* 'this', *kŭ* 'that' and *cə* 'that over there'. The same triple system is found in demonstrative locative nouns, e.g. *yəki* 'here', *kəki* 'there' and *cəki* 'yonder'.

Korean predicates do not agree in number, person or gender with their subjects. However, predicates show agreement with honorificness and politeness in different styles of speech. Three main levels of speech are distinguished with respect to politeness: plain, polite and deferential. Many other speech levels can also be represented among these three basic speech levels by different endings. The three main speech levels of declarative sentences have the following ending forms: plain: *ta*; polite: *yo*; deferential: *(sŭ)pnita*. Thus, when the speaker expresses his politeness toward the hearer, either the polite or the deferential speech level is used, e.g. *sənsæŋnim i cip e ka-yo* 'the teacher is going home'; *sənsæŋnim i cip e ka-pnita*. In contrast to this, when the speaker does not express any particular politeness toward the hearer, the plain speech level is used; e.g. *sənsæŋnim i cip e ka-n-ta*.

If the speaker wants to express his respect toward the referent of the subject, the honorific marker *si* is inserted between verbal bases and endings: e.g. *sənsæŋnim i cip e ka-si-əyo; sənsæŋnim i cip e ka-si-pnita; sənsæŋnim i cip e ka-si-n-ta*. In the last example, the insertion of the honorific marker *si* is possible in the predicate of a sentence ending in the plain speech level, since the honorificness is expressed to the subject, but not to the hearer. In the above example, if the subject is a student instead of a teacher, then unacceptable sentences are produced: **haksæŋ i hakkyo e ka-si-əyo; *haksæŋ i hakkyo e ka-si-pnita; *haksæŋ i hakkyo e ka-si-nta*. The ungrammaticality of the last examples is due to the violation of agreement between the subject and the predicate with respect to honorificness. In other words, the subject *haksæŋ* 'student' cannot occur with the predicate containing the honorific marker *si*, because *haksæŋ* belongs to the class of nouns which cannot be referred to with the honorific marker *si*.

Let us now turn to negation. Korean has three different negative morphemes: *an*, *ma* and *mos*. The morpheme *an* occurs in declarative and interrogative sentences and the morpheme *ma* occurs in propositive and imperative sentences, e.g. declarative: *cip e an ka-n-ta* 'I do not go home'; interrogative: *cip e an ka-ni?* 'don't you go home?'; propositive: *cip e ka-ci mal-ca* 'let's not go home'; imperative: *cip e ka-ci ma-la* 'don't go home'. The remaining negative morpheme *mos* has the meaning 'cannot', e.g. *cip e mos ka-n-ta* 'I cannot go home'. There are three types of negation in Korean. In the first type, the negative morphemes *an* and *mos* occur immediately before the main verb, as in the declarative and interrogative, as in the last example. The other two types involve more complicated operations. In the second type, the negative behaves like the main predicate and the complementiser *ci* is incorporated, as in the propositive and imperative. The third type of negation involves the main predicate *ha* 'do' in addition to *ci* complementation; *cip e ka-ci ani ha-n-ta* 'I don't go home'; *cip e ka-ci mos ha-n-ta* 'I cannot go home'. From these three types of negation, we can observe different occurrences of negative morphemes. That is, while the negative morpheme *an* appears in all three types of negation, the morpheme *mos* appears in the first and third types of negation. The remaining negative morpheme *ma* appears only in the second type of negation.

As a final example of Korean syntactic characteristics, Korean sentential complements will be briefly discussed. Sentential complements are marked with the nominalisers *kəs*, *ki*, *ŭm* and *ci* and with the complementiser *ko*. Several differences exist between nominalisers and complementisers: first, case particles occur after nominalisers but cannot occur after complementisers: e.g. in the sentence *na nŭn i cʰæk i cæmiis'-nŭn kəs ŭl a-n-ta* 'I know that this book is interesting', the accusative particle *ŭl* occurs right after the nominaliser *kəs*, but in the sentence **na nŭn i cʰæk i cæmiis'ta ko lŭl sæŋkakha-n-ta* 'I think that this book is interesting', the variant accusative particle *lŭl* cannot occur after the complementiser *ko*. Secondly, while the nominaliser is preceded by non-finite modifier forms *-nŭn-* and *-n/ŭn-*, the complementiser is preceded by the finite verbal ending form *-ta*. Thirdly, the nominaliser occurs in both the subject and object positions, but the complementiser occurs only in object position. Sentential complements containing the nominaliser have different syntactic behaviour from sentential complements containing the complementiser. Sentential complements containing the nominaliser behave like regular noun phrases. Thus, whereas sentential complements with the nominaliser undergo syntactic processes such as topicalisation, pseudo-cleft formation, passivisation, noun phrase deletion and pronominalisation, sentential complements with the complementiser do not undergo the same syntactic processes. Of the above nominalisers and complementisers, *ci* is used as a question nominaliser and *ko* is used as quotative complementiser: *na nŭn John i ənce o-nŭn ci molŭ-n-ta* 'I do not know when John will come'; *na nŭn John i næil o-n-ta ko malha-yəs'-ta* 'I said that John would come tomorrow'.

Sentential complements containing *ki* can be differentiated from sentential complements containing *ŭm/m* by syntactic and semantic characteristics. In the majority of cases, *ŭm/m* is used for factive complements (i.e. complements whose truth is presupposed), but *ki* is used for non-factive complements. A given predicate will take only one of these two nominalisers, e.g. *na nŭn John i cip e ka-l-kəs ŭl wənha-n-ta* 'I want John to go home'; **na nŭn John i cip e ka m ŭl wənha-n-ta*; *na nŭn John i cip e ka m ŭl al-as'-ta* 'I knew that John was going home'. **na nŭn John i cip e ka ki lŭl al-as'-ta*. The examples show that the non-factive predicate *wənha* 'want' occurs only with *ki* and the factive predicate *al* 'know' occurs with *ŭm/m*. The nominaliser *kəs* occurs with both factive and non-factive complements: *na nŭn John i cip e ka-nŭn kəs ŭl wənha-n-ta* 'I want John to go home'; *na nŭn John i cip e ka-nŭn kəs ŭl al-as'-ta* 'I knew that John was going home'.

Bibliography

For discussion of the origins and history of Korean, reference may be made to Chin-Wu Kim (1974) and Ki-Moon Lee (1967), the latter also available in a German translation. Ho (1965), a monograph treatment of Korean phonology, is available only in Korean, but two studies are available in English: Martin (1954), a classic treatment of Korean morphophonemics, and B.K. Lee (1977), from the generative viewpoint. Among descriptive grammars, Choi (1954) is available only in Korean and in the absence of a comparable descriptive grammar in English, the most useful sources of general information on Korean grammar are the pedagogical texts by Martin (1969) and Lukoff (1982). Nam-Kil Kim (1984) is a study of Korean sentence complementation from a generative viewpoint.

References

Choi, Hyon Bae. 1954. *Uli Malbon* (Jŏngŭmsa, Seoul)
Ho, Woong. 1965. *Kukŏ Umunhak* (Jŏngŭmsa, Seoul)
Kim, Chin-Wu. 1974. *The Making of the Korean Language* (Center for Korean Studies, University of Hawaii, Honolulu)
Kim, Nam-Kil. 1984. *The Grammar of Korean Complementation* (Center for Korean Studies, University of Hawaii, Honolulu)
Lee, B.K. 1977. *Korean Generative Phonology* (Iljisa, Seoul)
Lee, Ki-Moon. 1967. 'Hankukŏ Hyŏngsŏngsa', in *Hankuk Munhwasa Taekye*, vol. 5 (Korea University Press, Seoul; also available in German translation, *Geschichte der koreanischen Sprache*, translated by B. Lewin, Dr Ludwig Reichert Verlag, Wiesbaden, 1977.)
Lukoff, F. 1982. *An Introductory Course in Korean* (Yonsei University Press, Seoul)
Martin, S. 1954. *Korean Morphophonemics* (Linguistic Society of America, Baltimore)
—— 1969. *Beginning Korean* (Yale University Press, New Haven)

9 AUSTRONESIAN LANGUAGES

Ross Clark

1 Membership, Distribution and Status

The name 'Austronesian' is made up of Greek formatives meaning 'southern islands' and the languages of this family are spoken, with few exceptions, on a range of islands stretching more than halfway around the world from east to west and from the northern fringes of the tropics to the sub-Antarctic south. The number of languages in the family is estimated at somewhere between 500 and 1,000. 'Austronesia' includes Madagascar, Indonesia, the Philippines, Formosa and the Pacific island groups of Melanesia, Micronesia and Polynesia. Apart from recent intrusions, the only non-Austronesian languages in this domain are found on the island of New Guinea (where Austronesian speakers are confined to coastal areas) and some islands near it, including Timor and Halmahera to the west and New Britain, Bougainville and the Santa Cruz group to the east.

It is convenient to divide Austronesia geographically at about 130° east longitude, a line running just to the west of the Caroline Islands and New Guinea. The western area has about 300 languages, with a total of over 170 million speakers. Among these Javanese has pride of place in more than one respect, with the largest number of speakers (over 60 million), the longest written tradition (early inscriptions dating from the eighth century AD) and one of the major literatures of Asia. Malay, with a much smaller number of native speakers, has nevertheless achieved wider currency, as the lingua franca of the Malay Archipelago for several centuries and now as the national language of both Indonesia and Malaysia. Other languages of regional importance in this area include Achinese, Batak and Minangkabau of Sumatra, Sundanese of western Java, Madurese, Balinese and Sasak on islands east of Java, Iban and Ngadju of Borneo and Macassarese and Buginese of Sulawesi.

About 70 Austronesian languages are spoken in the Philippines. Tagalog, with 10 million native speakers in southwestern Luzon, serves as the national language (officially called Pilipino). Other important languages include Ilokano and Bikol, also of Luzon, and Cebuano and Hiligaynon (Ilongo) of the central islands.

The indigenous people of Formosa (Taiwan) spoke a number of Austronesian languages, but as a consequence of continued Chinese settlement since the seventeenth century they are now a small minority of the population, living mainly in the mountainous interior, and subject to cultural and linguistic assimilation to the Chinese. About 20 Formosan languages have been recorded, of which half are now extinct, the remainder having perhaps 200,000 speakers in all.

The Austronesian presence on the Asian continent is confined to Malay (on the Malay Peninsula) and the Chamic group. There are about 10 Chamic languages, spoken by ethnic minorities in southern Vietnam and Cambodia, numbering half a million all together. A small community of Chamic speakers has also been reported on Hainan Island in southern China.

The people of the Malagasy Republic, the far western outpost of Austronesia, speak a group of dialects diverse enough to be considered several different languages, though they are all conventionally referred to as Malagasy. Merina, spoken by about a quarter of the population, is the national standard.

The most striking contrast between the western and eastern regions of Austronesia is in the scale of the speech communities. There are at least 400 languages in the eastern region, but the total number of speakers is not much over two million — a figure exceeded by several individual languages of Indonesia and the Philippines. In Melanesia, one of the world's major foci of linguistic diversity, a typical language has only a few thousand or even a few hundred speakers. Among the larger Austronesian language communities in Melanesia are the Tolai (50,000) at the eastern end of New Britain and the Motu (13,000) on the south coast of New Guinea. Both these languages have acquired greater importance as a result of close contacts with European colonial administration, Tolai being spoken around the old German capital of Rabaul and Motu in the vicinity of Port Moresby, now the capital of Papua New Guinea. A simplified form of Motu (earlier called 'Police Motu' and now 'Hiri Motu') serves as lingua franca in much of the southern half of the country and has been recognised as one of the official languages of the National Parliament — the only Melanesian language to achieve such an official status. Other languages in Melanesia, while not necessarily having large numbers of speakers, have achieved regional importance through missionary use. Examples are Yabem and Gedaged on the north coast of New Guinea, Roviana in the western Solomon Islands and Mota in Vanuatu. The last, while spoken originally by only a few hundred people on one tiny island in the Banks group, has been widely used by Anglicans in both northern Vanuatu and the south-east Solomons.

While the typical pattern in Melanesia is one or more languages per island, in Fiji, Polynesia and Micronesia languages commonly extend over several neighbouring islands and correspondingly larger speech communities are common. Samoan (with over 200,000 speakers), Tongan

(90,000) and Fijian (200,000) are now national languages of independent states. Other Polynesian languages in wide use are Tahitian (70,000), a lingua franca throughout French Polynesia, and Rarotongan or Cook Islands Maori (20,000). Several Polynesian languages are now also spoken by sizable communities of emigrants in New Zealand, the United States and elsewhere.

Hawaii and New Zealand have had a linguistic history very different from that of the rest of Polynesia. Until the end of the eighteenth century both were populated entirely by Polynesians, but over the following hundred years massive intrusion by Europeans (and Asians in the case of Hawaii) reduced the indigenous population to a relatively powerless minority, whose language was largely excluded from public life and actively suppressed in the schools. In the twentieth century, the erosion of Polynesian-speaking rural communities by migration to the cities and the spread of English-language mass communications have accelerated the decline. There are now no more than a few hundred native speakers of Hawaiian and its extinction as a living language seems imminent. The Maori language of New Zealand is in a less desperate situation, with an estimated 70,000 native speakers. But very few of these are children and the number of communities using Maori as an everyday language has declined sharply in the last 40 years. It is unclear whether current programmes being undertaken in support of the language have any chance of reversing this trend. Both Maori and Hawaiian, however, are being studied more widely than ever in schools and universities and even if both should cease to exist as living vernaculars, they would continue to be cultivated as vehicles for the arts of oratory and poetry and as symbols of Polynesian identity in their respective countries.

The small and scattered islands of Micronesia have about a dozen languages among them. Some of these are spread over wide areas, such as the chain of dialects occupying most of the western Caroline Islands, with about 40,000 speakers, which has recently been termed 'Trukic' after its major population centre, Truk Island; Chamorro, spoken on Guam and the Marianas Islands to the north (52,000); and the languages of the Marshall Islands (21,000) and Kiribati (50,000). Others are restricted to single islands or compact groups, such as the languages of Belau (Palau), Yap, Ponape, Kosrae (Kusaie), Nauru and the Polynesian atolls Nukuoro and Kapingamarangi.

2 Comparative Austronesian

The existence of the Austronesian family was first recognised in the early seventeenth century, when the earliest Polynesian word lists collected by Dutch explorers were compared with Malay, which was already known to many Europeans as the lingua franca of the East Indies. These languages are fairly conservative in phonology and lexicon and any basic vocabulary will show many words that are obviously similar and, in some cases, identical:

	Malay	Futuna (Polynesian)
'two'	dua	lua
'five; hand'	lima	lima
'eye'	mata	mata
'ear'	telinga	talinga
'stone'	batu	fatu
'fish'	ikan	ika
'louse'	kutu	kutu
'weep'	tangis	tangi
'die'	mati	mate

The connection of Malagasy with Malay was noted at about the same time and the major languages of Indonesia and the Philippines were readily seen to belong to the same family, as were Tongan, Hawaiian, Maori and the other Polynesian languages that became known to Europeans during the eighteenth century. Many Melanesian and Micronesian languages, however, had undergone such extensive phonological and lexical changes that their Austronesian origins were much less apparent and it was not until the early twentieth century that the full extent of the family was understood.

The German scholar Otto Dempwolff, in the 1920s and 30s, laid the foundations of comparative Austronesian linguistics. He demonstrated the regular sound correspondences between many of the better known languages and reconstructed a large number of words of the ancestral language, Proto-Austronesian. Dempwolff also made an important advance in subgrouping (the establishment of the successive stages of differentiation from the ancestral language to the present diversity) by showing that almost all the languages of eastern Austronesia form a single subgroup. Earlier classifications had followed the geographical division into Indonesia, Melanesia, Micronesia and Polynesia and had been strongly influenced by the cultural and racial differences among Austronesian speakers. Dempwolff's group (now known as Oceanic) comprises all the languages of the eastern region with the exception of Palauan and Chamorro in Micronesia (which appear to have their closest connections in the Philippine area) and the languages of the western end of New Guinea, which group with Halmahera in eastern Indonesia.

Research since Dempwolff's time has greatly increased the amount of descriptive information on Austronesian languages from all areas and some consensus has emerged on the general outlines of the subgrouping of the family. Figure 45.1 shows a recent proposal by R. Blust. Atayalic, Tsouic and Paiwanic are three groups of Formosan languages. There is general agreement that the primary division within Austronesian is between Formosan languages and the rest. For the residual, non-Formosan group, Blust has proposed the term Malayo-Polynesian (formerly used as a synonym for Austronesian). Malayo-Polynesian in turn is divided into four subgroups, related as shown in the diagram. Central Malayo-Polynesian consists of about 50 languages of the Lesser Sunda Islands and the Moluccas, while South Halmahera-West New Guinea includes about 45 languages, extending as far east as Cenderawasih Bay. This leaves two very large subgroups: Oceanic, as defined above, and Western Malayo-Polynesian, which comprises all the remaining languages of western Austronesia, along with Chamorro and Palauan. Since these two groups between them account for at least 80 per cent of Austronesian languages, including all the well known ones, the earlier view of Austronesian as divided into an 'eastern' and a 'western' group now appears as an understandable simplification.

Figure 9.1: Subgrouping of Austronesian (after Blust)

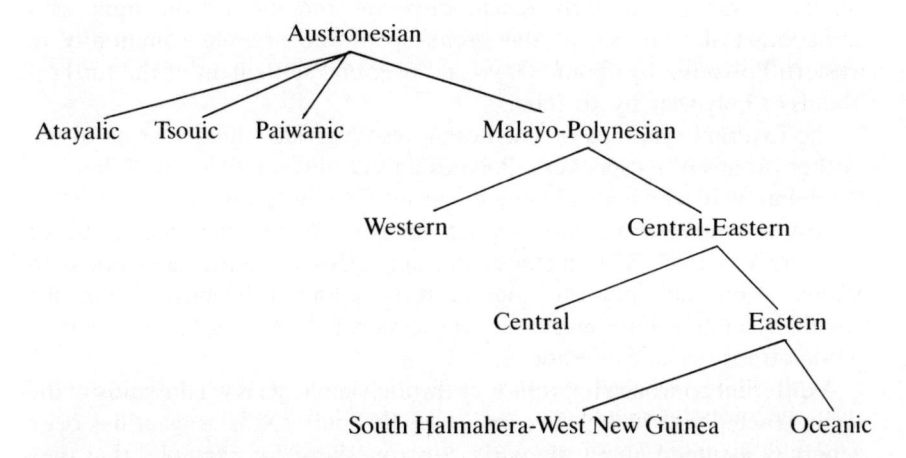

```
                        Austronesian
          ┌──────┬──────┬──────┴──────────┐
       Atayalic Tsouic Paiwanic     Malayo-Polynesian
                                    ┌──────┴──────┐
                                 Western      Central-Eastern
                                              ┌──────┴──────┐
                                           Central       Eastern
                                                      ┌──────┴──────┐
                                            South Halmahera-West New Guinea  Oceanic
```

Within Western Malayo-Polynesian and Oceanic, further subgrouping is a matter for much current research and argument. In each case, 30 or so local groupings can be defined, usually geographically coherent and ranging in size from a single language to several dozen. This lowest level of subgrouping seems fairly clear, but what the intermediate units of classification are — or indeed whether there are any — is much less agreed upon.

A great deal of the comparative research on Austronesian languages has been inspired by curiosity as to the origins and migrations of the far-flung Austronesian-speaking peoples. The subgrouping just outlined has certain implications for these questions of prehistory. First, it supports the generally assumed progression of Austronesian speakers from somewhere in the south-east Asian islands, eastward by stages further and further into the Pacific. The view, popular with many nineteenth-century theorists, that particular areas of Oceania were peopled by long-distance migrations from particular islands in Indonesia, finds no support in the linguistic evidence.

Language relationships also shed some light on the remoter fringes of the Austronesian family. In the 1950s, O.C. Dahl showed that the closest relative of Malagasy was the Ma'anyan language of south-east Borneo. This gives a fairly precise homeland for the Austronesian traders who first settled Madagascar, apparently early in the Christian era.

At the other end of Austronesia, the migrations of the Polynesians have been a tempting subject for both science and fantasy. Linguistically, Polynesian is a clearly-defined subgroup consisting of about 20 languages in the triangle defined by Hawaii, New Zealand and Easter Island, plus a further 15 small enclaves in Melanesia and Micronesia. These latter 'outliers' have been shown to be most closely related to Samoan and its near neighbours in western Polynesia, from which they apparently dispersed westward over a long period of time. The close relatedness of all Polynesian languages suggests a fairly recent dispersal and this is consistent with archaeological evidence of the break-up of the original community in western Polynesia by about 500 BC and eventual settlement of the furthest islands of Polynesia by AD 1000.

The external relations of Polynesian also provide some clues as to the further origins of its speakers. Polynesian's closest relatives are Fijian and Rotuman, with which it makes up the Central Pacific group. Central Pacific, in turn, is a member of a group which has been called 'Eastern Oceanic' or 'Remote Oceanic'. This includes the languages of central and northern Vanuatu and possibly the southeastern Solomon Islands. Again the linguistic relationships suggest a progression by short moves rather than sudden trans-oceanic migrations.

A different approach to prehistory through language is via the study of the reconstructed vocabulary. In some cases this only confirms what has been generally assumed about the early Austronesians: for example, that they cultivated crops such as taro and yams and were familiar with sailing outrigger canoes. Recent work by Blust, however, has advanced more controversial hypotheses about material culture (rice cultivation, metal-working) and has combined linguistic with ethnographic data to reconstruct aspects of the social structure of the Proto-Austronesian community.

Is Austronesian related to any other language family? Certainly suggestions have not been wanting, but proposed links with Japanese or Indo-European have not been supported by any significant evidence. The 'Austro-Tai' hypothesis, linking Austronesian with the Kadai languages, has been argued rather more seriously, but still must be considered only a somewhat more promising conjecture.

3 Structural Characteristics

Any generalisation about a large and diverse language family must be taken with caution, but certain structural features are sufficiently widespread to be considered typically Austronesian. These are shared by at least the more conservative languages in all regions, and were probably features of Proto-Austronesian.

The phonemic systems of Austronesian languages range from average complexity to extreme simplicity. Hawaiian, with just 13 phonemes ($p, k, ʔ, h, m, n, l, w, i, e, a, o, u$), was long considered the world's simplest, but it now appears that non-Austronesian Rotokas of Bougainville (North Solomons Province, Papua New Guinea) has only 11. Austronesian languages commonly allow only a restricted range of consonant clusters. Nasal + stop is the most widespread type, though in many Oceanic languages such phonetic sequences are treated as single prenasalised consonants. Final consonants were present in Proto-Austronesian, but have been categorically lost in many of the Oceanic languages. Lexical morphemes are typically bisyllabic.

Morphological complexity is likewise average to low. Nouns are suffixed for pronominal possessor in almost all Austronesian languages, though in Oceanic languages this is restricted to one category of possession. (See the description of Fijian below.) Verbs are prefixed, infixed or suffixed to indicate transitivity, voice and focus and to produce nominalised forms. Reduplication is extensively used to mark such grammatical categories as number and aspect. Pronouns have an 'inclusive' category for groups including both speaker and hearer, contrasting with the first person ('exclusive'), which definitely excludes the hearer.

Word order in Austronesian is predominantly verb-initial or verb-second and prepositional. (A number of languages in the New Guinea area have become verb-final and postpositional under the influence of neighbouring non-Austronesian languages.) Articles, which often distinguish a 'proper' from a 'common' class of nouns, precede the noun; adjectives and relative clauses follow.

Since two representative Western Malayo-Polynesian languages (Malay and Tagalog) are described elsewhere in this volume, I will conclude this chapter with a brief sketch of some features of a typical Oceanic language, Fijian.

The dialects of Fiji, like those of Madagascar, are sufficiently diverse to be considered at least two, if not several, distinct languages. Standard Fijian, the national language, is based on the speech of the southeastern corner of the island of Viti Levu. This area has long been politically powerful and it is likely that its dialect was widely understood even before it was selected as a standard by Protestant missionaries in the 1840s. The examples given here are in the formal type of standard Fijian described in the grammars, which differs in some ways from colloquial usage.

Fijian has the following consonants (given in Fijian orthography, with unexpected phonetic values shown in square brackets):

Voiceless stops: t, k
Voiced (prenasalised) stops: b [mb], d [nd], q [ŋg]
Fricatives: v [β], s, c [ð]
Nasals: m, n, g [ŋ]
Liquids: l, r, dr [nr̃]
Semi-vowels: w, y

The vowels are *i*, *e*, *a*, *o* and *u*, all of which may be either long or short. Vowel length is not normally indicated in writing Fijian, but here it will be shown by doubling the vowel letter. This treatment makes it possible to state the position of the main word stress very simply: it falls on the second-last vowel of the word.

Fijian nouns can be divided into common and proper. Common nouns are preceded by the article *na* (*na vale* 'the house'). Proper nouns, which include names of persons and places as well as personal pronouns, are preceded by the article *ko* (*ko Viti* 'Fiji', *ko ira* 'they'). Certain expressions referring to persons, however, though they involve common nouns, may optionally be preceded by *ko*, sometimes with *na* following: *na ganequ* or *ko na ganequ* 'my sister'. This choice provides for subtle distinctions of intimacy and respect.

The Fijian personal pronouns express four categories of number and four of person. In standard Fijian the independent pronoun forms are as follows:

	Singular	Dual	Paucal	Plural
First Person ('exclusive')	au	keirau	keitou	keimami
Inclusive	–	kedaru	kedatou	keda
Second Person	iko	kemudrau	kemudou	kemunii
Third Person	koya	rau	iratou	ira

The paucal category refers to a small number, greater than two. (These pronouns are misleadingly termed 'trial' in Fijian grammars.) As explained above, the inclusive category is used when both speaker and hearer are included, whereas first person and second person definitely exclude the other. Thus *kedatou* could be paraphrased 'a small group of people including both you and me', and *keimami* as 'a large group of people including me but not including you'. It will be seen from the definitions that the inclusive singular form is missing because such a combination is logically self-contradictory.

Like most Oceanic languages, Fijian distinguishes more than one relation within what is broadly called 'possession'. In standard Fijian there are four possessive categories. Familiar (inalienable) possession includes the relation between whole and part, including parts of the body, and most kin relations. With a pronominal possessor, familiar possession is indicated by suffixing the possessor directly to the noun: *na yava-qu* 'my leg', *na tama-na* 'her father'. In each of the other three possessive categories, the possessor is suffixed not to the noun but to a distinctive possessive base which precedes it. Edible and drinkable possession, not surprisingly, include the relation of a possessor to something which is eaten or drunk: *na ke-mu dalo* 'your taro', *na me-dra tii* 'their tea'. Eating and drinking are of course culturally defined, so that tobacco counts as edible, whereas various watery foods such as oysters, oranges and sugar cane are drinkable. The edible category also includes certain intrinsic properties and relations of association: *na ke-na balavu* 'its length, his height', *na ke-na tuuraga* 'its (e.g. a village's) chief'. (This appears to be the result of the merger of two historically distinct categories, rather than any conceptual association of such relations with eating.) The fourth category, *neutral*, includes relations not covered by the three more specific types: *na no-qu vale* 'my house', *na no-mu cakacaka* 'your work'.

Certain nouns tend to occur typically with certain possessive types because of their typical relation to possessors in the real world. And there are certain cases of apparently arbitrary assignment: *na yate-na* 'his liver', but *na no-na ivi* 'his kidneys'. Nevertheless, the system cannot be explained as a simple classification of nouns. There are numerous examples of the same noun in two different possessive relations, with the appropriate difference of meaning: *na no-qu yaqona* 'my kava (which I grow or sell)', *na me-qu yaqona* 'my kava (which I drink)'; *na no-na itukutuku* 'her story, the story she tells', *na ke-na itukutuku* 'her story, the story about her'.

The essential elements of the Fijian verb phrase are the verb itself and a preposed pronoun: *daru lako* (incl.-du. go) 'let's go', *e levu* (3 sg. big) 'it's big'. Most verb phrases also include one or more particles preceding or following the verb, which mark such categories as tense, aspect, modality, direction and emphasis: *keimami aa lako tale gaa mai* (1 pl. past go also just hither) 'we also came'; *era dui kanakana tiko* (3 pl. separately eat imperfective) 'they are eating each by himself'.

Transitivity is a highly developed lexical-semantic category in Fijian. A plain verb stem is normally intransitive and can be made transitive by the addition of a suffix: *lutu* 'fall', *lutu-ka* 'fall on (something)'; *gunu* 'drink', *gunu-va* 'drink (something)'; *boko* 'go out (of a fire, etc.)', *boko-ca* 'extinguish (something)'. As the examples show, the subject of the intransitive verb may correspond to the subject of the transitive (as with *lutu* and *gunu*) or to the object (as with *boko*).

The transitive suffixes just illustrated are all of the form -C*a*, where C is a consonant (or zero). Which consonant is used must in general be learned as a property of a particular verb, though there is some correlation with semantic classes. There are also transitive suffixes of the form -C*aka* and many verbs may occur with either type of suffix. In such cases, the two transitive forms generally differ as to which additional participant in the action is treated as the object of the verb. Thus: *vana* 'shoot', *vana-a* 'shoot, shoot at (a person, a target, etc.)', *vana-taka* 'shoot with (a gun, a bow, etc.)'; *masu* 'pray', *masu-ta* 'pray to', *masu-laka* 'pray for'.

When the verb phrase is accompanied by a full noun phrase subject or object, the normal order is verb phrase–object–subject:

```
era    aa    rai-ca        na yalewa  na gone
3 pl.  past  see-trans.    the woman  the child
'The children saw the woman.'
```

In this sentence the word order identifies *na yalewa* as object and *na gone* as subject. Note also that *na gone* is specified as plural not by marking on the noun phrase itself, but by its coreference with the subject pronoun *era* in the verb phrase.

When the object is proper (in the sense defined above), it occurs within the verb phrase, immediately following the verb, the proper article *ko* is dropped and the final vowel of the transitive suffix changes from *a* to *i*:

```
era    aa    rai-ci        Viti kece gaa  na gone
3 pl.  past  see-trans.    Fiji all  just the child
'The children all saw Fiji.'
```

A non-singular human object requires a coreferent object pronoun in this position, which provides another possibility for number marking:

```
era    aa    rai-ci        rau    na yalewa  na gone
3 pl.  past  see-trans.    3 du.  the woman  the child
'The children saw the two women.'
```

The transitive suffix in *-i* also appears in reciprocal and passive constructions:

```
era    vei-rai-ci            na gone
3 pl.  recip.-see-trans.     the child
'The children look at each other.'
```

```
e      aa    rai-ci        ko    Viti
3 sg.  past  see-trans.    art.  Fiji
'Fiji was seen.'
```

Note that in the last example the appearance of *ko* indicates that 'Fiji' is subject and not object.

It will be seen that *-Ci* is the more general form of the transitive suffix and that *-Ca* occurs only with third person objects which are either singular or non-human. If we take *-Ca* to be a reduced form of *-Ci-a*, where *-a* is a third person singular/non-human object pronoun, we see that the general rule is that all external object noun phrases must be accompanied by a coreferent object pronoun. This analysis is confirmed by the majority of Fijian dialects and other Oceanic languages.

Finally, Fijian has one verb-object structure where transitive marking does not appear. A generic or non-specific object immediately follows the verb, without suffix or article:

erau rai vale   tiko   na yalewa
3 du. see house imperf.   the woman
'The two women are looking at houses.'

Bibliography

Pawley (1974) is a detailed survey article, while Blust (Forthcoming) promises to be a major monograph treatment. For the geographical distribution of Austronesian languages, Wurm and Hattori (1981–4) is an indispensable work, covering all of Austronesia and several neighbouring families; in addition to excellent maps there is much information on subgrouping and numbers of speakers, as well as references to more detailed studies. Sebeok (1971) contains survey articles on all Austronesian areas; some are simply chronicles of research, but others contain considerable linguistic information.

For comparative phonology, Dempwolff (1934–8) is still the fundamental work on comparative Austronesian; Dahl (1973) is a reexamination of Dempwolff's conclusions by one of his students, mainly concerned with comparative phonology. For the linguistic evidence concerning early Austronesian culture history, reference should be made to Blust (1976; 1980).

Grammars of Fijian include Churchward (1941), a concise but perceptive missionary grammar, and Milner (1972), ostensibly pedagogical but usable as reference; however Schütz (1986) is the most comprehensive and systematic description to date, covering not only grammar and phonology but also the history of the study of the language, the development of the writing system, etc. Geraghty (1983) is the definitive study of Fijian linguistic diversity.

References

Blust, R. 1976. 'Austronesian Culture History: Some Linguistic Inferences and Their Relations to the Archaeological Record', *World Archaeology*, vol. 8, pp. 19–43.
────── 1980. 'Early Austronesian Social Organization: The Evidence of Language', *Current Anthropology*, vol. 21, pp. 205–47.
────── Forthcoming. *Austronesian Languages* (Cambridge University Press, Cambridge)
Churchward, M.C. 1941. *A New Fijian Grammar* (reprinted by Government Press, Suva, 1973)
Dahl, O.C. 1973. *Proto-Austronesian* (Studentenlitteratur, Lund)
Dempwolff, O. 1934–8. *Vergleichende Lautlehre des austronesischen Wortschatzes*, 3 vols. (Dietrich Reimer, Berlin)
Geraghty, P.A. 1983. *The History of the Fijian Languages* (University Press of Hawaii, Honolulu)
Milner, G.B. 1972. *Fijian Grammar*, 3rd ed. (Government Press, Suva)

Pawley, A.K. 1974. 'Austronesian Languages', in *The New Encyclopaedia Britannica, Macropaedia* (Encyclopaedia Britannica, Chicago)

Schütz, A.J. 1986. *The Fijian Language* (University Press of Hawaii, Honolulu)

Sebeok, T.A. (ed.) 1971. *Current Trends in Linguistics*, vol. 8: *Linguistics in Oceania* (Mouton, The Hague)

Wurm, S.A. and S. Hattori (eds.) 1981–4. *Language Atlas of the Pacific Area*, 2 parts (Australian Academy of the Humanities, Canberra)

10 Malay (Indonesian and Malaysian)

D.J. Prentice

1 Introduction

A form of the Malay language constitutes the national language in four countries of South-East Asia. In descending order of size of population these are: the Republic of Indonesia (160 million), the Federation of Malaysia (15 million), the Republic of Singapore (three million) and the Sultanate of Brunei (250,000). The variant of Malay used in the first-named state, which is officially termed *Bahasa Indonesia* (Indonesian language), will be referred to here as 'Indonesian'. The second variant, known in Malaysia as *Bahasa Malaysia* (Malaysian language) and in Singapore and Brunei as *Bahasa Melayu* (Malay language) or *Bahasa Kebangsaan* (national language), will be referred to as 'Malaysian'.

As can be seen from the accompanying map, native speakers of Malay are concentrated in the area of the Malacca Straits, a highly strategic location, since the Malacca Straits was the route through which the extensive maritime trade between India and Arabia in the west and China in the east had to pass. Moreover, the monsoon pattern made it impossible to complete the voyage without a pause of some months in the Malay-speaking region, a fact which resulted in Malay eventually acquiring the status of lingua franca throughout the Archipelago. Although this expansion of the language has not been historically documented, it is known that Malay was already in use in eastern Indonesia in the sixteenth century and it was considered quite normal for Francis Xavier to preach in Malay when he was in the Moluccas.

Outside the Malacca Straits area, Malay dialects are also found along the southern and western coasts of Borneo, in the southernmost provinces of Thailand and in the Mergui Archipelago of Burma. Malay-based creoles are found not only among the originally Chinese-speaking inhabitants of the old Straits Settlements of former British Malaya, but also in various ports of eastern Indonesia and on Christmas Island and the Cocos Islands in the Indian Ocean.

Despite this wide geographic distribution, Malay is by no means the mother tongue of the majority of the region's inhabitants. In fact this status is only achieved in Brunei, where it is the language of 60 per cent

Map 10.1

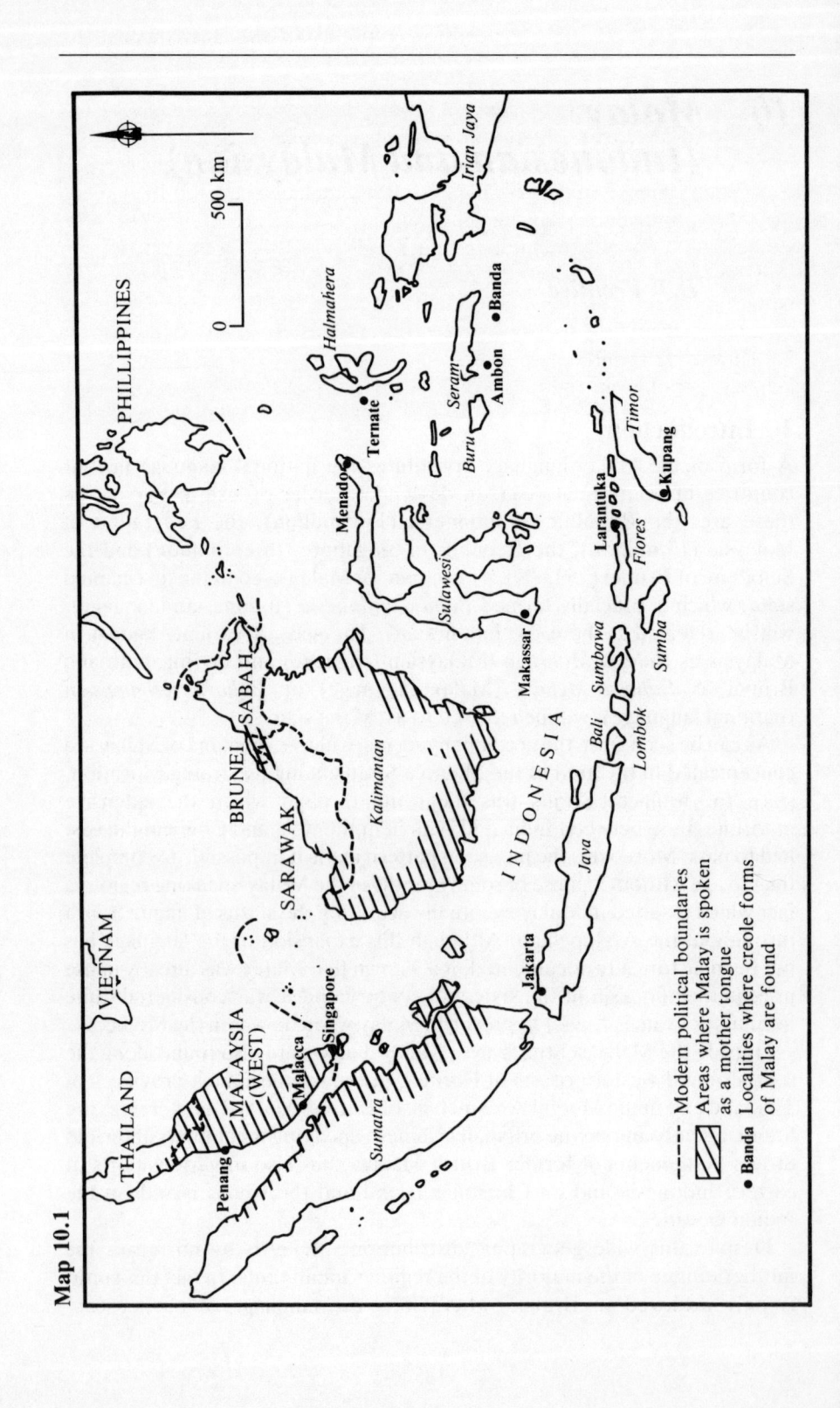

population (30 per cent speaking Chinese and the remainder non-Malay indigenous languages). In the other three countries the Malay-speaking proportion of the population is as follows: Malaysia 45 per cent (35 per cent speak Chinese languages, 10 per cent Indian languages and 10 per cent non-Malay indigenous languages), Singapore 15 per cent (70 per cent Chinese, 10 per cent Indian languages) and Indonesia 7 per cent (90 per cent non-Malay indigenous languages, 3 per cent Chinese). In terms of native speakers, the most important language of the whole region is Javanese (60 million speakers in central and eastern Java), followed by Sundanese (20 million speakers in western Java). Other important languages spoken in Indonesia (all with more than one million speakers) are Achinese (northernmost Sumatra), Batak (north-central Sumatra), Minangkabau (south-west Sumatra, regarded by many as a dialect of Malay), Buginese, Macassarese (both in southern Celebes), Madurese (Madura and eastern Java) and Balinese (Bali). The exact number of languages in the region is not known but can be safely estimated at around 300, of which the vast majority belong to the Austronesian language family. Non-Austronesian languages are found only in furthest eastern Indonesia and the interior of the Malay Peninsula.

The most important means of inter-ethnic communication in this multi-lingual situation has for centuries been provided by various forms of Malay, a fact which played a decisive role in the choice of Malay as the national language of Indonesia. Except in Singapore, where English is predominant, the language is today the main vehicle of communication for a population of almost 200 million, not only in areas of business and government but also in the mass media and at all levels of education.

The oldest known Malay text is to be found in a stone inscription dating from AD 683. This inscription and a few others of later date originate from the Hindu-Buddhist maritime empire of Srivijaya which had its capital near Palembang (southern Sumatra) and which at the height of its power (ninth to twelfth centuries) ruled over most of what is now Malaysia and western Indonesia. The inscriptions, written in a Pallava script originating from southern India, contain laws and accounts of military expeditions. They show that Malay was the administrative language of the empire, even in areas outside the Malay-speaking region (as shown by a tenth-century Malay inscription from West Java). Since Srivijaya was known far afield as a religious, cultural and commercial centre, it can be assumed that the language was used in these domains too. It was probably in this period that the first form of pidginised Malay (later known as Bazaar Malay) arose as a contact language among traders. Bazaar Malay still exists but is gradually disappearing as more people become familiar with the standard language.

From the late fourteenth to the early sixteenth century, the region was dominated by the powerful sultanate of Malacca, the rulers of which had at an early date been converted to Islam. The courts of this and other Malay sultanates possessed a rich literary tradition which produced many works, the most famous being the *Sejarah Melayu* or 'Malay Annals', a court history probably written in the sixteenth century but known only from a later manuscript. The language used in these literary and religious works, written in an adapted form of the Arabic script, is now termed 'Classical Malay'. It remained the golden standard for written Malay for the next 400 years, i.e. until the first quarter of the twentieth century in Indonesia and until the 1950s in Malaysia.

After the conquest of Malacca by the Portuguese in 1511, the court fled to the south and eventually established a polity which embraced Johore (the southern tip of the Malay Peninsula) and the island groups of Riau and Lingga in modern Indonesia. The literary tradition of the Malacca sultanate survived the upheavals of the colonial period and continued at the court of the Sultans of Riau-Johore. After the Napoleonic wars, the Treaty of London in 1824 regulated the division of the area into spheres of influence for the British and the Dutch (who had previously driven out the Portuguese). The boundary between the two spheres split the Riau-Johore sultanate into two. The literary Malay of the court continued, however, to be regarded as the standard on both sides of the new frontier and served in both areas as the basis for the future national language. Indonesian and Malaysian are therefore much closer to each other than they might have been if the boundary had been set elsewhere. On the other hand, for the whole of the nineteenth and part of the twentieth century the language was exposed to different influences in the two areas: from Dutch and Javanese in the Netherlands East Indies and from English and local Malay dialects in the British-controlled areas. During the crucial period of the Industrial Revolution, with all its new technological developments, advanced education was only available (if at all) through the language of the colonial power, which meant that the few Malay-speaking intellectuals had more contact with their Dutch or British counterparts than with each other. The language therefore lacked a common technical vocabulary. This divergence did not end with the independence of Indonesia and Malaysia: each country plotted its own course in rehabilitating the lexicon of the language to enable it to cope with twentieth-century technology. Not until the late 1970s was a joint Indonesian-Malaysian policy developed for the creation and adaptation of technical terms.

As a result, the major differences between Indonesian and Malaysian are lexical rather than grammatical in nature. The language described in the remainder of this chapter is the majority variant (i.e. Indonesian), although occasional references are made to significant Malaysian differences.

2 Phonology

The segmental phonemes of Indonesian are presented in table 10.1. Most of the symbols used in table 10.1 are also used for the same phonemes in the

Table 10.1: Segmental Phonemes

		Contoids					Vocoids		
		Labial [1]	Dental[2] + Alveolar	Palatal	Velar	Glottal	Front	Central	Back
Consonants	Stops	p b	t d	c j	k g	ʔ			
	Nasals	m	n	ñ	ŋ				
	Fricatives	f[3] v[3]	s z[3]	š[3]	x[3]	h			
	Lateral		l						
	Trill		r[4]						
Vowels	Semi-Vowels			y					w
	High						i		u
	Mid						e	ə	o
	Low							a	

Note: [1] f and v are labio-dental, the remainder bilabial. [2] t (and n preceding t) are dental, the remainder alveolar. [3] f, v, z, š and x occur only in loanwords. [4] In Malaysia r is a uvular fricative word-initially and medially, and is elided word-finally.

standard orthography. The vowels ə (frequently called pəpət) and e are not distinguished, however, both being spelt with 'e'. Dictionaries and grammars generally indicate the difference by using 'é' for e and 'e' for ə. The same convention will be followed in this chapter. The consonants š, x, ñ, ŋ are written 'sy', 'kh', 'ny', 'ng' respectively, while the diphthongs aw and ay are written 'au' and 'ai'. The phonemic status of ʔ is disputed. Some linguists maintain that it is an allophone of k in syllable-final position (kakak [kakaʔ] 'elder sibling', rakyat [raʔyat] 'people') and a predictable, non-phonemic transitional phenomenon between two vowels of which the first is a or e or between two identical vowels (seumur [səʔumur] 'of the same age', seékor [səʔekor] 'one (animal)', keenam [kəʔənam] 'sixth', maaf [maʔaf] 'pardon', cemooh [cəmoʔoh] 'mock'). Although this undoubtedly represents the original situation, the picture has changed under the influence of loanwords which do not conform to the pattern just described: fisik [fisik] 'physical' versus bisik [bisiʔ] 'whisper', maknit [maknit] 'magnet' versus makna [maʔna] 'meaning'. Summarising, it can be said that orthographic 'k' in word-initial and intervocalic position always represents k, while elsewhere (i.e. syllable-finally) it represents either ʔ or, less frequently, k.

The present orthography, which is used in both Indonesia and Malaysia, dates only from 1972, before which time each country had its own spelling system. Since so much written material is only available in the obsolete orthographies and since many proper names retain their original spellings, the major differences are presented in table 10.2.

A cursory inspection of an Indonesian dictionary reveals a strong predominance of disyllabic lexemes. Monosyllabic forms are without

Table 10.2: Spelling Systems

Post-1972 Common orthography	Pre-1972 Indonesia	Malaysia
c	tj	ch
j	dj	j
kh	ch	kh
ny	nj	ny
sy	sj	sh
y	j	y
e (ə)	e	e, ĕ
e (e)	e, é	e
i (before word-final h, k)	i	e
i (elsewhere)	i	i
u (before word-final h, k, ng, r)	u, oe*	o
u (elsewhere)	u, oe*	u

Note: *The spelling 'oe' was replaced by 'u' in 1947.

exception (1) bound morphemes, clitics or particles (e.g. -*ku* 'my', *se-* 'one, same', *ke* 'to(wards)', -*kah* (interrogative), *dan* 'and'); (2) loanwords (e.g. *cat* 'paint' from Chinese, *sah* 'authorised' from Arabic, *bom* 'bomb' from Dutch); (3) interjections (e.g. *cih!* 'poo!', *dor!* 'bang! (of gunshot)'); or (4) abbreviations of names and terms of address (e.g. *pak* from *bapak* 'father, sir', *bu* from *ibu* 'mother, madam', *Man* from *Suleiman* (male name)). Polysyllabic forms are usually the result of (1) morphological derivation (e.g. *beberapa* 'some, several' from *berapa* 'how many ?' + reduplication, *seumur* 'of the same age' from *se-* 'one, same' + *umur* 'age', *Merapi* (name of two volcanoes, one in Sumatra, the other in Java) from *mer-* (fossilised prefix) + *api* 'fire'); (2) of compounding (e.g. *matahari* 'sun' from *mata* 'eye' + *hari* 'day', *kacamata* 'spectacles' from *kaca* 'glass' + *mata* 'eye'); or (3) of borrowing (e.g. *jendéla* 'window' from Portuguese, *sandiwara* 'play, drama' from Sanskrit, *sintaksis* 'syntax' from Dutch). A small number of polysyllabic forms, however, appear to be inherited and not explicable as the result of one of these processes (e.g. *telinga* 'ear', *belakang* 'back').

Most Indonesian lexemes can be said to conform to the following canonical form:

$(C_1) V_1 (C_2) V_2 (C_3)$

The minimal free form consists of V_1V_2 (e.g. *ia* 'he, she'). In the inherited vocabulary, the following conditions apply:

C_1 = any consonant except *w* and *y*;
V_1 = any vowel;
C_2 = (1) any consonant; (2) a combination NC, i.e. a consonant preceded by a homorganic nasal (the normal combinations are *mp*, *mb*; *nt*, *nd*; *nc*, *nj*,

where the nasal is palatal despite the spelling; *ngk*, *ngg*; and *ngs*, where the nasal is alveolar for some speakers); or (3) a combination *r*C (only when V₁ = *e*);
V₂ = any vowel except *e*;
C₃ = any consonant except a palatal or a voiced stop (i.e. *c*, *j*, *ny*, *b*, *d* and *g*).

Large numbers of loanwords such as *kompleks* and *struktur* do not of course conform to this pattern.

Stress in Indonesian is non-phonemic and purely a matter of pitch (volume and quantity do not play a role in neutral speech). It regularly falls on the penultimate syllable (e.g. *'barat* 'west', *'tidur* 'sleep', *'péndék* 'short'), except when that syllable contains *e* followed by a single consonant, in which case it falls on the final syllable (e.g. *be'rat* 'heavy', *te'lur* 'egg'). In the case of *e* in the penultimate followed by two consonants, speakers fall into two groups differing in usage: group A, speakers originating from Java and the island to its east and group B, those originating from Sumatra and the Malay Peninsula. Group A displaces the stress to the final syllable while group B retains it on the penultimate *e* (e.g. A:*cer'min*, B:*'cermin* 'mirror', A:*leng'kap*, B:*'lengkap* 'complete'). In the case of suffixation, speakers of group A place the stress on the new penultimate, while those of group B retain it on the original syllable (A:*kepén'dékan*, B:*ke'péndékan* 'shortness, abbreviation', A:*keleng'kapan*, B:*ke'lengkapan* 'completeness').

Evidence from the Srivijayan inscriptions indicates that Malay, like its proto-language, originally had only four vowels: *i*, *u*, *e* and *a*. The phonemes *é* and *o* result from lowering of original *i* and *u*, universally in final closed syllables and unpredictably in non-final syllables. In the former environment, where the distinctions *i*/*é* and *u*/*o* are still subphonemic, the choice of an orthographic 'i' and 'u' is arbitrary, as indicated by the pre-1972 spelling systems. However, the existence of a vowel harmony rule (by which a non-central vowel in a non-final syllable may not be followed by a higher vowel in the final syllable) has led to the development not only of doublets (*bungkuk* and *bongkok* 'bow, stoop', *kicuh* and *kécoh* 'cheat, trick') but also of minimal pairs (*burung* 'bird' versus *borong* 'wholesale purchase', *giling* 'crush, grind' versus *géléng* 'shake the head'). Furthermore, the addition to the vocabulary of large numbers of neologisms in which the *i*/*é* and *u*/*o* distinctions are maintained in final closed syllables (*palét* 'palette' (from Dutch) versus *palit* 'smear', *kalong* 'fruitbat' (from Javanese) versus *kalung* 'garland, necklace') means that the distinctions have become phonemic in all environments.

3 Morphology

Indonesian has about 25 derivational affixes, but only two inflectional affixes (*meN₂*- and *di*-, see page 205). In this respect the standard language is more complex than the Malay dialects and the Malay-based creoles, which have far fewer affixes. In comparison with related Western Austronesian languages such as Javanese or Tagalog, however, the Indonesian affix system can be described as impoverished. The derivational affixes consist of not only prefixes and suffixes but also infixes and simulfixes. The infixes, four in number, are placed between the initial consonant of a base and the following adjective. They are restricted to a limited number of fossilised forms, e.g. *-em-* (cognate with Tagalog-*um*- in *gemetar* 'tremble' ← *getar* (idem), *tali-temali* 'rigging, cordage' ← *tali* 'rope'; *-el-* in *telunjuk* 'index finger' ← *tunjuk* 'point', *jelajah* 'explore' ← *jajah* 'colonise'; *-en-* in *senantan* '(of fighting cocks) milk-white' ← *santan* 'coconut-milk'; *-er-* in *seruling* 'flute' ← *suling* (idem). Another quite common fossilised affix is the prefix *mer-* (cognate with the highly productive *mag-* of Tagalog), which survives in *Merapi* (see page 190 above), *mertua* 'parent-in-law' ← *tua* 'old', *mersiul* 'crested wood-quail (bird species)' ← *siul* 'whistle' and other species names of flora and fauna.

Before describing the role of the living affixes, it is necessary to explain the Indonesian word-class system, the classification of which is based on a combination of morphological, syntactic and semantic factors. Indonesian lexical (as opposed to functional) bases are divisible into nominals (including nouns, pronouns and numerals) and verbals. The latter are divided into intransitive verbs and transitive verbs, according as they can cooccur with a grammatical object. The intransitive verbs, finally, can be classified as stative verbs, denoting qualities and states of affairs, or dynamic verbs, denoting changes of state, processes and actions. Examples are:

nominals: *rumah* 'house', *sapu* 'broom', *saya* 'I', *banyak* 'many, much';
stative verbs: *bagus* 'beautiful', *banyak* 'numerous', *mati* 'dead', *rusak* 'damaged';
dynamic verbs: *pergi* 'go', *duduk* 'sit (down)', *mati* 'die', *tahu* 'know';
transitive verbs: *bunuh* 'kill', *sapu* 'sweep', *rusak* 'damage'.

As shown by the examples *sapu*, *banyak*, *mati* and *rusak*, some bases are members of more than one word class. On the other hand, there are also bases without class membership (termed 'precategorials' and marked with a hyphen before the base) which occur only in derivations, reduplications and compounds (e.g. *-temu* → *bertemu* (d.v.) 'meet'; *-layan* → *layani* (t.v.) 'serve, wait on'; *-tari* → *menari* (d.v.) 'dance' and *tata tari* (nm.) 'choreography'; *-kupu* → *kupu-kupu* (nm.) 'butterfly'). Furthermore, it should be noted that colloquial spoken Indonesian is characterised by (among other things) extensive use of non-affixed forms instead of derivations which results in a greater degree of overlapping between word classes than in the standard (i.e. written, formal) language.

In table 10.3 the inflectional affixes and the most important derivational affixes are presented in the order in which they will be treated in the following pages. Secondary derivation, in which a derived form serves as the basis for a further derivation, is very frequent and is almost invariably

Table 10.3: Inflectional and Derivational Affixes

Derivational	Verb-forming	ber- meN₁- per- -i -kan ter- ke--an₁	Stative and dynamic verbs Dynamic verbs Transitive verbs Stative and accidental dynamic verbs
	Noun-forming	peN- -an ke--an₂ per--an peN--an	Deverbal and other nominals
Inflectional		meN₂- di- ∅-	Agent-orientation Object-orientation Imperative (*inter alia*)

accompanied by elision of the affix(es) employed in the primary derivation. For instance, the noun *obat* 'medicine', when suffixed with *-i* 'apply [BASE] to', produces *obati* (t.v.) 'treat (medically)'. This transitive verb in turn serves as the basis for derivations with *-kan* 'cause to undergo the action of [BASE]' (producing *obatkan* (t.v.) 'have treated') and with *peN--an* 'act of performing [BASE]' (producing *pengobatan* (nm.) '(medical) treatment'), in which the suffix *-i* of the underlying form is elided.

The prefix *ber-*, which is realised as *be-* when the base begins with *r...* or *CerC...*, forms large numbers of intransitive verbs, many of which occur without the prefix in informal speech. This is indicated by placing the prefix between brackets. Although it occurs with some precategorials to form dynamic verbs (*-main* → *(ber)main* 'play', *-nyanyi* → *(ber)nyanyi* 'sing'), it is most productive with nominal bases (including compounds of nominal + numeral and nominal + stative verb), when it forms intransitive verbs with a great variety of meanings: 'possess, wear, use etc. [BASE]'. Examples are: *mobil* 'car' → *bermobil* 'go by car', *sekolah* 'school' → *(ber)sekolah* 'go to school', *bapak* 'father, sir, you' → *berbapak* 'have a father, use *bapak* as a term of address', *ékor* 'tail' + *panjang* 'long' → *berékor panjang* 'long-tailed', *kaki* 'foot, leg' + *empat* 'four' → *berkaki empat* 'four-legged, four-footed'. With verbal bases, *ber-* is less productive. When affixed to a dynamic verb base indicating motion (always in combination with the suffix *-an*), it adds the semantic element 'diffuseness', i.e. plurality of actor, of action or of direction, e.g. *terbang* 'fly' → *beterbangan* 'fly in all directions', *pergi* 'go' → *bepergian* 'go on a journey, go to various places', *keluar* 'come/go out' → *berkeluaran* 'come/go out in large numbers'. When attached to transitive verb bases, *ber-* produces reciprocal verbs. In this case it is frequently accompanied by the suffix *-an* and/or complete reduplication of the base, e.g. *ganti* 'replace' → *berganti(-ganti)* 'succeed each other, take turns', *kejar* 'chase' → *berkejar(-kejar)an* 'chase each other', *kepit* 'squeeze between arm and body' → *berkepit(an)* 'walk/stand arm-in-arm', *tikam* 'stab' → *bertikam-tikaman* 'stab each other'.

In the case of the prefix meN_1-, N represents a nasal consonant homorganic with the initial phoneme of the base. As can be seen from table 46.4, the general pattern is that the nasals are preposed to voiced initials and substituted for voiceless initials. Nasal substitutions are indicated in the table by the capital letters *M, N, NG, NY*. The similar but more complicated

Table 10.4: Morphophonemics of meN_1

Initial phoneme of base	Form of prefix
b	mem-
p	meM-
d, j, c	men-
t	meN-
(vowel), h, g	meng-
k	meNG-
s	meNY-
(other phonemes)	me-

morphophonemics of the functionally distinct meN_2- are discussed on page 205 below. Verbs formed with meN_1- are always dynamic verbs and are less numerous than those formed with *ber-*. As with the latter, certain meN_1- verbs occur without the prefix in informal speech. Affixed to nominals (including compounds) and to precategorials, meN_1- has a great variety of meanings: 'behave like, resemble, move towards, collect, produce, consume etc. [BASE]', e.g. *gajah* 'elephant' → *menggajah* 'loom large', *darat* 'mainland' → *mendarat* 'go ashore', *seberang* 'other side (of road, river)' → *menyeberang* or colloquially *seberang* 'cross over', *rumput* 'grass' → *merumput* 'cut grass, (of cattle) graze', *tujuh* 'seven' + *bulan* 'month' → *menujuh bulan* 'hold a ceremony in the seventh month of pregnancy', *-amuk* → *mengamuk* 'run amuck, rage', *-jadi* → *(men)jadi* 'become'. When affixed to a stative verb, meN_1- forms a dynamic verb with the meaning '(gradually) become [BASE]' or 'behave in a [BASE] manner', e.g. *jauh* 'far, distant' → *menjauh* 'withdraw', *sombong* 'arrogant' → *menyombong* 'put on airs', *kurang* 'less' → *mengurang* 'diminish'.

The affixes *per-*, *-i* and *-kan* produce transitive verbs both from nominals and from other transitive or intransitive verbs, but are infrequently found with precategorials. Of the three affixes, *per-* was originally an important transitivising and causative prefix (as *pag-*, its cognate in Tagalog, still is — see page 223), but its functions have been usurped by *-kan*, which developed out of the preposition *akan* 'towards, with respect to'. As a result, *per-* as a transitivising prefix no longer has a function that is not also expressed by *-kan* or *-i*. In the formation of transitive verbs in the modern language, the prefix *per-* and the common simulfix *per--kan* always have one of the functions of the suffix *-kan* alone, while the now rare simulfix *per--i* always has one of the functions of *-i*. Accordingly, the following descriptions of *-kan* and *-i* also treat cases of *per-* and *per--kan* and of *per--i* respectively.

The suffix *-kan* is arguably the commonest and most productive of all derivational affixes in Indonesian and is frequently found in neologisms. When the base is a nominal denoting an animate being, a transitive verb derived with *-kan* has the meaning 'cause to become [BASE]' or 'regard, treat as [BASE]': *raja* 'king' → *rajakan* 'crown', *budak* 'slave' → *budakkan*, *perbudak* 'enslave, treat like a slave', *tuhan* 'god' → *pertuhan(kan)* 'deify, treat like a god', *istri* 'wife' → *peristri* 'take as one's wife, marry'. When the base denotes an inanimate object, various semantic patterns are found, the most frequent being 'place in/on [BASE]': *penjara* 'prison' → *penjarakan* 'imprison', *izin* 'permission' → *izinkan* 'permit, allow', *ladang* 'unirrigated field' → *perladang(kan)* 'open up (land) for cultivation', *proklamasi* 'proclamation' → *proklamasikan* 'proclaim'. With a stative verb base, verbs derived with *-kan* have the meaning 'cause to become [BASE]' or 'regard as [BASE]', e.g. *basah* 'wet' → *basahkan* 'wet', *dalam* 'deep' → *dalamkan*, *perdalam* 'deepen', *panjang* 'long' → *panjangkan* 'lengthen, extend' and *perpanjang* (idem) + 'extend the validity of', *kecil* 'small' → *kecilkan* 'reduce (garment, photo)' and *perkecil* 'belittle'. Semantic differentiation between *per-* and *-kan* is not uncommon, as seen in the derivatives of *panjang* and *kecil* above. Some Indonesian speakers, especially those with Javanese as their mother tongue, also maintain a distinction between such pairs as *dalamkan* 'make deep something which is shallow' and *perdalam* 'make deeper something which is already deep'. These distinctions are much less clear-cut in Malaysian, which prefers the simulfix *per--kan* in all the examples just given. Affixation of *-kan* to a dynamic verb produces three categories of transitive verbs: (1) those which mean 'cause to perform the action of [BASE]', e.g. *jatuh* 'fall' → *jatuhkan* 'drop', *berkumpul* 'gather' → *kumpulkan* 'gather, collect', *bekerja* 'work' → *pekerjakan* 'put to work, employ', *menyusu* 'suck at the breast' → *susukan* 'suckle, breast-feed'; (2) those which mean 'produce by the action of [BASE]', e.g. *muntah* 'vomit' → *muntahkan* 'regurgitate', *berkata* 'say, speak' → *katakan* 'say', *menari* 'dance' → *tarikan* 'perform (dance)'; and (3) transitive verbs of emotion, perception or speech which are semantically equivalent to [BASE] + preposition, e.g. *lupa* (± *akan*) 'forget (about)' → *lupakan* 'forget (about)', *mimpi* (+ *tentang*) 'dream (about)' → *mimpikan* 'dream about', *berbicara*

(+ *tentang*) 'talk (about)' → *bicarakan* 'discuss', *berjuang* (+ *untuk*) 'strive, fight (for)' → *perjuangkan* 'strive, fight for'. Derivations with *-kan* based on transitive verbs are divisible into two main groups: those in which object-replacement does not occur (in which case both the base transitive verb and the transitive verb with *-kan* have the direct object or 'goal' of the action as their object) and those in which object-replacement does occur, where a function other than 'goal', i.e. 'beneficiary' or 'instrument', is promoted to object of the verb with *-kan*. The former category can be further divided into causative and non-causative verbs. The non-causative are synonymous (or almost so) with their bases, the only difference being that the form with *-kan* usually connotes a more purposeful or more intense action than the base form. Examples are: *tulis* 'write' → *tuliskan* 'write (down)', *kirim* 'send' → *kirimkan* 'send (off), dispatch', *dengar* 'hear, listen to' → *dengarkan* 'listen to', *antar* 'bring, convey' → *antarkan* (idem). The causative verbs with *-kan* all have the meaning 'cause to undergo the action of [BASE]', e.g. *lihat* 'see' → *(per)lihatkan* 'cause to be seen, show', *dengar* 'hear, listen to' → *perdengarkan* 'cause to be heard, play (tune, record)', *séwa* 'hire' → *séwakan* 'cause to be hired, rent out', *obati* 'treat (medically)' → *obatkan* 'have treated (medically)'. Derivatives with *-kan* which have a beneficiary or instrumental object are more frequent in formal than in colloquial Indonesian. They occasionally give rise to competing forms, e.g. *tulis* 'write' → *tuliskan* 'write for (someone)' and 'write with (something)' (both differing from *tuliskan* 'write (something) down', see above), *beli* 'buy' → *belikan* 'buy for' and 'buy with, spend (money)', *cari* 'look for, seek' → *carikan* 'seek for, find for (someone)', *témbak* 'shoot' → *témbakkan* 'shoot with, fire (gun)'. Use of a derived verb with an instrumental object usually results in the original 'goal' object acquiring a new preposition, as in *témbak babi dengan senapang* 'shoot the pigs with a rifle' versus *témbakkan senapang (ke)pada babi* 'fire the rifle at the pigs', whereas this is usually not the case with verbs with a beneficiary object: *cari rumah untuk Ali* 'look for a house for Ali' versus *carikan Ali rumah* 'find Ali a house'.

The suffix *-i* is much less productive than *-kan*. There is, moreover, one phonologically determined constraint on its occurrence: it cannot be affixed to bases ending with the phonemes *i* or *y*, i.e. bases ending in orthographic 'i'. Combined with a nominal base, *-i* produces transitive verbs with one (or more) of the following meanings: 'apply [BASE] to', 'remove [BASE] from' or 'function as [BASE] of/for', e.g. *obat* 'medicine' → *obati* 'put medicine on, treat medically', *air* 'water' → *airi* 'irrigate', *tanda tangan* 'signature' → *tandatangani* 'sign', *kulit* 'skin' → *kuliti* 'peel (fruit), skin (animal), cover (book)', *bulu* 'fur, feather' → *bului* 'pluck (bird), fletch (arrow)', *ketua* 'chairman' → *ketuai* 'preside over, chair (meeting)', *dalang* 'puppet-master' → *dalangi* 'mastermind (conspiracy)'. In combination with a stative verb denoting a quality, *-i* produces a causative transitive verb with the meaning 'cause to be/become [BASE]'. The few surviving examples of the simulfix *per--i*, all of which have less common variants without *per-*, are confined to this group. Examples: *basah* 'wet' → *basahi* 'wet', *takut* 'afraid' → *takuti* 'frighten', *baik* 'good' → *(per)baiki* 'improve, repair'. Such forms as these can be synonymous with verbs derived with *-kan* from the same stative verb base. Usually, however, there is a subtle semantic distinction: the forms with *-i* imply the application of the quality of [BASE] to the object, an implication which is absent from the *-kan* forms. Thus *basahkan* means 'make wet (by any means, including soaking in liquid)', whereas *basahi* can only mean 'make wet by applying liquid' and not 'by placing in liquid'. When the base is a stative verb denoting emotion or perception or a dynamic verb denoting movement or location, the derivative with *-i* is semantically equivalent to [BASE] + preposition, e.g. *marah* (+ *pada*) 'angry (with)' → *marahi* 'scold', *suka* (± *akan*) 'fond (of something)', and (± *(ke)pada*) 'fond (of someone)' → *sukai* 'like', *hormat* (+ *kepada/terhadap*) 'respectful (towards)' → *hormati* 'respect', *duduk* (+ *di*) 'sit (on)' → *duduki* 'occupy', *berkunjung* (+ *ke(pada)*) 'pay a visit (to)' → *kunjungi* 'visit', *menjauh* (+ *dari*) 'go away, withdraw (from)' → *jauhi* 'avoid'. As with *-kan*, when *-i* is attached to a transitive verb object-replacement may or may not occur. When it does not occur, *-i* denotes plurality of object and/or intensification or repetition of the action: *pukul* 'strike' → *pukuli* 'beat up', *makan* 'eat' → *makani* 'devour', *angkat* 'lift' → *angkati* 'lift many (objects), lift repeatedly'. With object-replacement, the *-i* derivative has the location or direction of the action as its object. The base transitive verb frequently has a synonymous or nearly synonymous form with *-kan*, e.g. *tulis(kan)* 'write (down)' → *tulisi* 'inscribe (with something), write on', *kirim(kan)* 'send (off)' → *kirimi* 'send something to', *tanam(kan)* 'plant (e.g. seed)' → *tanami* 'plant (e.g. field) (with something), plant something in'.

The so-called 'accidental' verbs are formed by the prefix *ter-* or the simulfix *ke--an*₁, of which the former is more common. When affixed to dynamic verb bases, *ter-* indicates sudden or involuntary action: *duduk* 'sit (down)' → *terduduk* 'fall on one's backside', *tidur* 'sleep' → *tertidur* 'fall asleep', *memekik* 'scream' → *terpekik* 'scream involuntarily'. With transitive verb bases, *ter-* yields three kinds of verbs. Firstly it can produce accidental dynamic verbs which in Indonesian (but not in Malaysian) are exclusively object-oriented, i.e. the subject of the *ter-* predicate is the object of the underlying base verb. Examples are: *pukul* 'strike' → *terpukul* 'be struck accidentally', *makan* 'eat' → *termakan* 'be eaten by mistake'. Secondly, and most frequently, *ter-* produces stative verbs indicating the state resulting from the action of the base transitive verb. These verbs are object-oriented in both Indonesian and Malaysian. Examples are: *singgung* 'offend' → *tersinggung* 'offended', *hormati* 'respect' → *terhormat* 'respected', *dapati* 'find, encounter' → *terdapat* 'occur, be found', *letakkan* 'put, place' → *terletak* 'situated, located', *organisasi(kan)* 'organise' → *terorganisasi* 'organised, regimented'. Thirdly, *ter-* can yield object-oriented stative verbs with a semantic element of potentiality. These verbs occur most frequently in negative sentences, preceded by *tidak* 'not', and form an exception to the general rule that in secondary derivations all primary derivational affixes are elided. Examples: *angkat* 'lift' → *tidak terangkat* 'cannot be lifted', *makan* 'eat' → *tidak termakan* 'inedible', *dalami* 'explore in depth' → *tidak terdalami* 'unfathomable', *selesaikan* 'solve' → *tidak terselesaikan* 'insoluble'. The final function of *ter-* is to form superlatives, a function in which it is restricted to occurrence with monomorphemic stative verb bases, e.g. *baik* 'good' → *terbaik* 'best', *tinggi* 'high' → *tertinggi* 'highest'.

Of the much rarer accidental verbs formed with ke--an_1, four are object-oriented dynamic verbs or stative verbs based on transitive verbs of perception: *lihat* 'see' → *kelihatan* 'be seen; be visible; appear, seem', *dengar* 'hear' → *kedengaran* 'be heard; be audible; sound', *dapati* 'find, encounter' → *kedapatan* 'be found (doing something)', *ketahui* 'know, find out' → *ketahuan* 'be found out, come to light'. The remainder, which can have bases of any word class, all share the meaning 'be adversely affected by [BASE]': *hujan* (nm.) 'rain' → *kehujanan* 'be caught in the rain', *malam* (nm.) 'night' → *kemalaman* 'be overtaken by nightfall', *takut* (s.v.) 'afraid' → *ketakutan* 'be overcome by fear', *mati* (s.v.) 'dead' and (d.v.) 'die' → *kematian* 'be bereaved', *curi* (t.v.) 'steal' → *kecurian* 'be robbed', *datangi* (t.v.) 'come to, arrive at' → *kedatangan* 'receive (unexpected) visitors'.

The nasal element of the prefix *peN-* combines with the initial phoneme of the base in the same way as that of meN_1- (see page 194 above). With a dynamic or transitive verb base *peN-* forms a nominal with the meaning 'person who (customarily) performs [BASE]': *(ber)nyanyi, (me)nyanyi* 'sing' → *penyanyi* 'singer', *menangis* 'weep' → *penangis* 'cry-baby', *duduki* 'occupy' → *penduduk* 'occupant, inhabitant', *kumpulkan* 'collect' → *pengumpul* 'collector'. Less frequently the derived nominal has the meaning 'instrument with which [BASE] is performed': *buka* 'open' → *pembuka botol* 'bottle-opener'. A *peN-* derivative from a stative verb base is both a nominal and a stative verb and has the meaning '(person who is) characterised by [BASE]', e.g. *takut* 'afraid' → *penakut* 'coward(ly)', *marah* 'angry' → *pemarah* 'bad-tempered (person)'.

The suffix *-an*, which occurs either alone or as an element of the simulfixes ke--an_2, *per--an* and *peN--an*, is the commonest noun-forming affix. Deverbal nouns formed with *-an*, which (unlike the simulfixes) is no longer productive, refer to the object, instrument, location or action of the base verb, which can be a dynamic or transitive verb: *(ber)nyanyi, (me)nyanyi* 'sing' → *nyanyian* 'song, singing', *makan* 'eat' → *makanan* 'food', *timbang* 'weigh' → *timbangan* 'weighing-scales', *berlabuh* 'drop anchor' → *labuhan* 'anchorage', *pukul* 'strike' → *pukulan* 'blow'. The formation of deverbal nouns through the productive simulfixes is linked to the morphology of the underlying verb: ke--an_2 occurs with non-derived intransitive verbs, *per--an* with intransitive verbs derived with *ber-* and transitive verbs derived with *per-*, and *peN--an* with all other transitive verbs. All these derived nominals denote 'quality, process or activity of [BASE]': *indah* 'beautiful' → *keindahan* 'beauty', *datang* 'come' → *kedatangan* 'coming, arrival', *bersekutu* 'be allied' → *persekutuan* 'alliance, federation', *perbaiki* 'repair, improve' → *perbaikan* 'repair, improvement', *satu* 'one' → *kesatuan* 'unit, unity', *bersatu* 'united' → *persatuan* 'union, association', *satukan* 'unify' → *penyatuan* 'unification'. The simulfixes *ke--an*$_2$ and *per--an* also occur with nominal bases, producing nouns denoting collectivity, e.g. *pulau* 'island' → *kepulauan* 'archipelago', *air* 'water' → *perairan* '(territorial) waters'. They are frequently found in modern Indonesian as the formatives of nouns used almost exclusively in attributive position, as the equivalents of English and Dutch denominal adjectives, e.g. *agama* 'religion' → *keagamaan* '(affairs) pertaining to religion, religious', as in *latar-belakang keagamaannya* 'his/her/its religious background' as opposed to *latar-belakang agamanya* 'the background of his/her/its religion'. Frequently, however, the denominal adjective is borrowed along with the underlying noun, as *géografi* 'geography' and *géografis* 'geographical' from Dutch. Intensive borrowing of foreign derivatives combined with use of indigenous derivational mechanisms often leads to synonymy. From Dutch has been borrowed both the verb *organisir* 'organise' and the noun *organisasi* 'organisation'. As already seen, the latter gives rise to a second verb *organisasi(kan)* 'organise' while both verbs can further serve as bases for nominal derivations: *pengorganisiran* and *pengorganisasian*, both of which mean 'organisation' in the sense of 'the act of organising'.

Another morphological process which is almost as important as affixation and furthermore very characteristic for Indonesian and related languages is reduplication, of which there are three forms. Full reduplication, which involves repetition of the whole lexeme, is used grammatically as one way of indicating plurality with nouns (see page 200 below) but has also numerous lexical uses (e.g. *kuda* 'horse' → *kuda-kuda* 'saw-horse'). In altered reduplication, the whole base is also doubled, but one or more of its phonemes are at the same time replaced (e.g. *balik* 'go back' → *bolak-balik* 'go back and forth'). Partial reduplication can be summarised in the formula $C_1 e C_1 V_1 ...$, i.e. repetition of the initial consonant of the base followed by the vowel *e*, e.g. *laki* 'husband' → *lelaki* (also *laki-laki*) 'man, male'. It does not occur with vowel-initial bases and is not very common in Indonesian. In Malaysian on the other hand, not only do all cases of lexical full reduplication have alternatives with partial reduplication (thus *kuda-kuda* and *kekuda* 'saw-horse'), but it is also frequently used for the coinage of new terms: *pasir* 'sand' → *pepasir* 'granule', *bola* 'ball' → *bebola* 'ball-bearing'. Full and altered reduplication are found with bases of all word classes (including precategorials), in combination with various affixes and with diverse functions, of which only a few can be exemplified here: (1) diversity and collectivity, e.g. *daun* 'leaf' → *daun-daunan* or *dedaunan* 'foliage', *sayur* 'vegetable' → *sayur-mayur* 'various vegetables'; (2) similarity, e.g. *anak* 'child' → *anak-anakan* 'doll' (see also *kuda-kuda* above); (3) vagueness, e.g. *mérah* 'red' → *kemérah-mérahan* 'reddish'; (4) aimlessness, e.g. *duduk* 'sit' → *duduk-duduk* 'sit around (doing nothing)', *ikut* 'follow' → *ikut-ikutan* 'follow blindly'; (5) reciprocity, e.g. *hormati* 'respect' → *hormat-menghormati* 'respect each other', see also examples with *ber-(-an)* on page 922 above; (6) continuousness or repetition, e.g. *turun* 'descend' → *turun-temurun* 'from generation to generation' (cf. also *bolak-balik* above); and (7) intensity, e.g. *cabik* 'tear' → *cabik-cabik* 'tear to pieces', *habis* 'finished, used up' → *habis-habisan* 'all-out, total (war, destruction)'.

4 Syntax

Nouns are not marked for number, gender or definiteness, nor are verbs marked for person or tense. A sentence such as *harimau makan babi* 'tiger + eat + pig' has therefore an infinite number of meanings, varying from 'tigers eat pigs' to 'the tigresses have eaten a boar', according to the context. There exist mechanisms for making the distinctions mentioned, but these are only used when the distinction is important and not conveyed by the context. Full reduplication of nouns, for instance, can be used to indicate miscellany, variety or simple plurality: *babi* '(the, a) pig, (the) pigs', *babi-babi* '(the) pigs, various pigs'. Definiteness can be indicated by (among other things) a deictic (*itu* 'the, that') or a personal pronoun (*-nya* 'his/her/its/the') after a noun: *babi itu* 'that/those/the pig(s)', *babi-babinya* 'his/her/its/the (various) pigs'. Gender can be shown by the use of modifiers *lelaki/jantan* 'male' and *perempuan/betina* 'female' (for humans and non-humans respectively) after the noun: *cucu* 'grandchild', *cucu lelaki* 'grandson', *cucu perempuan* 'granddaughter'; *babi* 'pig', *babi jantan* 'boar', *babi betina* 'sow'.

As will be evident from the examples just given, modifiers in noun phrases usually follow the element which they modify. Immediately following the head noun can occur a noun used attributively or possessively (*rumah* 'house', *batu* 'rock, stone', *rumah batu* 'stone house'; *guru* 'teacher', *rumah guru* 'teacher's house') or a monomorphemic stative verb (*baru* 'new', *rumah baru* 'new house'). In second place can occur one or more relative clauses, introduced by the relative linker *yang*, and one or more prepositional phrases (*terbakar* 'burnt', *rumah yang terbakar* 'the house which was burnt down'; *di* 'in, at', *rumah di Jakarta* 'house(s) in Jakarta'). Final position is reserved for the deictics *ini* 'this' and *itu* 'that, the' (*rumah yang terbakar ini* 'this house which has been burnt down', *saya* 'I', *rumah saya di Jakarta yang terbakar itu* 'that house of mine in Jakarta which was burnt down'). When the position immediately following the head noun is occupied, any further attributive modifier must be placed in a *yang*-clause in second position (*rumah batu yang baru* 'new stone house'). This occasionally yields ambiguity: *rumah guru yang baru* can mean 'the teacher's new house' (in which *yang baru* modifies *rumah*) or 'the house of the new teacher' (in which it modifies *guru*). Similarly, an attributive consisting of a qualified or polymorphemic stative verb is placed in a *yang*-clause (*rumah yang terbaru* 'newest house', *rumah yang cukup baru* 'fairly new house').

The most important exception to the general word order rule in noun phrases is the quantifier, which precedes the noun (but can also follow it, especially in lists). The quantifier consists of a numeral (or other quantifying term such as 'several', 'many', etc.) followed by an optional 'classifier'. The numerals from 'one' to 'ten' are: *satu* 'one', *dua* 'two', *tiga* 'three', *empat* 'four', *lima* 'five', *enam* 'six', *tujuh* 'seven', *delapan* 'eight', *sembilan* 'nine' and *sepuluh* 'ten'. The numerals between 'ten' and 'twenty' are formed with *belas*: *sebelas* 'eleven', *dua belas* 'twelve', *tiga belas* 'thirteen' etc. Higher numerals are formed with *puluh* 'tens', *ratus* 'hundreds', *ribu* 'thousands' and *juta* 'millions'. In combination with these forms, as with *belas* and all nouns of measurement, *satu* 'one' takes the form of a prefix *se-*: *sepuluh* 'ten', *seratus tujuh puluh* 'one hundred and seventy', *seribu sembilan ratus delapan puluh lima* '1985', *sejuta* 'one million'. Except for 'first', which is expressed by the Sanskrit loanword *pertama*, ordinals are formed with the prefix *ke-* (e.g. *ketujuh* 'seventh', *kedua puluh lima* 'twenty-fifth'), while fractions are formed with *per-* (e.g. *sepertujuh* 'one seventh', *tiga pertujuh* 'three sevenths').

The classifier is a morpheme-type found in many Asian languages (including non-Austronesian languages such as Vietnamese and Chinese). It occurs between a numeral and a noun and gives information about the form, size or character of the latter. Classical Malay possessed dozens of classifiers, such as *butir* (lit. 'grain') for small round objects and *batang* ('stick') for long, solid cylindrical objects. Although some of these are still in use in fixed expressions, in modern Indonesian membership of this subclass is for all practical purposes reduced to three: *buah* ('fruit') for inanimate nouns, *ékor* ('tail') for animate non-human nouns and *orang* '(person') for human nouns (*tiga buah rumah* 'three houses', *tiga ékor babi* 'three pigs', *tiga orang guru* 'three teachers'). With classifiers, the numeral *satu* is abbreviated to *se-* when it has the meaning 'a, an'; this is the usual way of marking a noun for indefiniteness, thus *sebuah rumah* 'a house' versus *satu (buah) rumah* 'one house'. Similar in their syntactic behaviour to classifiers are metrical nouns, which include not only names for units of measurement such as *jam* 'hour', *méter* 'metre' but also all nouns denoting objects which can be used or regarded as containers, e.g. *sebotol bir* 'a bottle of beer' (as opposed to *sebuah botol bir* 'a beer-bottle'); with *gerobak* 'cart' and *kayu* 'wood', *segerobak kayu* 'a cartload of wood' versus *sebuah gerobak kayu* 'a wooden cart', *tiga gerobak kayu* 'three cartloads of wood' versus *tiga (buah) gerobak kayu* 'three wooden carts'.

Indonesian is particularly rich in pronouns (a subclass of nominals), the majority of which are marked for varying degrees of familiarity or formality. There are only five unmarked pronouns: *saya* 'I', *kami* 'we (exclusive)' (i.e. 'I + he/she/they'), *kita* 'we (inclusive)' (i.e. 'I + you'), *dia* (also *ia* in formal Indonesian) 'he, she' and *meréka* 'they'. For the first person, *aku* 'I' is marked as intimate, while the third person *beliau* 'he, she' is marked as respectful. In the third person, traditionally only the bound form *-nya* can refer to inanimate entities. In recent years, however, the forms *ia* and *dia* are increasingly common in this function. There are no unmarked pronouns for the second person: (*eng*)*kau* and *kamu*, historically the unmarked singular and plural forms respectively, have not only lost the number distinction but are also marked as intimate. In all non-intimate situations various appellatives are used as second person (and under certain circumstances also first person) pronouns: personal names (to friends and acquaintances of the same age), kinship terms (to blood-relations or people regarded as such) and titles (to strangers, to older or more senior people and to colleagues in formal situations). Indonesian is therefore one of the few languages in the world in which pronouns are an open class, with an infinite membership. In the late 1950s an attempt was made to simplify the situation by propagating the use of *anda* (originally an honorific termination for kinship terms used in letters, e.g. *anakanda* 'dear child', from *anak* 'child') as an unmarked pronoun, intended to be as universal as English *you*. Although in some intellectual circles it is now so used, *anda* has only added to the complexity: it is now commonly used when addressing the general public via the mass media, where the age, status etc. of the reader, listener or viewer is unknown. Three pronouns (*aku*, (*eng*)*kau/kamu* and *dia/ia*) have inflected (or cliticised) forms for various functions, as shown in table 10.5. All the forms listed in the table for the function 'subject' can also be used for the other functions.

Table 10.5: Inflected (Cliticised) Pronouns

	Free forms Subject	Object	Bound forms Object	Agent	Possessive
1st	aku	*daku	*-ku	ku-	-ku
2nd	(eng)kau kamu	*dikau	*-kau, *-mu	kau-	-kau, -mu
3rd	*ia, dia	dia	-nya	-nya	-nya

Note: * = literary forms

Prepositional phrases consist of a noun phrase or a (nominalised) verb phrase preceded by a relator, which itself can be either simple or compound. A simple relator is either one of the three indigenous clitics (*di* (location), *ke* (movement towards) or *dari* (movement from)) or a word originally belonging to a different word class (nominal or verb), or borrowed from another language. Examples are: *dengan* 'with (accompaniment, instrument)', originally a nominal 'companion'; *melalui* 'through', also an agent-oriented transitive verb 'go/pass through'; *terhadap* 'towards, with regard to', originally a stative verb 'facing, directed towards'; *sebab* 'because of', also a nominal 'cause', borrowed from Arabic; *tanpa* 'without', borrowed from Javanese. A compound relator usually consists of one of the clitics *di/ke/dari*, followed by one of a class of locative words (originally nominals), e.g. *dalam* 'interior', *atas* 'upper surface', *antara* 'interval, space between', as in *di rumah* 'in/at the house, at home', *di dalam rumah* 'in/inside the house', *ke dalam rumah* 'into the house', *dari dalam rumah* 'from (inside) the house'. Before animate nouns and expressions of time, *di*, *ke* and *dari* are replaced by *pada*, *(ke)pada* and *dari(pada)* respectively: compare *di rumah itu* 'at that house' and *pada waktu itu* 'at that time', *ke Jakarta* 'to Jakarta' and *(ke)pada Ali* 'to Ali'. One or both parts of certain compound relators may be omitted, especially with verbs which contain a notion of direction or location, such as *masuk* 'come/go in': *Ali masuk ke dalam rumah*, *Ali masuk ke rumah*, *Ali masuk dalam rumah* or in colloquial style simply *Ali masuk rumah* 'Ali comes/goes into the house'.

In verb phrases with a dynamic or transitive verb as head, a three-way aspect distinction can be made by the markers *telah* (action completed), *sedang* (action commenced but not completed) and *akan* (action not commenced), which precede the verb: *Ali telah berpindah* 'Ali has (had, will have etc.) moved house', *Ali sedang berpindah* 'Ali is (was etc.) moving house', *Ali akan berpindah* 'Ali will (was going to etc.) move house'. In the spoken language *telah*, *sedang* and *akan* are replaced by *sudah*, *masih* or *lagi* and *mau* respectively, which can also co-occur with stative verbs and (under certain conditions) with nouns and numerals. Other tense-aspect distinctions can be indicated outside the verb phrase by temporal adverbs such as *bésok* 'tomorrow', *ésoknya* 'the next day', *nanti* 'soon', *sekarang* 'now', *tadi* 'just now', *tadinya* 'up to now, until then' etc. Adverbs of degree, which occur mostly but not exclusively with stative verbs, have a fixed position vis-à-vis the head: some occur before the stative verb (*paling* 'most', *terlalu* 'too'), some after the stative verb (*sekali* 'very') and some in either position (*amat* 'very', *benar* 'truly, really'). All verbs can be preceded by modals (e.g. *harus* 'must, have to', *boléh* 'may, be allowed to', *bisa* or *dapat* 'can, be able to', *ingin* 'wish to') and by negatives (e.g. *tidak* 'not', *jangan* (vetative), *bukan* (contrastive negative)). The combination of [negative] + [completed action] is expressed by *belum*: *Ali telah pergi* 'Ali has gone' is negated by *Ali belum pergi* 'Ali hasn't gone (yet)'. Changes in word order reflect semantic differences: *Ali tidak harus hadir* 'Ali doesn't have to be present' versus *Ali harus tidak hadir* 'Ali mustn't be present (must be 'not present')'

The unmarked word order within the sentence is subject–predicate, as seen in all the sentences used as examples above. The order predicate–subject is, however, very frequent and, except when the predicate is an object-oriented transitive verb, indicates focus on the predicate. When the predicate is an agent-oriented transitive verb (see page 933 below) with an object, the latter must always follow the verb; otherwise word order within the sentence is flexible and determined by factors of style and prominence. A copulative verb does not exist: *Ali guru* 'Ali is a teacher', *Ali marah* 'Ali is angry', *Ali di Jakarta* 'Ali is in Jakarta', *Ali (sedang) mendengar radio* 'Ali is listening to the radio'; and with predicate–subject order (with focus on the predicate): *guru Ali* 'Ali is **a teacher**', *marah Ali* 'Ali is **angry**', *di Jakarta Ali* 'Ali is **in Jakarta**', *(sedang) mendengar radio Ali* 'Ali is **listening to the radio**'. Nominal predicates can only be negated by *bukan* (*Ali bukan guru* 'Ali isn't a teacher'), whereas other predicates are negated either by *tidak* 'not (neutral negative)' or by *bukan* 'not (contrastive negative)', e.g. *Ali tidak marah* 'Ali isn't angry' and *Ali bukan marah* 'Ali isn't **angry** (he's **pleased**)'. In the written language an equational sentence, in which both subject and predicate are nominal phrases or nominalised verbal phrases, often has the structure 'subject–*adalah*–predicate'. The marker *adalah* (or *ialah* with third person subjects) is used when structural complexity of subject and/or predicate renders the boundary between the two sentence elements doubtful. In the spoken language this function is performed by intonation (rising intonation on the subject, slight caesura between subject and predicate and falling intonation on the predicate). The following sentences can only be differentiated in written Indonesian by the use of the predicate marker *adalah* in the second:

```
Subject     Predicate  Object
kerja-nya   menarik    mahasiswa
work-his    attract    student
```
'His work attracts students.'

```
Subject               Predicate
kerja-nya  (adalah)   menarik   mahasiswa
work-his              attract   student
```
'His work (i.e. job, task) is to attract students.'

The subject of an Indonesian sentence is always definite, i.e. it represents either a unique entity or an entity already known from the linguistic or non-linguistic context or a particularised item or class. Given the general tendency towards limitation of redundancy (see page 200 above), it is not surprising that the subject is frequently not expressed. Thus, when the subject of a subordinate clause is identical to that of the main clause, usually only the latter is expressed, regardless of the order in which the clauses appear:

Ali tinggal di rumah karena (dia) sakit
Ali stay   at house because he   ill
'Ali stayed at home because he was ill.'

This sentence could also appear as: *karena (dia) sakit, Ali tinggal di rumah* 'because he was ill, Ali stayed at home'. Whenever the subject is an inanimate entity known from the context, it is obligatorily absent, as in:

Jangan masuk rumah itu. Berbahaya.
don't go-in house that dangerous
'Don't go into that house. (It's) dangerous.'

When the predicate is a nominal, a stative verb or a dynamic verb, the subject represents the entity which respectively is equivalent to, is characterised by or performs the action of the predicate. When the predicate is a transitive verb, however, the subject can represent either the entity which performs the action of the predicate or that which undergoes it. This distinction between agent-orientation and object-orientation is marked on the transitive verb by the only inflectional affixes in the Indonesian verb system, *meN₂-* and *di-* respectively. The agent-oriented form is also frequently used as a nominal with the meaning 'the act (or activity) of verb-ing (tr.)', as in the sentence *kerjanya (adalah) menarik mahasiswa* above.

The morphophonemics of *meN₂-* are similar to those of *meN₁-* (see table 10.4). The differences include prenasalisation (rather than nasalisation) of initial voiceless consonants with some bases and the occurrence of an allomorph *menge-* with monosyllabic bases. Thus the initial *p* of the derivational prefix *per-* is never replaced by the nasal of *meN₂-*: *perlihatkan* 'show' → *memperlihatkan*. The same occurs irregularly with verbs which begin with the sequence *per...*, even though this is not a prefix: *percayai* 'trust' (from Sanskrit *pratyaya*) → *mempercayai*. Preservation of initial voiceless consonants is moreover frequent among verbs based on loanwords: *khianati* 'betray' → *mengkhianati, takhtakan* 'enthrone' → *mentakhtakan*. Competing forms sometimes arise: *terjemahkan* 'translate' → *menterjemahkan* and *menerjemahkan*. Monosyllabic bases and transitive verbs derived from them take either the regular allomorph of *meN₂-* (with or without deletion of initial voiceless consonants) or the allomorph *menge-* or (in most cases) both: *lém* 'glue' → *mengelém, bom* 'bomb' → *mengebom* or *membom, sahkan* 'authorise' (from *sah* 'valid') → *mengesahkan* or *mensahkan*.

An object-oriented verb takes the prefix *di-* when the agent is not expressed by a pronoun. The agent often directly follows the verb and is then optionally marked by the preposition *oléh* 'by'. In other positions *oléh* is obligatory: *Ali memukul Zainal kemarin* 'Ali struck Zainal yesterday', *Zainal dipukul (oléh) Ali kemarin* or *Zainal dipukul kemarin oléh Ali* 'Zainal was struck by Ali yesterday'. When the agent is expressed by a pronoun, two constructions are found. With a third person agent the *di-* form of the verb can be suffixed with the clitic pronoun *-nya* 'he, she' or directly followed by the pronoun *meréka* 'they' (in other positions the marker *oléh* must be used: *oléhnya, oléh meréka*): *Zainal dipukulnya kemarin* or *Zainal dipukul kemarin oléhnya* 'he struck Zainal yesterday'. When the agent is first or second person and increasingly in modern usage also when it is third person, the agent pronoun (or a cliticised form thereof, see table 10.5) is placed immediately preceding the zero-form of the verb, i.e. the verb without prefix. In the following examples the agent-oriented sentence is given first: *dia tidak harus membeli buku ini* or *buku ini tidak harus dibelinya* or *buku ini tidak harus dia beli* 'he doesn't have to buy this book', *engkau tidak harus membeli buku ini* or *buku ini tidak harus kaubeli* 'you don't have to buy this book'. The zero-form of a transitive verb is also frequently used in imperative sentences, where it is likewise object-oriented: *Buku ini baik sekali. Beli(lah)!* 'This book's very good. Buy (it)!' (The clitic *-lah* is used with imperatives to soften a command.)

At first glance the distinction between agent-orientation and object-orientation seems comparable to that between active and passive in various Indo-European languages. There are many differences, however. Firstly, as already mentioned, the subject of the sentence is always definite, so that the English sentence 'a dog has bitten Ali's child' would be expressed in Indonesian with an object-oriented construction: *anak Ali digigit anjing*. Secondly, there are numerous grammatical constraints on verb orientation. The relativiser *yang*, for instance, must always be linked to the subject of the verb in the relative clause: *buku yang dibeli Ali mahal sekali* 'the book which Ali bought is very expensive' (*buku yang Ali membeli* is ungrammatical). The same phenomenon is seen in *wh*-questioning and in contrastive focusing, which usually involve relativisation, equationalisation (or clefting) and a predicate–subject word order: *siapa (yang) membeli buku ini?* 'who bought this book?', *apa yang dibeli Ali?* 'what did Ali buy?', *Ali(lah) yang membeli buku ini* 'Ali (not Zainal) was the one who bought this book' or '**Ali** bought this book', *buku ini(lah) yang dibeli Ali* 'this book (not that one) is the one that Ali bought' or 'Ali bought **this** book', *buku(lah) yang dibeli Ali* 'books (not something else) are what Ali bought' or 'Ali bought **books**'. With the subject–predicate order the contrastive element is absent: *yang dibeli Ali (adalah) buku* 'what Ali bought was books'. Finally, choice of verb-orientation can also be governed by stylistic considerations. In written narrative style, for instance, a series of actions is frequently represented by a series of object-oriented constructions with a predicate–subject word order. One example will suffice to bring this chapter to a close: *dia berbaring di tempat tidur, diperbaikinya letak bantalnya, dimatikannya lampu dan dipejamkannya matanya* 'he lay down on the bed, adjusted his pillow, switched off the lamp and closed his eyes'.

Bibliography

Among descriptive grammars of Malay, the following are particularly to be recommended: Lombard (1977), Macdonald and Dardjowidjojo (1967), Alieva et al. (1972) and Kähler (1956). For syntax, reference may be made to Fokker (1951), while Amran Halim (1974) deals with the important question of intonational correlates of syntactic structure. Teeuw (1959) is an important contribution on the history of the language, while Tanner (1967) examines the relations between Bahasa Indonesia and other languages among educated Indonesians. Fuller bibliographical sources are provided by Teeuw (1961) and Uhlenbeck (1971). Adelaar (1985) makes a preliminary reconstruction of the ancestor-language of Standard Malay and five other Malay dialects (or languages very closely related to Malay) and presents information on the history of the language, revealed by the techniques of modern comparative linguistics.

References

Adelaar, K.A. 1985. *Proto-Malayic: the reconstruction of its phonology and parts of its lexicon and morphology*. (Ph.D. thesis, University of Leiden; to appear in the series *Verhandelingen*, Royal Institute of Linguistics and Anthropology (K.I.T.L.V.), Leiden)

Alieva, N.F. et al. 1972. *Grammatika indonezijskogo jazyka* (Nauka, Moscow)

Amran Halim. 1974. *Intonation in Relation to Syntax in Bahasa Indonesia* (Djambatan and Department of Education and Culture, Jakarta)

Fokker, A.A. 1951. *Inleiding tot de studie van de Indonesische syntaxis* (J.B. Wolters, Groningen and Jakarta)

Kähler, H. 1956. *Grammatik der Bahasa Indonesia* (Otto Harrassowitz, Wiesbaden)

Lombard, Denys. 1977. *Introduction à l'indonésien* (S.E.C.M.I., Paris)

Macdonald, R.R. and S. Dardjowidjojo. 1967. *A Student's Reference Grammar of Modern Formal Indonesian* (Georgetown University Press, Washington, DC)

Tanner, N. 1967. 'Speech and Society Among the Indonesian Élite: A Case Study of a Multilingual Community', *Anthropological Linguistics*, vol. 9, no. 3, pp. 15–40.

Teeuw, A. 1959. 'The History of the Malay Language', *Bijdragen tot de Taal-, Land- en Volkenkunde*, vol. 115, no. 2, pp. 138–56.

────── 1961. *A Critical Survey of Studies on Malay and Bahasa Indonesia* (Martinus Nijhoff, The Hague)

Uhlenbeck, E.M. 1971. 'Indonesia and Malaysia', in T.A. Sebeok (ed.) *Current Trends in Linguistics*, vol. 8, *Linguistics in Oceania* (Mouton, The Hague and Paris), pp. 55–111.

11 Tagalog

Paul Schachter

1 Historical Background

Tagalog is a member of the Hesperonesian (West Indonesian) branch of the Austronesian language family. Native to the southern part of the island of Luzon in the Philippines, it has in recent years spread as a second language over virtually the entire Philippine archipelago. Thus, while only about a quarter of the population of the Philippines were Tagalog-speaking in 1940, by 1970 over half were (approximately 20 million out of 35 million), and it has been estimated that by the year 2000 over 98 per cent of all Filipinos will speak Tagalog as either a first or a second language.

The remarkable recent diffusion of Tagalog reflects its selection in 1937 as the Philippine national language. Under the name of Pilipino (or Filipino), Tagalog — with a lexicon enriched by borrowings from other Philippine languages — is now taught in schools throughout the Philippines. The spread of the language has also been favoured by urbanisation — Tagalog is native to the largest city of the Philippines, Manila, and it is used as a lingua franca in many cities with mixed populations — as well as by its prominence in the mass media.

The dialect of Tagalog which is considered standard and which underlies Pilipino is the educated dialect of Manila. Other important regional dialects are those of Bataan, Batangas, Bulacan, Tanay-Paete and Tayabas. The lexicon of educated Manila Tagalog contains many borrowings from Spanish and English, the former reflecting over three centuries of colonial domination of the Philippines by Spain, the latter reflecting the period of American hegemony (1898–1946), as well as the current status of English as both the language of higher education in the Philippines and a lingua franca second in importance only to Pilipino itself. Spanish and English have also had some impact on the phonology of Tagalog (see section 2, below), but little if any on the syntax and morphology. (See section 4, however, for some instances of borrowed Spanish gender distinctions.)

2 Phonology and Orthography

Tagalog phonology has been significantly affected by the incorporation into the language of many loanwords from Spanish, English and other languages. One effect of this incorporation has been an expansion of the phonemic inventory of the language, an expansion that has influenced both the vowel and the consonant systems.

Contemporary Tagalog has the five vowel phonemes shown in table 11.1.

Table 11.1: Tagalog Vowel Phonemes

	Front	Central	Back
High	i		u
Mid		e	o
Low		a	

This five-vowel system no doubt developed out of a three-vowel system in which [i] and [e] were allophones of a single phoneme and [u] and [o] were allophones of another. Contrasts between /i/ and /e/ and between /u/ and /o/ are, however, well established in contemporary Tagalog, not only in borrowed vocabulary (*misa* /mi:sah/ 'mass' vs. *mesa* /me:sah/ 'table', *bus* /bu:s/ 'bus' vs. *bos* /bo:s/ 'boss') but, albeit less commonly, in native vocabulary as well (*iwan* /ʔi:wan/ 'leave' vs. *aywan* /ʔe:wan/ 'not known', *babuy* /ba:buy/ 'pig-like person' vs. *baboy* /ba:boy/ 'pig'). Vowel length in non-word-final syllables is phonemic, as the following examples illustrate: *aso* /ʔa:soh/ 'dog', *aso* /ʔasoh/ 'smoke', *maglalakbay* /magla:lakbay/ 'will travel', *maglalakbay* /maglalakbay/ 'travel a lot'. In word-final syllables of native words, vowel length is not phonemic: the general rule is that *phrase*-final syllables are long, non-phrase-final syllables short. Thus *sibat* /sibat/ 'spear' is pronounced [siba:t] phrase-finally, but not in *sibat ba?* /sibat bah/ [sibat ba:h] 'is it a spear?'. Word-final syllables of *non*-native words may, however, show phonemic length. For example, borrowed monosyllabic names have a long vowel in any context: e.g. *si Bob ba?* /si ba:b ba/ [si ba:b ba:h] 'is it Bob?'.

There are sixteen consonant phonemes that occur in native words. These are displayed in table 11.2. Probably [d] and [r] were once allophones of a single phoneme, as is evidenced by a good deal of free or morphophonemically-conditioned alternation between them (e.g. *daw* /daw/ ~ *raw* /raw/ 'they say', *dalita* /da:litaʔ/ 'poverty' vs. *maralita* /mara:litaʔ/ 'poor'). There is no doubt, however, that they now contrast, not only in loanwords (*dos* /do:s/ 'two' vs. *Rose* /ro:s/ 'Rose') but in native words as well (*maramdamin* /maramda:min/ 'sensitive' vs. *madamdamin* /madamda:min/ 'moving').

In addition to the consonant phonemes shown in table 11.2, there are two others, the labio-dental fricative /f/ and the alveolar affricate /tʃ/, that occur

Table 11.2: Tagalog Consonant Phonemes

	Labial	Dental	Alveolar	Palatal	Velar	Glottal
Voiceless stop	p	t			k	ʔ
Voiced stop	b	d			g	
Nasal	m	n			ŋ	
Fricative			s			h
Lateral			l			
Tap or trill			r			
Glide				y	w	

in loanwords only: e.g. *Flora* /flo:rah/ 'Flora', *chief* /tʃi:f/ 'chief', *kotse* /ko:tʃeh/ 'car'.

In native words tautosyllabic consonant clusters are restricted to syllable-initial clusters in which the second consonant is a glide: e.g. *diyan* /dyan/ 'there', *buwan* /bwan/ 'month'. In loanwords syllable-initial clusters whose second consonant is /l/ or /r/ are also common: e.g. *plato* /pla:toh/ 'plate', *grado* /gra:doh/ 'grade'; and various syllable-final clusters are found in borrowings from English: e.g. *homework* /ho:mwo:rk/, *dimples* /di:mpols/, *bridge* /bri:ds/.

The most common syllable patterns are CVC, in both final and non-final syllables, and CV(:), in non-final syllables only. When two CVC syllables abut within a word, a very wide range of medial CC clusters is attested. Word-internal geminate clusters do not, however, occur.

Stress is closely tied to vowel length. Syllables with phonemically long vowels are always stressed. Syllables with vowels that are not phonemically long but that are phonetically long as a result of their occurrence in phrase-final position are also stressed if there are no phonemically long vowels in the phrase-final word. Thus the final syllable of *magaling* /magaliŋ/ [magali:ŋ] 'excellent' is stressed in citation, but in *magaling na* /magaliŋ nah/ [magaliŋ na:h] 'it's excellent now', the stress falls on *na* instead. Unstressed vowels are not reduced and the language is syllable-timed rather than stress-timed.

Significant morphophonemic alternations across word boundaries include the deletion of word-final /h/ in non-phrase-final position (*maganda* /magandah/ 'beautiful', *maganda pa* /maganda pah/ 'it's still beautiful', *maganda pa ba?* /maganda pa bah/ 'is it still beautiful?') and the replacement of word-final /ʔ/ by vowel length under the same circumstances (*maputi* /maputiʔ/ 'white', *maputi nga* /maputi: ŋaʔ/ 'it's really white', *maputi nga po* /maputi: ŋa: poʔ/ 'it's really white, sir/madam'. Significant morphophonemic alternations *within* the word include a 'rightward' shift of vowel length — and hence of stress — before the verbal suffixes *-an* and *-in* (*tasa* /ta:sah/ 'assessment' + *-an* → *tasahan* /tasa:han/ 'assess', *pala* /pa:lah/ 'shovel' + *-in* → *palahin* /pala:hin/ '(to) shovel') and a set of assimilations involving prefixes that end in nasals, such as the verbal prefix /maN/ (where /N/ represents an unspecified nasal consonant): e.g. /maN/ + /p/ → /mam/,

/maN/ + /t/ → /man/, /maN/ + /k/ → /maŋ/, as in *mamili* (/maN/ + /pi:li?/ → /mami:li?/) 'choose', *manakot* (/maN/ + /ta:kot/ → /mana:kot/) 'frighten', *mangailangan* (/maN/ + ka?ilaŋan/ → /maŋa?ilaŋan/) 'need'.

Tagalog is not a tone language. It does, however, have a complex intonational system. As in English, intonation may be used to distinguish pragmatically different sentence types (e.g. requests for information vs. requests for repetition), to express speaker attitudes (e.g. cordiality), to indicate contrast or emphasis etc.

Prior to the Spanish colonisation of the Philippines, a syllabary, probably of Indian origin, had been used for writing Tagalog, but under the Spanish this was supplanted by a version of the Roman alphabet. Nowadays Tagalog uses the same 26 letters that are used for writing English, although the seven letters *c, f, j, q, v, x* and *z* are used chiefly in proper names of foreign origin and in certain other borrowings from English or Spanish. These seven letters are not included in the conventional Tagalog alphabet, or *abakada*, which consists of 20 letters (including the digraph *ng*, used for /ŋ/), in the following order: *a b k d e g h i l m n ng o p r s t u w y*. The writing system does not indicate vowel length (or stress), marks /h/ only syllable-initially and does not mark /?/ at all. Thus words that differ from one another only in vowel length (see examples above) or only in that one ends in /h/ and the other in /?/ (e.g. *bata* /ba:tah/ 'bathrobe' and *bata* /ba:ta?/ 'child') are spelled identically. There is also some inconsistency — as well as some debate — with regard to the spelling of loanwords: e.g. *molecule* vs. *molikyul*. And there are two very common words, the case particle /naŋ/ and the plural particle /maŋah/, whose conventional spellings, respectively *ng* and *mga*, are non-phonemic. With these and a few other exceptions, however, there is a fairly good match between spelling and pronunciation.

3 Syntax

Tagalog is a predicate-initial language. That is, in the most common and basic type of clause, words or phrases that express predicates precede words or phrases that express arguments. Predicates belong to one of two classes: verbal and non-verbal. The structures of basic clauses containing these two types of predicates are discussed in turn below.

Clauses with verbal predicates consist of a verb followed by one or more argument expressions (noun phrases, pronouns etc.). These argument expressions do not in general occur in a fixed order and word order is not used in distinguishing the roles that are assigned to the various arguments, e.g. in distinguishing an actor argument (see below) from a patient argument. Instead these roles are indicated by the form of the verb and/or the form of the argument expressions themselves.

The verb always contains an affix — which may be a prefix, an infix or a suffix — that indicates the semantic role of one particular argument expression. This expression has been variously referred to in descriptions of Tagalog as the subject, the topic or the focus, but all of these terms are misleading in one way or another and it seems better to refer to this argument expression as the *trigger*, a term that reflects the fact that the semantic role of the argument in question triggers the choice of the verbal affix. If, for example, the trigger designates the actor (the participant whose role is presented as central: the agent of an action predicate, the experiencer of an experiential predicate etc.), one affix is used; if the trigger designates the patient, another affix is used. The trigger itself has the same form, whatever the semantic role of its referent: for example, it is preceded by the particle *ang* if it is expressed by a common noun and by the particle *si* if it is expressed by a personal name. The semantic roles of any *other* argument expressions in the clause, however, are indicated by the forms of these expressions themselves: for example, a non-trigger argument that expresses the actor is preceded by the particle *ng* if it is expressed by a common noun, by the particle *ni* if it is expressed by a personal name.

On the basis of what has been said thus far, it might appear that variations in the choice of the trigger could reasonably be described in terms of the familiar grammatical category of *voice*, with actor-trigger clauses being identified as active, patient-trigger clauses as passive and the trigger being identified as the (active or passive) subject. There are, however, important differences between the Tagalog trigger system and familiar voice systems. In the first place, the arguments that can be chosen as trigger show a much wider range of semantic roles than the arguments that can be chosen as subject in typical voice systems and consequently there are many more distinct verb forms than a voice system's typical two. In addition to actor and patient, the trigger argument in a Tagalog clause may have the semantic role of direction (goal or source), beneficiary, instrument, location or reason, among others and each of these choices determines a different choice of verbal affix. Secondly, in voice systems the active can generally be regarded as the unmarked voice by virtue of its frequency, unrestricted distribution and the like. But Tagalog actor-trigger clauses are not unmarked in relation to their non-actor-trigger counterparts. Indeed, the latter turn out to be generally more frequent in texts and to have fewer distributional restrictions. For these reasons, it seems best not to describe the Tagalog trigger system as a voice system.

The following examples illustrate part of the trigger system. In each case the verbal affix that indicates the semantic role of the trigger and the trigger itself are italicised. (All of the verbs in these examples contain a reduplicating aspectual affix — the first *a* of *aalis* — and the actor-, beneficiary- and instrument-trigger verbs also contain certain other affixes whose functions will be explained in section 4.)

As the English translations show, the trigger is normally interpreted as definite, a non-trigger patient as indefinite and other non-trigger arguments

Mag-aalis		*ang tindero*		ng bigas	sa	sako	para sa babae.
AT-cont.-take:out		tg. storekeeper		pat. rice	drc.	sack	ben. woman

'The storekeeper will take some rice out of a/the sack for a/the woman.'

Aalis*in* ng tindero *ang bigas* sa sako para sa babae.
cont.-take:out-PT acr. storekeeper tg. rice drc. sack ben. woman
'A/the storekeeper will take the rice out of a/the sack for a/the woman.'

Aalis*an* ng tindero ng bigas *ang sako* para sa babae.
cont.-take:out-DT acr. storekeeper pat. rice tg. sack ben. woman
'A/the storekeeper will take some rice out of the sack for a/the woman.'

*I*pag-aalis ng tindero ng bigas sa sako *ang babae*.
BT-cont.-take:out acr. storekeeper pat. rice drc. sack tg. woman
'A/the storekeeper will take some rice out of a/the sack for the woman.'

*I*pangaalis ng tindero ng bigas sa sako *ang sandok*.
IT-cont.-take:out acr. storekeeper pat. rice drc. sack tg. scoop
'A/the storekeeper will take some rice out of a/the sack with the scoop.'

as either definite or indefinite. Note also that some of the particles have more than one function. Thus *ng* occurs in these examples as both a patient marker and an actor marker, while *sa* occurs as both a direction marker and as part of the beneficiary marker *para sa*.

As noted previously, the order of post-verbal arguments is generally free. Thus in addition to the orderings shown above, any other ordering of the arguments in the examples would also be grammatical (although some would be unusual). There is, however, a general preference for the actor as the first argument in a non-actor-trigger clause and for either the (actor) trigger or the patient as the first argument in an actor-trigger clause.

There is also one set of argument expressions whose order in relation to other argument expressions and to one another is not free. These are the actor and trigger personal pronouns, which are *enclitics*: i.e. they occur in a fixed position immediately after the clause-initial constituent. If there are two enclitic pronouns in the same clause, they observe the rule that monosyllabic pronouns precede disyllabic pronouns. Thus in the following sentence the order of all the words is fixed:

Nakita mo siya kahapon.
PT-perf.-see you-acr. he-tg. yesterday
'You saw him yesterday.'

This contrasts with the variable ordering observable in the following sentences, which show that argument expressions are freely ordered in relation not only to one another but also to adverbs such as *kahapon* 'yesterday':

{ Nakita ni Juan si Maria kahapon.
PT-perf.-see acr. Juan tg. Maria yesterday
Nakita ni Juan kahapon si Maria.
Nakita si Maria ni Juan kahapon.
Nakita si Maria kahapon ni Juan.
Nakita kahapon ni Juan si Maria.
Nakita kahapon si Maria ni Juan. }
'Juan saw Maria yesterday.'

In addition to enclitic pronouns, Tagalog also has a set of enclitic *particles* that occur in a fixed position in relation to other sentence elements. Note, for example, the position of the interrogative particle *ba* in the following sentence:

Nakita mo ba siya kahapon?
PT-perf.-see you: acr. Q he:tg. yesterday
'Did you see him yesterday?'

Clauses with non-verbal predicates are in many cases translated into English by sentences with the main verb *be*, which has no Tagalog counterpart. These clauses consist of a predicate expression followed by a trigger expression. The predicate expression may be a noun (phrase), an adjective (phrase) or a prepositional phrase. Some examples are:

Abogado ang bunso.
lawyer tg. youngest:child
'The youngest child is a lawyer.'

Hinog ang mga mangga.
ripe tg. pl. mango
'The mangoes are ripe.'

Nasa kusina si Nene.
in kitchen tg. Nene
'Nene is in the kitchen.'

A construction consisting of a non-verbal predicate and a trigger is also used to express possession, as in:

May trak si Ben.
ex. truck tg. Ben
'Ben has a truck.'

The same type of non-verbal predicate is also used to express existence. In this case, however, the predicate is not followed by a trigger, but is instead often followed by an adverbial: e.g.

is linked to it by a *ligature*. The ligature has two morphophonemically conditioned alternants: if the citation form of the preceding word ends in /h/, /ʔ/ or /n/, the ligature takes the form of an /ŋ/ (*ng*) replacing the final consonant; in all other cases, the ligature takes the form /na/ (*na*). (Ligatures also occur in certain other constructions, such as constructions involving auxiliary verbs like *dapat* 'must'.) For example, when the demonstrative *ito* /itoh/ 'this' precedes the ligature, the /ŋ/ form occurs and when the noun *galang* /galaŋ/ 'bracelet' precedes, the /na/ form occurs: thus *itong galang* /itoŋ galaŋ/, *galang na ito* /galaŋ na itoh/ 'this bracelet'. Similarly, the noun *bata* /ba:taʔ/ 'child' and the adjective *gutom* /gutom/ 'hungry' respectively require the /ŋ/ and /na/ forms of the ligature in *batang gutom* /ba:taŋ gutom/ 'hungry child' and *gutom na bata* /gutom na ba:taʔ/.

Although a demonstrative and the noun it modifies may occur in either order, the alternative orderings are generally not in free variation, but are, rather, conditioned by discourse factors. The constituent that comes second typically represents the more salient information and may, for example, be contrastive. Thus:

Mahal   itong   galang.   (Pero mura   itong   singsing.)
expensive this-lig.   bracelet   but   cheap   this-lig.   ring
'This bracelet is expensive. (But this ring is cheap.)'

Mahal   ang   galang   na ito.   (Pero mura   ang   galang   na iyan.)
expensive tg.   bracelet lig. this but   cheap tg.   bracelet lig. that
'This bracelet is expensive. (But that bracelet is cheap.)'

(As the first example illustrates, when a trigger expression begins with a demonstrative, no trigger particle is used.) The alternative orderings of *adjectives* and the nouns they modify, on the other hand, often do appear to be a matter of free variation.

Possessive pronouns, as noted, may also either precede or follow the noun, but in this case a difference in form is associated with the difference in order. When the possessive pronoun precedes, it takes a form that may be called the *sa* form and it is obligatorily linked to the following noun by a ligature. (The *sa* form is so called because it also occurs after the particle *sa*.) When the possessive pronoun follows, it takes a form that may be called the *ng* form, and there is no ligature. (The *ng* form occurs in essentially the same contexts as common-noun phrases introduced by the particle *ng*.) For example, 'my house' may be expressed as either *aking bahay* (the *sa* form first person singular pronoun *akin* + ligature + *bahay* 'house') or *bahay ko* (*bahay* + the *ng* form first person singular pronoun *ko*). The orderings are both very common and there is no obvious difference in usage between them.

Yes-no questions in Tagalog are characterised by rising intonation, as opposed to the characteristic falling intonation of statements. A yes-no

> May trak doon.
> ex. truck there
> 'There's a truck over there.'

Although Tagalog is basically predicate-initial, there are certain fairly common constructions in which some other constituent precedes the predicate. In one such construction, the clause-initial constituent — which may be the trigger, an adverbial or one of certain types of non-trigger arguments — is immediately followed by the particle *ay*. Some examples are:

> Ang sulat ay tinanggap ko kahapon.
> tg. letter inv. PT-perf.-receive I:acr. yesterday
> 'I received the letter yesterday.'

> Doon ay ipinagbili niya ang kalabaw.
> there inv. PT-perf.-sell he:acr. tg. carabao
> 'There he sold the carabao.'

> Saanman ay makakaabot ang koreyo.
> to-any:place inv. AT-cont.-can-reach tg. mail
> 'The mail can reach any place.'

Ay constructions are more common in writing and in formal speech than they are in ordinary conversation. It has been suggested that in narratives the referent of the constituent preceding *ay* is often one that has been referred to at some earlier point and that *ay* is typically used to reintroduce such a referent.

In other types of non-predicate-initial constructions, the pre-predicate constituent may have a special discourse function, such as contrast or emphasis. Some examples are:

> Bukas, magpapahinga ako. Ngayon, dapat akong magtrabaho.
> tomorrow AT-cont.-rest I:tg. today must I:tg.-lig. AT-work
> 'Tomorrow, I'll rest. Today, I've got to work.'

> Bukas aalis si Pedro
> tomorrow AT-cont.-leave tg. Pedro
> 'It's tomorrow that Pedro is leaving.'

Just as the ordering of clause constituents shows considerable variability, so does the ordering of constituents of noun phrases. Although certain modifiers, such as numbers and other quantifiers, regularly precede the head noun and others, such as possessive noun phrases, regularly follow it, there are also several types of modifiers that may either precede or follow the head noun: e.g. demonstratives, adjectives and possessive pronouns.

A demonstrative or an adjective, whether it precedes or follows the noun, question may be distinguished from the corresponding statement by intonation alone or it may, in addition, be marked by the enclitic interrogative particle *ba*. This particle also occurs optionally in question-word questions. The latter, however, have their own distinctive intonation patterns, which differ from those of both yes-no questions and statements. (The most common intonation patterns for both question-word questions and statements are falling patterns, but the patterns differ in detail: the question-word questions start with high pitch and fall steadily throughout; the statements start with mid pitch, rise to high pitch on the last stressed syllable and then fall.)

The questioned constituent normally comes first in a question-word question. If this constituent is an adverbial or a non-trigger argument, any enclitic pronouns and/or particles contained in the clause attach to it and hence precede the predicate, e.g.

> Kailan mo (ba) siya nakita?
> when you-acr. Q he:tg. PT-perf.-see
> 'When did you see him?'

> Sa aling parti ka (ba) pumunta?
> drc. which-lig. party you:tg. Q AT-perf.-go
> 'Which party did you go to?'

(Role-marking particles and prepositions in general are never 'stranded' in Tagalog. Thus in the last example, *sa* must precede the question word and cannot be left in post-predicate position as *to* is in the English translation.)

If the questioned constituent is a trigger argument, the rest of the clause must be put into the form of a headless relative clause (see below) and preceded by the trigger particle *ang*. Under these circumstances, the enclitic particle *ba* still follows the questioned constituent, but any enclitic actor pronoun follows the predicate. Some examples are:

> Ano (ba) ang ginawa mo kahapon?
> what Q tg. PT-perf.-do you-acr. yesterday
> 'What did you do yesterday?'

> Sino (ba) ang gumawa ng sapatos na iyon?
> who Q tg. AT-perf.-make pat. shoe(s) lig. that
> 'Who made those shoes?'

Imperative sentences of the most common type have a falling intonation pattern like that of question-word questions. Syntactically they are just like statements with verbal predicates and second-person actors (which may but need not be triggers), except that the verb is in the infinitive form, rather than one of the finite forms that are found in statements. Some examples are:

Mag-alis   ka   ng   bigas sa   sako.
AT-take:out you:tg. pat.   rice   drc. sack
'Take some rice out of a/the sack.'

Basahin   mo   nga   ang   librong   ito.
read-PT   you:acr. please tg.   book-lig. this
'Please read this book.'

(*Nga* 'please' in the last example is an enclitic particle.)

Hortative sentences are identical to imperatives, except that the actor is a first person plural inclusive pronoun (see section 4). For example:

Mag-alis   tayo   ng   bigas sa   sako.
AT-take:out we:incl:tg. pat. rice   drc. sack
'Let's take some rice out of a/the sack.'

Basahin nga   natin   ang   librong   ito.
read-PT please we:incl.:acr.   tg.   book-lig. this
'Please let's read this book.'

Tagalog has distinct ways of negating imperative/hortative clauses, existential/possessive clauses and clauses of other types. Imperatives and hortatives are negated with a clause-initial *huwag*, which is immediately followed by any enclitic pronouns and particles, then by a ligature and then by the verb. Examples are:

Huwag kang   mag-alis   ng   bigas sa   sako.
neg.   you:tg.:lig.   AT-take:out pat. rice   drc. sack
'Don't take any rice out of a/the sack.'

Huwag nga   nating   basahin ang librong   ito.
neg.   please we:incl.:lig.   read-PT tg. book-lig. this
'Please, let's not read this book.'

Existential and possessive clauses are negated with a clause-initial *wala*. *Wala* replaces the affirmative existential/possessive particle *may(roon)*, and is followed by a ligature. Any enclitics in the clause come between *wala* and the ligature. Examples are:

Wala   akong   pera.
neg.   I:tg.-lig. money
'I don't have any money.'

Walang   bahay doon.
neg.-lig. house there
'There isn't a house there.'

Clauses of other types are negated with a clause-initial *hindi*. Again, any enclitics immediately follow the negative particle. *Hindi* is not, however, followed by a ligature.

    Hindi   ko   nakita   si   Rosa.
    neg.   I:acr.   PT-perf.-see   tg.   Rosa
    'I didn't see Rosa.'

    Hindi   mayaman   si   Rosa.
    neg.   rich   tg.   Rosa
    'Rosa isn't rich.'

As suggested previously, it does not seem to be appropriate to identify the Tagalog grammatical category trigger with the traditional grammatical category subject. One reason is that there are certain subject-like properties that are associated not with the trigger but, rather, with the actor. For example, as we have already seen, the actor, whether or not it also happens to be the trigger, always represents the addressee of an imperative sentence. It is also the actor that controls the reference of a reflexive (expressed by a possessive pronoun and the nominal *sarili* 'self'), as illustrated by the following sentences:

    Mag-aalaala   ang   lolo   sa   kaniyang   sarili.
    AT-cont.-worry:about   tg.   grandfather   drc.   he-L   self
    'Grandfather will worry about himself.'

    Aalalahanin   ng   lolo   ang   kaniyang   sarili.
    cont.-worry:about-DT   acr.   grandfather   tg.   he-L   self
    'Grandfather will worry about himself.'

Since the first of these sentences has an actor-trigger verb, the actor, which is the reflexive controller, happens to be the trigger as well. The second sentence, however, has a direction-trigger verb and here we can see clearly that the reflexive controller is the actor and *not* the trigger, since in this case it is the trigger itself that is reflexivised.

On the other hand, there *are* certain subject-like properties that are associated with the trigger. One such property is relativisability. Only trigger arguments (and certain constituents of trigger arguments) may be relativised in Tagalog. Thus if one wishes to relativise an actor, an actor-trigger clause must be used; if one wishes to relativise a patient, a patient-trigger clause must be used; etc. The following examples illustrate this. (As the examples show, relativisation in Tagalog involves the deletion of the relativised argument — the trigger — from the relative clause. The head of the relative clause and the clause itself may occur in either order, but head-first is the more common ordering. A ligature occurs between the head and the relative clause.)

Iyon ang babaeng magluluto ng isda.
that tg. woman-lig. AT-cont.-cook pat. fish
'That's the woman who will cook some fish.'

Iyon ang isdang iluluto ng babae.
that tg. fish-lig. PT-cont.-cook acr. woman
'That's the fish that a/the woman will cook.'

In the first sentence the actor is relativised, so the verb in the relative clause must be actor-trigger; in the second sentence the patient is relativised, so the verb in the relative clause must be patient-trigger. Similarly, if a directional argument is relativised, the verb in the relative clause must be direction-trigger, and if a beneficiary is relativised, the verb in the relative clause must be beneficiary-trigger, as in:

Iyon ang sakong aalisan ko ng bigas.
that tg. sack-lig. cont.-take:out-DT I:acr. pat. rice
'That's the sack that I'll take some rice out of.'

Iyon ang batang ipagluluto ko ng pagkain.
that tg. child-lig. BT-cont.-cook I:acr. pat. food
'That's the child I'll cook some food for.'

(If one attempts to relativise a *non*-trigger argument, the result is ungrammatical: e.g.:

*Iyon ang babaeng iluluto ang isda.
that tg. woman-lig. PT-cont.-cook tg. fish)

Although verbs, adjectives and nouns are clearly distinguished from one another on a *morphological* basis in Tagalog (see section 4), distributionally or syntactically they are all rather similar. We have already seen that all three can serve as predicates. In addition, all three can serve as (heads of) arguments or as modifiers. A verbal or adjectival argument may be analysed as a headless relative clause. For example, compare the following with the last grammatical example cited:

Iyon ang ipagluluto ko ng pagkain.
that tg. BT-cont.-cook I:acr. pat. food
'That's the one I'll cook some food for.'

Here the phrase headed by the verb *ipagluluto*, which has the form of a relative clause, is functioning as the trigger argument of the sentence. Some relevant examples involving adjectives are:

Sino ang batang pinakamatalino sa klase?
who tg. child-lig. most-smart in class
'Who is the smartest child in the class?'

Sino ang pinakamatalino sa klase?
who tg. most-smart in class
'Who is the smartest one in the class?'

We have already seen both adjectives and verbs (in relative clauses) serving as modifiers, in highly similar constructions involving a ligature between the head and the modifier. Nouns too occur as modifiers in this type of construction: e.g. *gulay na repolyo* 'vegetable dish made from cabbage' (cf. *gulay* 'vegetable (dish)', *repolyo* 'cabbage'), *laruang kalan* 'toy stove' (cf. *laruan* 'toy', *kalan* 'stove'). Thus the syntactic similarities among nouns, verbs and adjectives in Tagalog are quite striking, although, as we shall see, there are clear morphological grounds for distinguishing them.

4 Morphology

Tagalog verb morphology is quite complex. The verb stem may be polymorphemic and there are obligatory trigger-marking and aspectual affixes — which may be prefixes, suffixes or infixes — as well as affixes with a wide range of other functions. The following selective summary of Tagalog verb morphology treats, in order: stem formation, trigger affixation, other non-aspectual affixation and aspectual affixation.

Many Tagalog verb stems consist of a single morpheme: e.g. *abot* (cf. *umabot* 'reach for', which consists of the actor-trigger affix *-um-* plus *abot*), *iyak* (cf. *umiyak* 'cry'), *uwi* (cf. *umuwi* 'go home'). However, there are also a great many verb stems that are analysable as consisting of two or more morphemes. Of these, the most common are those involving the stem-forming prefixes *pag-* and *paN-*.

Pag- combines very productively with nouns to form verb stems that denote characteristic activities involving the referents of the nouns. For example, *pagbus* is the stem of the actor-trigger verb *magbus* 'ride a bus', *pag-Ingles* (cf. *Ingles* 'English') is the stem of *mag-Ingles* 'speak English', *pagtsinelas* (cf. *tsinelas* 'slippers') is the stem of *magtsinelas* 'wear slippers', and *pag-ingat* (cf. *ingat* 'care') is the stem of AT *mag-ingat*/DT *pag-ingatan* 'be careful of'. (In actor-trigger verbs, the initial /p/ of *pag-* and *paN-* is assimilated to the actor-trigger prefix *m-*. For some purposes — see below — it is convenient to refer to the resultant forms, *mag-* and *maN-*, as if they were single affixes rather than composites.)

In addition, *pag-* combines with certain simple verb stems to form the stems of 'intensive' verbs: i.e. verbs that designate intense, frequent or prolonged performance of the activity designated by the simple stem. For example, *pag-* combines with *kain* 'eat' to form the stem of *magkain* 'eat (repeatedly etc.)' and with *lakad* 'walk' to form the stem of *maglakad* 'walk (repeatedly etc.)'. *Pag-* also forms verb stems with adjectives, which may themselves be morphologically complex — e.g. *pagmabait* (cf. *mabait* 'kind', *bait* 'kindness'), which is the stem of AT *magmabait*/DT *pagmabaitan* 'pretend to be kind to' — and even with certain phrases — e.g. *pagmagandang-gabi* (cf. *magandang gabi* 'good evening (the greeting)'), which is the stem of *magmagandang-gabi* 'wish good evening'.

Like *pag-*, but less productively, *paN-* combines with nouns to form stems that denote characteristic activities involving the referents of the nouns. For example, *pamangka* (cf. *bangka* 'boat' — see section 2 for the assimilation of certain morpheme-initial consonants to prefixal /N/) is the stem of the actor-trigger verb *mamangka* 'go boating', and *panganak* (cf. *anak* 'child, offspring') is the stem of AT *manganak*/PT *ipanganak* 'give birth to'. *PaN-* also combines with certain nouns and simple verb stems to form stems that denote destructive or harmful activity and with certain other simple verb stems to form stems that denote activity directed toward multiple objects. For example, *paN-* combines with *walis* 'broom' to form the stem of *mangwalis* 'hit with a broom' and with *kain* 'eat' to form the stem of *mangain* 'devour'; it also combines with *kuha* 'get' to form the stem of *manguha* 'gather' and with *tahi* 'sew' to form the stem of *manahi* 'sew (a number of things, or professionally)'.

There is also a *paN-* stem-forming prefix — distinguishable from the one just discussed on the basis of a different pattern of morphophonemic alternations — that forms the stem of instrument-trigger verbs. This type of stem may occur independently as a noun with instrumental meaning. Examples are *pam(p)unas* 'something to wipe with' (cf. *punas* 'sponge bath'), which is the stem of the instrument-trigger verb *ipam(p)unas* 'wipe with', and *pan(s)ulat* 'something to write with' (cf. *sulat* 'letter'), which is the stem of the instrument-trigger verb *ipan(s)ulat* 'write with'.

Among the other stem-forming affixes that deserve mention are two different reduplicating prefixes, one monosyllabic, the other disyllabic. The monosyllabic reduplicating prefix is in general a copy of the first consonant and vowel of the following simple verb stem (but see the discussion of aspectual reduplication below). In one of its uses it combines with *pag-* to form certain additional intensive verbs: e.g., *pagtatapak* the stem of DT *pagtatapakan* 'step on (repeatedly etc.)' (cf. DT *tapakan* 'step on') and *pagbabagsak*, the stem of PT *ipagbabagsak* 'drop (repeatedly etc.)' (cf. PT *ibagsak* 'drop').

The disyllabic reduplicating prefix generally consists of a copy of the first two (usually the only two) syllables of the following simple stem. One use of the disyllabic reduplicating prefix is to form the stem of 'moderative' verbs, i.e. verbs that designate activities performed in moderation, occasionally, at random etc. Some examples are *hiya-hiya*, the stem of AT *mahiya-hiya* 'be a little ashamed' (cf. AT *mahiya* 'be ashamed') and *linis-linis*, the stem of PT *linis-linisin* 'clean a little' (cf. PT *linisin* 'clean').

As indicated above, trigger affixes mark the semantic role of the trigger phrase. Among the roles that may be affixally marked are: actor, patient, direction, beneficiary and instrument. (Others, which will not be discussed here, include location, reason and referent ('about' object).) That affixes that most commonly mark these roles are shown in table 11.3.

Table 11.3: Trigger-marking Affixes

AT:	-um-, m-, ma-, maka-
PT:	-in, i-, -an, ma-
DT:	-an, -in
BT, IT:	i-

The forms of the affixes given in the table are those that occur in infinitives. Some trigger affixes assume different forms in certain finite (i.e. aspect-marked) verbs. These forms will be presented later, in connection with the discussion of aspectual affixation.

As table 11.3 shows, there are several different actor-, patient- and direction-trigger affixes. The choice among these affixes is lexically determined and to some extent idiosyncratic, although there are certain generalisations that can be made.

The actor-trigger affixes, all of which involve the phoneme /m/, are the infix *-um-* and the prefixes *m-*, *ma-* and *maka-*. *-um-* is infixed between the first consonant and first vowel of the stem: e.g. *humingi* 'borrow' (stem: *hingi*), *sumulat* 'write' (stem: *sulat*), *tumakbo* 'run' (stem: *takbo*). (In the written form of verbs whose stem-initial consonant is /ʔ/, *-um-* appears as a prefix, since /ʔ/ is not represented in the standard orthography: e.g. *umabot* /ʔumabot/ 'reach for' (stem: *abot* /ʔabot/).) *-um-* is the most common affix in actor-trigger verbs with single-morpheme stems and its occurrence in certain subclasses of actor-trigger verbs is predictable, e.g. in verbs of 'becoming' where the stem also occurs as the stem of a *ma-* adjective — cf. *gumanda* 'become beautiful' – *maganda* 'beautiful', *tumaas* 'become tall' – *mataas* 'tall'.

The prefix *m-* replaces the initial *p-* of the stem-forming prefixes *pag-* and *paN-*, resulting in the forms *mag-* and *maN-* respectively, as in *magbigay* 'give', *magluto* 'cook', *mangisda* 'fish' (cf. *isda* 'fish (noun)'), *mangailangan* 'need' (cf. *kailangan* 'need (noun)'). As indicated above, *mag-* occurs productively in verbs that express a characteristic activity involving the referent of the noun that underlies them (e.g. *mag-Ingles* 'speak English'). There are also certain regular correspondences between *-um-* and *mag-* verbs formed with the same stem, e.g. cases in which the *-um-* verb takes two arguments and the *mag-* verb three, such as: *pumasok* 'come/go into' and *magpasok* 'bring/take into', *lumabas* 'come/go outside' and *maglabas* 'bring/take outside'. *MaN-* too has certain characteristic uses — e.g. in verbs indicating destructive activity, such as *mangwalis* 'hit with a broom' (cf. *magwalis* 'sweep') — but it is considerably less common than *mag-*.

AT *ma-* (there is also a PT *ma-*) occurs productively in verbs of 'becoming' whose stems are unaffixed adjectives — e.g. *mabingi* 'become deaf ' (cf. *bingi* 'deaf '), *mamahal* 'become expensive' (cf. *mahal* 'expensive') — and idiosyncratically in a relatively small number of other common verbs: e.g. *matulog* 'sleep', *matuto* 'learn'. *Maka-* occurs idiosyncratically in a few common verbs: e.g., *makakita* 'see', *makarinig* 'hear'. (*Maka-* also occurs productively in ability verbs — see below.)

The most common patient-trigger affixes are *-in* and *i-*. *-in* is the most frequent patient-trigger counterpart of AT *-um-* in corresponding patient- and actor-trigger verbs formed with the same stem (e.g. AT *humuli*/PT *hulihin* 'catch') and *i-* is the most frequent patient-trigger counterpart of AT *m-* (though there are also a good many AT *m-*/PT *-in* correspondences, including some cases where *-in* and *i-* are apparently in free variation, e.g. AT *magluto*/PT *iluto* ~ *lutuin* 'cook'). The stem-forming prefix *pag-* that occurs in AT *m-* verbs is often obligatorily absent — less often optionally absent — from the corresponding patient-trigger verbs. (This is also true of direction-trigger verbs formed with *-in*, and of both patient- and direction-trigger verbs formed with *-an* — see below.) For example, the patient-trigger counterpart of AT *magbigay* 'give' is *ibigay* and the patient-trigger counterpart of AT *magkaila* 'deny' is either *ikaila* or *ipagkaila*. (On the other hand, the patient-trigger counterpart of AT *magbili* 'sell' is *ipagbili*, in which *pag-* is obligatorily retained.) Much less commonly, a stem-forming prefix *paN-* that occurs in an actor-trigger verb is omitted from the patient-trigger counterpart, e.g. the patient-trigger counterpart of AT *mangailangan* 'need' is *kailanganin*.

The suffix *-an*, which is the most common direction-trigger affix, occurs less frequently as a patient-trigger affix, often in verbs that express actions involving surface contact with, or surface effect on, the patient: e.g. *labhan* 'launder', *pintahan* 'paint', *walisan* 'sweep', *hawakan* 'hold'. *Ma-* is the patient-trigger counterpart of AT *maka-* and occurs idiosyncratically in a few verbs: e.g. *makita* 'see', *marinig* 'hear'.

Some examples of DT *-an* are: *puntahan* 'go to', *up(u)an* 'sit on', *masdan* 'look at', *bilhan* 'buy from', *pagbilhan* 'sell to'. The suffix *-in* occurs idiosyncratically as direction-trigger affix in a few verbs — e.g. *pupuin* 'use *po* (sir/madam) in addressing' — and more systematically in certain other cases, among them cases in which DT *-an* is, as it were, preempted. These are cases in which *-an* is used as the direction-trigger affix of a three-argument verb and *-in* as the direction-trigger affix of a two-argument verb formed with the same stem: e.g. *pasukan* 'bring/take into' vs. *pasukin* 'come/go into', *labasan* 'bring/take outside' vs. *labasin* 'come/go outside'.

Beneficiary-trigger verbs are formed with *i-*. Any stem-forming *pag-* or *paN-* in the corresponding actor-trigger verb is retained. Examples are: *ipirma* 'sign for' (cf. AT *pumirma* 'sign'), *ipaglaba* 'launder for' (cf. AT *maglaba* 'launder'), *ipanguha* 'gather for' (cf. *manguha* 'gather').

Instrument-trigger verbs are also formed with *i-*, but in this case the stem must usually be formed with the prefix *paN-*, as in *ipam(p)unas* 'wipe with', *ipan(s)ulat* 'write with'. However, if the simple stem itself designates an instrument, alternative instrument-trigger formations without any stem-forming prefix or with the stem-forming prefix *pag-* also occur. Thus, the stem *suklay* 'comb' occurs in IT *isuklay* and *ipagsuklay* as well as *ipan(s)uklay* 'comb with', and the stem *gunting* 'scissors' occurs in IT *igunting* and *ipaggunting* as well as *ipanggunting* 'cut with'.

Apart from trigger affixes, there are a good many other non-aspectual affixes, among them affixes with ability and causative meanings. The ability affixes are *maka-* and *ma-*. *Maka-* occurs in actor-trigger verbs, in which it replaces *-um-* or *m-*: e.g. AT *makaawit* 'be able to sing' (cf. *umawit* 'sing'), AT *makapagluto* 'be able to cook' (cf. *magluto* 'cook'), AT *makapangisda* 'be able to fish' (cf. *mangisda* 'fish'). *Ma-* occurs with non-actor-trigger verbs. It replaces *-in*, but occurs together with *i-* or *-an*: e.g. PT *magamit* 'be able to use' (cf. *gamitin* 'use'), BT *maibili* 'be able to buy for' (cf. *ibili* 'buy for'), DT *mapuntahan* 'be able to go to' (cf. *puntahan* 'go to').

Causative verbs are all formed with the causative-stem-forming prefix *pa-*, which occurs in addition to a trigger affix. Causative verbs, in a sense, have two actors, one causing the other to act. However, morphologically (as well as syntactically), only the 'causer' is treated as an actor, while the 'causee' is treated as a kind of patient. Thus, when the causer is the trigger, the actor-trigger affix *mag-* (*m-* + *pag-*) is invariably used, but when the causee is the trigger the patient-trigger affix *-in* is invariably used: e.g., A(causer)T *magpapunta*/P(causee)T *papuntahin* 'cause to go' (cf. non-causative AT *pumunta* 'go'), A(causer)T *magpatsinelas*/P(causee)T *papagtsinelasin* 'cause to wear slippers' (cf. AT *magtsinelas* 'wear slippers').

There are also causative verbs in which the trigger is some argument other than the causer or the causee. Under these circumstances, the same trigger affix that occurs in the corresponding non-causative verb is ordinarily used, except that *-in* (which is, as it were, preempted, to mark the causee as trigger) is replaced by *i-* in patient-trigger verbs and by *-an* in direction-trigger verbs. Thus PT *ipalinis* 'cause to clean' (cf. PT *linisin* 'clean') selects as trigger the object cleaned, while P(causee)T *palinisin* selects as trigger the causee, the one caused to do the cleaning. Similarly, DT *papasukan* 'cause to enter' (cf. DT *pasukin* 'enter') selects as trigger the place entered, while P(causee)T *papasukin* selects as trigger the one caused to enter. Some other relevant examples are: PT *papintahan* 'cause to paint' (cf. PT *pintahan* 'paint'), DT *pasulatan* 'cause to write to' (cf. DT *sulatan* 'write to'), BT *ipabili* 'cause to buy for' (cf. BT *ibili* 'buy for').

Turning now to aspectual affixation, let us begin with a brief overview of the Tagalog aspect system. Tagalog, then, makes no true tense distinctions like the English past–non-past distinction, but instead makes a distinction between events viewed as actual and events viewed as hypothetical and, among the actual events, between those viewed as complete and those viewed as incomplete. Events viewed as complete are in the *perfective* aspect, those viewed as incomplete are in the *imperfective* aspect and those viewed as hypothetical are in the *contemplated* aspect. The perfective aspect is often translated into English by the past or the present perfect, the imperfective aspect by the simple present or by the present or past progressive and the contemplated aspect by the future: e.g. perf. *nagwalis* 'swept, has swept', imperf. *nagwawalis* 'sweeps, is/was sweeping', cont. *magwawalis* 'will sweep'. There are, however, other translation equivalents in certain cases. For example, the imperfective rather than the perfective form is used for the equivalent of the English negative perfect: thus 'hasn't swept yet' is expressed by *hindi pa nagwawalis*, not *hindi pa nagwalis. (*Hindi* is a negator, *pa* an enclitic particle.)

From a morphological point of view, aspect is marked in Tagalog by two patterns of affixation, one of which is common to imperfective and contemplative verbs, the other to imperfective and perfective verbs. The pattern that is common to imperfective and contemplated verbs can be called 'incompleteness' marking (since hypothetical events are necessarily incomplete), while the pattern common to imperfective and perfective verbs can be called 'actuality' marking.

Incompleteness marking involves a monosyllabic reduplicating prefix. This prefix normally consists of a copy of the first consonant and first vowel of the following syllable, except that the vowel of the reduplicating prefix is always long, whatever the length of the vowel in the following syllable. (Vowel length distinguishes this aspectual reduplication from the stem-forming reduplication mentioned above, which always involves a *short* vowel. Compare, for example, the aspectual reduplicating prefix /la:/ in *maglalakbay* /magla:lakbay/ 'will travel' and the stem-forming (intensive) reduplicating prefix /la/ in *maglalakbay* /maglalakbay/ 'travel (repeatedly etc.)'.)

The rules for the placement of the aspectual reduplicating prefix in relation to other prefixes are rather complex. Some other prefixes always precede the reduplicating prefix, but others may either precede or follow it, resulting in the possibility of alternative orderings. For example, in the contemplated and imperfective forms of the verb *maipabili* 'be able to cause to buy', the reduplicating prefix follows the ability prefix *ma-* but may either precede or follow the patient-trigger prefix *i-* and the causative prefix *pa-*; thus cont. *maiipabili*, *maipapabili* and *maipabibili* 'will be able to cause to buy' are all well formed.

Actuality marking, which is common to imperfective and perfective verbs, in most cases involves an affix that contains the phoneme /n/. The sole exceptions to this generalisation are verbs whose infinitives are formed with the actor-trigger infix *-um-*, in which actuality marking consists simply in the retention of this infix. The infix, in other words, is present in imperfective and perfective forms, but absent from contemplated forms. For example, the imperfective and perfective forms of the verb *pumunta* 'go' (stem: *punta*) are, respectively, *pumupunta* and *pumunta*, while the contemplated form is *pupunta*. (As these examples illustrate, the perfective forms of *-um-* verbs are identical with the infinitives.)

There are three actuality-marking affixes that contain /n/: the prefix *n-*, the prefix *ni-* and the infix *-in-*. The prefix *n-* occurs as a replacement of *m-* in all prefixes that begin with the latter in the infinitive. For example, *nagwalis* and *nagwawalis* are the perfective and imperfective forms corresponding to the infinitive *magwalis* 'sweep'. Similarly, *nangisda* is the perfective form of *mangisda* 'fish', and AT *nakakita*/PT *nakita* are the perfective forms of AT *makakita*/PA *makita* 'see'. The prefix *ni-* and the infix *-in-* occur in all other cases as either free or morphophonemically conditioned alternants. For example, the perfective form corresponding to the infinitive *lagyan* 'put on' may be either *nilagyan* or *linagyan*, but the perfective form corresponding to *iabot* 'hand to' must be *iniabot* and that corresponding to *hiraman* 'borrow from' must be *hiniraman*.

If the verb marked by *ni-* or *-in-* contains the prefix *i-*, this always precedes the *ni-* or *-in-*, as in *iniyuko* ~ *iyinuko*, the perfective forms of *iyuko* 'bend', or *ibinigay*, the perfective form of *ibigay* 'give'. Otherwise, *ni-* is always word-initial and *-in-* always follows the first consonant of the word. A special property of verbs whose infinitives are formed with the suffix *-in* is the loss of this suffix in the actuality-marked forms. Thus, corresponding to the infinitive *yayain* 'invite', we find perfective *niyaya* ~ *yinaya* and imperfective *niyayaya* ~ *yinayaya* (cf. the contemplated form *yayayain*, in which the suffix *-in* is retained).

Adjective morphology in Tagalog is also rather complex. Probably the most common adjective formations are those involving the prefix *ma-*: e.g. *mabuti* 'good' (cf. *buti* 'goodness'), *masama* 'bad' (cf. *sama* 'badness'), *malaki* 'big' (cf. *laki* 'bigness'), *maliit* 'small' (cf. *liit* 'smallness'). There are also many unaffixed adjectives — e.g. *mahal* 'expensive', *mura* 'cheap', *hinog* 'ripe', *hilaw* 'raw' — as well as many adjectives formed with various other affixes — e.g. *-an*, as in *putikan* 'virtually covered with mud' (cf. *putik* 'mud'), *-in*, as in *lagnatin* 'susceptible to fever' (cf. *lagnat* 'fever'), and *maka-*, as in *makabayan* 'patriotic' (cf. *bayan* 'country').

In certain cases adjectives may be morphologically marked for number or gender. Many *ma-* adjectives are marked as plural by a monosyllabic reduplicating prefix occurring between *ma-* and the stem: e.g. *mabubuti* 'good (pl.)', *masasama* 'bad (pl.)'. Such plural marking is, however, optional, and the non-pluralised forms may in general be used with plural as well as with singular referents. Gender marking is restricted to certain adjectives borrowed from Spanish, which occur in two gender-marked forms, a feminine form ending in *-a* and a masculine form ending in *-o*: e.g. *komika* (f.)/*komiko* (m.) 'funny', *simpatika* (f.)/*simpatiko* (m.) 'pleasing', *tonta* (f.)/*tonto* (m.) 'stupid'.

Adjectives may also be morphologically marked as intensive or moderative. Intensive formations involve the prefix *napaka-* (which replaces the *ma-* of a *ma-* adjective), while moderative formations involve disyllabic reduplication. Examples are: *napakabuti* 'very good', *napakamahal* 'very expensive', *mabuti-buti* 'rather good', *mahal-mahal* 'rather expensive'.

The comparative of equality is marked by (*ka*)*sing-* — e.g. (*ka*)*singbuti* 'as good as', (*ka*)*singmahal* 'as expensive as' — and the superlative is marked by *pinaka-* — e.g. *pinakamabuti* 'best', *pinakamahal* 'most expensive'. (Note that the *ma-* of a *ma-* adjective such as *mabuti* 'good' is dropped after (*ka*)*sing-* but retained after *pinaka-*.) The comparative of inequality is, however, expressed syntactically (by a preceding *mas*, *lalong* or *higit na* 'more' and a following *kaysa* or (*kaysa*) *sa* 'than').

Tagalog noun morphology is relatively simple. Nouns are not inflected for case or number (there is, however, obligatory *syntactic* role marking involving particles like *ng* and *sa* — see above — as well as optional syntactic pluralisation, involving the particle *mga*), and only certain nouns borrowed from Spanish are marked for gender: e.g. *amiga* (f.)/*amigo* (m.) 'friend', *sekretarya* (f.)/*sekretaryo* (m.) 'secretary'. Nonetheless, a good many morphologically complex nouns occur and some of these reflect quite productive patterns of affixation. Among the latter are: affixation with -*an* to express a place associated with what the stem designates, as in *aklatan* 'library' (cf. *aklat* 'book'), *halamanan* 'garden' (cf. *halaman* 'plant'); affixation with -*in* to express the object of the action expressed by a verb formed with the same stem, as in *awitin* 'song' (cf. *umawit* 'sing'), *bilihin* 'something to buy' (cf. *bumili* 'buy'); and affixation with *taga-* to express the performer of the action of a verb formed with the same stem, as in *tagasulat* 'writer' (cf. *sumulat* 'write'), *tagapagbili* 'seller' (cf. *magbili* 'sell'), *tagapangisda* 'fisherman' (cf. *mangisda* 'fish').

The Tagalog personal pronoun system is summarised in table 11.4. The person-number categories that are distinguished are first, second and third person, singular and plural. There are, however, two distinct types of

Table 11.4: Personal Pronouns

	ng *form*	sa *form*	Unmarked *form*
Singular			
1st person	ko	akin	ako
2nd person	mo	iyo	ka/ikaw
3rd person	niya	kaniya	siya
Plural			
1st person-exclusive	namin	amin	kami
1st person-inclusive	natin	atin	tayo
2nd person	ninyo	inyo	kayo
3rd person	nila	kanila	sila

first person plural. When the addressee is not included in the group being referred to (i.e., when the meaning is 'he/she/they and I'), the *exclusive* forms are used. When, on the other hand, the addressee *is* included in the group being referred to (i.e. when the meaning is 'you (and he/she/they) and I'), the *inclusive* forms are used. Note that no gender distinctions are made: the same third person singular forms are used to refer to males and females. The Tagalog personal pronouns are, however, strictly *personal*, in the sense that they are used to refer only to human beings (and to humanised animals, such as pets or animals in folktales). Where English would use *it* (or *they* with a non-human referent), Tagalog uses either no pronoun at all or a demonstrative.

Each personal pronoun category is associated with three distinct forms, except for the second person singular, which is associated with four. The *ng* form is the form that occurs in the same contexts as common-noun phrases that are preceded by the particle *ng*: e.g. non-trigger actors. The *sa* form is the form that occurs after the particle *sa* or as a prenominal possessive pronoun. The unmarked form is the form that occurs in most other contexts, e.g. in isolation or when the pronoun functions as the trigger of the clause. In the case of the second person singular pronoun, there are two unmarked forms: *ka*, which functions exclusively as a trigger, and *ikaw*, which occurs in other unmarked contexts.

A similar three-way distinction is made in the demonstrative pronouns, as shown in table 11.5.

Table 11.5: Demonstrative Pronouns

	ng *form*	sa *form*	Unmarked *form*
'this'	nito	dito	ito
'that (near addressee)'	niyan	diyan	iyan
'that (not near addressee)'	niyon, noon	doon	iyon

Three demonstrative categories are distinguished, one equivalent to English 'this' and two that divide the range of English 'that', one of them used when the referent is near the addressee, the other when it is not. Again the *ng* forms are those that occur in the same contexts as *ng* phrases (*niyon* and *noon* are free variants). The *sa* forms of the demonstratives occur in the same contexts as *sa* phrases (including directional and locative *sa* phrases, in which case the demonstratives have the meanings 'here' and 'there'). And the unmarked forms occur in most other contexts.

Finally, it may be mentioned that there are also three contextually distinguished forms of the personal-name marker, i.e. the marker that is used when the head noun is a personal name: the *ng* form *ni*, the *sa* form *kay* and the unmarked form *si*. Such formal distinctions within the nominal system serve to identify the semantic and/or syntactic roles of arguments more or less unambiguously, thus allowing for the freedom of word order which, together with the trigger system and the complex verbal morphology, constitute perhaps the most striking typological features of Tagalog.

Bibliography

Tagalog grammar was first studied by Spanish missionaries in the sixteenth century, but it is only in the present century that the language has been analysed on its own terms, rather than on the basis of often inappropriate European models. Bloomfield's (1917) influential grammar, written from a classic structuralist perspective, served as the basis for the first grammar by a native speaker of the language, Lopez (1940). The most comprehensive grammar of the language written to date is Schachter and Otanes (1972). De Guzman (1978) is an innovative analysis of verbal morphology, so central to the language.

For the history of the diffusion of Tagalog as Pilipino, the Philippine national language, see Gonzales (1977). Constantino (1971) provides a historical survey of the linguistic analysis of Tagalog and seven other Philippine languages.

References

Bloomfield, L. 1917. *Tagalog Texts with Grammatical Analysis* (University of Illinois, Urbana)

Constantino, E. 1971. 'Tagalog and Other Major Languages of the Philippines', in T. A. Sebeok (ed.), *Current Trends in Linguistics*, vol. 8, *Linguistics in Oceania* (Mouton, The Hague)

De Guzman, V. 1978. *Syntactic Derivation of Tagalog Verbs* (= *Oceanic Linguistics*, Special Publication, no. 16)

Gonzales, A. 1977. 'Pilipino in the Year 2000', in B. Sibayan and A. Gonzales (eds.), *Language Planning and the Building of a National Language* (= *Philippine Journal of Linguistics*, Special Monograph, no. 5)

Lopez, C. 1940. *A Manual of the Philippine National Language* (Bureau of Printing, Manila)

Schachter, P. and F. Otanes. 1972. *Tagalog Reference Grammar* (University of California Press, Los Angeles)

Language Index

Abor Miri Dafla 72, 74
Achinese 173, 187
Afroasiatic 7, 15
Ahom 21, 23
Ainu 128, 132
Akha *see* Hani
Akkadian 15f.
Albanian 10
Aleut *see* Eskimo-Aleut
Altaic 7, 9, 12, 89, 128, 151, 154
Amerindian 7
Amharic 9f., 11
Amoy *see* Min
Andro 74
Angami 72
Anglo-Saxon *see* English
Annamese *see* Vietnamese
Annamite *see* Vietnamese
Arabic 4, 15, 132, 190, 203
Atayalic 176f.
Atsi *see* Zaiwa
Australian 5, 7, 8
Austric 7
Austro-Asiatic 7, 12, 49
Austro-Tai 29, 178
Austronesian 7, 11f., 13, 16, 29, 128, 153, 171–84, 187, 192, 208

Bahing 72
Bai 71
Balinese 173, 187
Balkan sprachbund 10
Balti Tibetan 77
Bangla *see* Bengali
Bantu 89
Baric 73–4
Basque 7
Batak 173, 187
Belau *see* Palauan
Be 22
Bengali 14
Bikol 173
Black Tai *see* Tai Dam
Bodic 73, 74

Bodish 71–4 *passim*
Bodo 72
Bodo-Garo 72, 74, 80
Bodo-Konyak 74
Boro *see* Bodo
Bouyei 21, 23
Buginese 173, 187
Bulgarian 10
Bunan 71
Burmese 12, 71f., 75–8 *passim*, 80, 106–26
Burmic 73–4
Burmish 72, 106
Burushaski 7
Buyi *see* Bouyei

Cambodian *see* Khmer
Cantonese *see* Yue
Castilian *see* Spanish
Caucasian 7, 9
Cebuano 14, 24, 173
Celtic 6
Central Pacific 178
Cham 12
Chamic 174
Chamorro 175–7 *passim*
Chang 72
Chepang 79
Chin *see* Kuki-Chin
Chinese 3, 8, 10f., 12, 13, 15, 21, 22, 25, 27, 49–52 *passim*, 54, 64–6 *passim*, 71, 75–8 *passim*, 81, 83–105, 107, 129–34 *passim*, 141, 151, 156, 165, 187, 190, 201
Chinese Shan *see* Tai Nuea
Chinghpo *see* Jinghpo
Congo-Kordofanian *see* Niger-Kordofanian
Cook Islands Maori *see* Rarotongan
Cushitic 10

Daco-Rumanian *see* Rumanian
Danish 2
Dari *see* Persian
Dehong Dai *see* Tai Nuea
Dravidian 7, 9, 13, 14, 15, 128, 153
Dutch 2, 3, 6, 134, 188, 190, 191, 199

231

232 LANGUAGE INDEX

East Himalayan 72–5 *passim*, 79
Egyptian 15
English 1, 3f., 5f., 8, 9, 10, 11, 13, 15, 17, 30, 42, 44, 46, 54, 59, 85, 91, 94, 97f., 102, 108, 109, 123–5, 127, 129, 132, 133–5, *passim*, 140, 143, 144, 146, 148, 149, 159, 165–7 *passim*, 187, 188, 199, 202, 206, 208–11 *passim*, 225, 226, 229
Erythraic *see* Afroasiatic
Eskimo-Aleut 7
Eurasiatic 7

Fijian 175–83
Filipino *see* Tagalog
Formosan 174, 176
French 1, 9, 15, 17f., 50, 51, 54, 66f., 127
Frisian 3, 6
Fukkianese *see* Min
Futuna 176

Garo 72
Gedaged 174
Gelao 22
Georgian 9
German 2, 3, 5f., 8, 10, 11, 14, 16, 18, 127, 144
Germanic 6, 9, 11, 16, 109, 134
Gilbertese (Kiribati) 175
Greek 4, 10, 18, 30, 108, 109
Gujarati 14
Gurung 71, 74, 76
Gyarong 73, 74, 78–80 *passim*

Hakka 84, 85, 104
Hamito-Semitic *see* Afroasiatic
Hani 72
Hausa 15
Hawaiian 175, 176
Hebrew 14f.
Hellenic *see* Greek
Hesperonesian 208
Hiligaynon 173
Hindi *see* Hindi-Urdu
Hindi-Urdu 14, 15, 108
Hindustani *see* Hindi-Urdu
Hiri Motu 174
Hmong-Mien 25
Hokkianese *see* Min

Iban 173
Ibero-Caucasian 7
Ilokano 173
Ilongo *see* Hiligaynon
Indic *see* Indo-Aryan
Indo-Aryan (Indic) 14, 30, 107–9 *passim*, 115, 119
Indo-European 6–8 *passim*, 10, 12–15 *passim*, 26, 64, 89, 93, 96, 98, 127, 128, 144, 165, 178, 206

Indo-Pacific 7
Indonesian *see* Malay
Iranian 6
Irish 6
Italian 54, 56

Japanese 7, 8, 9, 11, 12, 15, 50, 127–52, 165, 178
Javanese 14, 173, 187, 188, 191, 192, 203
Jinghpaw *see* Jinghpo
Jinghpo 72–5 *passim*, 78, 79, 81

Kachin *see* Jinghpo
Kachinic 72–4 *passim*
Kadai (Kam-Tai), 12, 21, 22, 24–7, 29, 178
Kadu 74
Kam-Tai *see* Kadai
Kam Muang 21, 23, 24, 31
Kam-Sui 22, 24, 27
Kamarup 73–4
Kanauri 71
Kapingamarangi 175
Karen 73, 78, 80, 106
Karenic 73
Ket 7
Kham-Magar 74
Khamti 21, 23, 27
Khmer (Cambodian) 12, 27, 31–3, 37, 109
Khoisan 7
Khuen 21, 23
Kiranti/Rai 72, 74, 78
Kiribati *see* Gilbertese
Konyak 72, 74
Korean 7, 9, 12, 15, 50, 128f., 132, 144, 153–70
Kosraean 175
Kuki-Chin 72, 74, 106
Kuki-Naga 74
Kusaie *see* Kosraean

Laha 22
Lahu 72
Lakher 72
Lakkja 22
Lamekhite *see* Afroasiatic
Lao 12, 21, 23, 27, 31
Laqua 22
Lati 22
Latin 1, 4, 9, 11, 14, 15, 17, 18, 30, 108, 109, 133f.
Lawng 72
Lepcha 75
Limbu 72
Lisramic *see* Afroasiatic
Lisu 72
Lolo *see* Yi
Lolo-Burmese 72–4 *passim*, 77, 78, 80, 106
Loloish 72, 74, 76, 107
Longzhou 26

LANGUAGE INDEX

Lotha 72
Lue *see* Tai Lue
Luish 72, 74
Lushai 72

Macassarese 173, 187
Macedonian 10
Madurese 173, 187
Malagasy 13, 174, 176, 178
Malay 12, 14, 173–7 *passim*, 180, 185–207
Malayo-Polynesian 12, 176f., *see also* Austronesian
Manchu 154
Mandarin *see* Chinese
Manipuri *see* Meithei
Maori 175, 176
Marathi 14
Marshallese 175
Maru *see* Lawng
Mbabaram 8
Meithei 72, 74, 75
Merina 174
Miao-Yao 12, 16, 71, 77
Mikir 72, 74
Min 84f., 87–90 *passim*
Minangkabau 173, 187
Minjia *see* Bai
Moldavian *see* Rumanian
Mon 106, 107, 111, 115, 117–9 *passim*
Mon-Khmer 49, 106, 107, 111, 117
Mongolian 7, 9, 13, 154
Moso *see* Naxi
Mota 174
Motu 174
Munda-Mon-Khmer *see* Austro-Asiatic

Na-Dene 7
Naga 72, 74, 76, 106
Nakhi *see* Naxi
Nauruan 175
Naxi 72–5 *passim*
Newari 71, 74, 75, 78
Ngadju 173
Niger-Kordofanian 7
Nilo-Saharan 7
Nocte 72, 79
Northeastern Thai *see* Lao
Northern Thai *see* Kam Muang
Norwegian 2
Nukuoro 175
Nung (Tai) 21
Nung (Tibeto-Burman) 73, 74, 80

Oceanic 176, 177, 179, 180
Old Saxon 16
Osmanli *see* Turkish

Padaung 106

Paiwanic 176f.
Palauan 175–7 *passim*
Pali 22, 30, 31, 107–11 *passim*
Panjabi 14
Papiamento *see* Papiamentu
Papiamentu 17
Papuan 7, 12
Pashto 6
Persian 6, 15, 132
Phuan 32
Phuthai 32
Pilipino *see* Tagalog
Polish 5, 6
Polynesian 154, 175–8 *passim*
Ponapean 175
Portuguese 15, 17, 54, 134, 190
Primi 73, 74
Pyu 107

Qiang 73, 74
Quechua 9

Rajasthani 14
Rarotongan 175
Rawang 73
Red Tai 21, 23
Rengma 72
Romance 4, 9, 10, 17, 22, 88, 109
Rotokas 180
Rotuman 178
Roviana 174
Rumanian 10
Rung 71, 73, 74, 79
Russian 5, 6, 8, 54, 144
Ryukyuan 128

Saek 21, 23, 27
Samoan 174, 178
Sanskrit 8, 14, 22, 30, 31, 36f., 190, 205
Sasak 173
Scandinavian languages 2, 6, 11
Sema 72
Semitic 9f., 15, 89
Semite-Hamitic *see* Afroasiatic
Shan *see* Tai Long
Siamese *see* Thai
Sifan 73
Sinitic 71
Sino-Tibetan 7, 10f., 12, 71–82, 83, 128
Slavonic 4, 6, 10, 88
South Halmahera-West New Guinea 177
Southern Thai 21
Spanish 8, 15, 17, 134, 144, 208, 209, 211, 227f.
Sui 24
Sumerian 1, 15
Sundanese 173, 187

234 LANGUAGE INDEX

Swahili 14
Swedish 2

Tagalog 14, 173, 180, 192, 195, 208–30
Tahitian 175
Tai, 7, 12, 19–27, 29–32 *passim*, 47, 50, 71, 77, 81, 107
Tai Dam 21, 23, 26
Tai Long (Shan) 21, 23, 106, 108
Tai Lue 21, 23, 31f.
Tai Nuea 21, 23
Tai Yuan *see* Kam Muang
Taiwanese *see* Min
Tajiki *see* Persian
Tamang 71, 74, 78
Tamil 14
Tangkhul 77
Tangut 73–5 *passim*
Tasmanian 7
Tay 21
Telugu 14
Thai 10f., 21–3 *passim*, 25–7 *passim*, 29–47, 106, 108, 109
Thakali 71, 74
Tho 21
Thulung 72
Tibetan 11, 12, 71, 73, 75–8 *passim*, 80, 81, 106
Tibeto-Burman 12, 25, 27, 71–82, 89, 106, 107, 109, 111, 112, 117
Tibeto-Kanauri 74
Tibeto-Karen 73
Tok Pisin 3, 16
Tolai 174

Tongan 174–6 *passim*
Trukic 175
Trung 73
Tsouic 176f.
Tungusic 7, 9, 154
Turkic 7, 9, 154
Turkish 15, 132

Uralic 7
Urdu *see* Hindi-Urdu

Vayu 72
Vedic *see* Sanskrit
Vietnamese 10f., 12, 15, 25, 49–67, 71, 77, 201

Wancho 72
Welsh 6
White Tai 21, 23
Wiyaw 8
Wu 83, 84, 87

Xishuangbanna Dai *see* Tai Lue
Xixia *see* Tangut

Yabem 174
Yap 175
Yay 21, 23, 26
Yi 72, 75, 107
Yue (Cantonese) 3, 84, 85, 89–92 *passim*

Zaiwa 72
Zhuang 21, 23